CW01648854

This book is dedicated to mam and dad, for their support and encouragement, to Pamela, Josie and Jessica and grandchildren Cerys, Owen and Anna.

Also to past students and friends, climbers and artists alike,including the Wanneys Climbing Club, my “Ford Castlers”, Craster painters - particularly the late lamented Roy Billen - my Monkseaton Art Historians and to members of the 3 out of 10 club.

ISBN 978-0-9934123-2-5
First published in the UK in 2016 by Wanney Books
Printed in the UK by Elanders, NE27 0QG

A Sense of Place

Gordon Highmoor

Paintings and Drawings

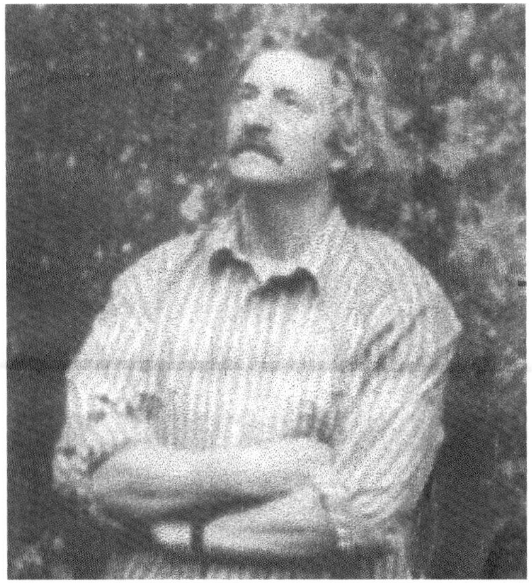

Gordon Highmoor was raised in Newbiggin by the Sea on the Northumberland coast where his father, a coal cutter in the local mine, was also Group Scoutmaster of the 1st Newbiggin Troop with its headquarters virtually on the beach at the south end of the village.

He attended Morpeth Grammar School where he showed a talent particuarly for English and Art and was also Newbiggin's first Queen Scout. On leaving school he worked for some years for a firm of architects in Newcastle until he changed direction and enrolled in the College of Art (later to become the University of Northumbria), taking his NDD in Illustration in 1964. Here his main tutors were Tom Bromly, Peter Bottomley and John Crisp.

A keen rock climber and mountaineer, he has worked as an instructor for the, then, CCPR including a summer in an Outward Bound School, then secured a lectureship in Art and Design in New College Durham where he rose to be senior lecturer and Head of the Department. He has shown his paintings and drawings in several exhibitions at various galleries in the region although he dislikes selling unless it is to friends who really want the work.

In 1966 he married Pamela, who he had met at art school, and they moved to Jesmond near to where she taught art at a local private school. They produced two talented daughters who, although not artists themselves, hold important positions in medicine and animal sciences. They in turn parented three grandchildren, Cerys (now 10), Owen (7) and Anna (5).

In 1995, after taking early retirement from lecturing, Gordon took a Diploma in Archaeology at Newcastle University in order to find out more about the landscape which informs his present work. He has taught summer schools in the Isle of Mull, Kindrogen in Perthshire and Ford Castle in Northumberland, run many workshops and very popular WEA classes in Painting and Drawing in Craster and Art Appreciation in Monkseaton, and was, for many years, secretary of the Friends of the Hatton Gallery in Newcastle University's Fine Art Department. He has collaborated with the archaeologist Stan Beckensall in the production of many books on the Archaeology of the North, designing the covers and illustrations in the text.

If pressed, he would list his other interests as good (ie "serious") music, British novels from Kingsley Amis onwards, old German air-cooled cars, English motor cycles, Irish Rugby and, of course, his grandchildren. He has a great respect for certain art critics including the late Brian Sewell, Robert Hughes, John Berger, Julian Spalding and David Lee. His list of hates is even longer, including as it does, “Artbollocks", all that is bad about young British Art, Electronic gadgetry, most "pop" and media people and so-called 'professional' sportsmen (particularly English).

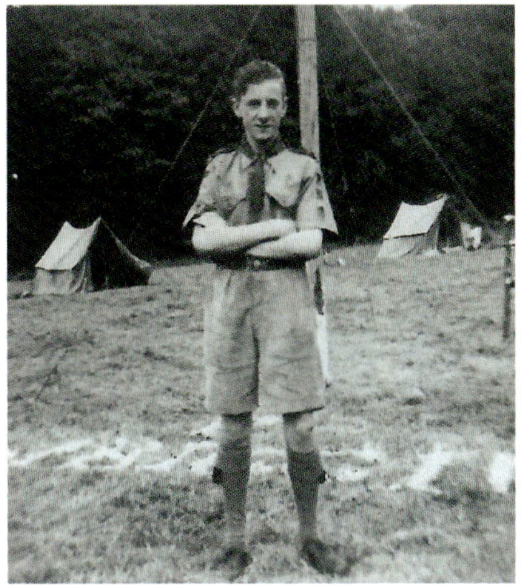

Newbiggin gets its first
Queen's Scout 1952

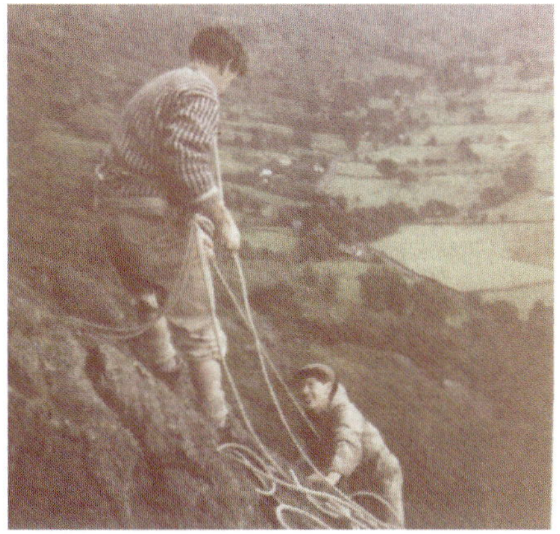

Outward Bound climbing
instructor in the Lake District
1963

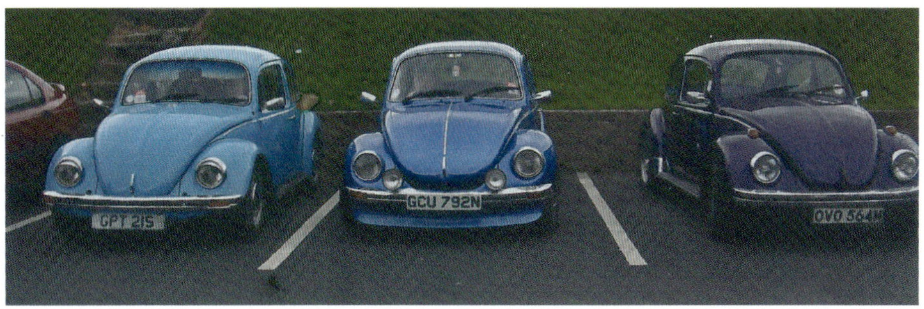

OUR VOLKSWAGENS

After motorbikes the obvious step seemed to be more air-cooled transport so we, as a family, became Beetle fanatics. As well as me, both daughters have one each and we've also had Camper Vans.

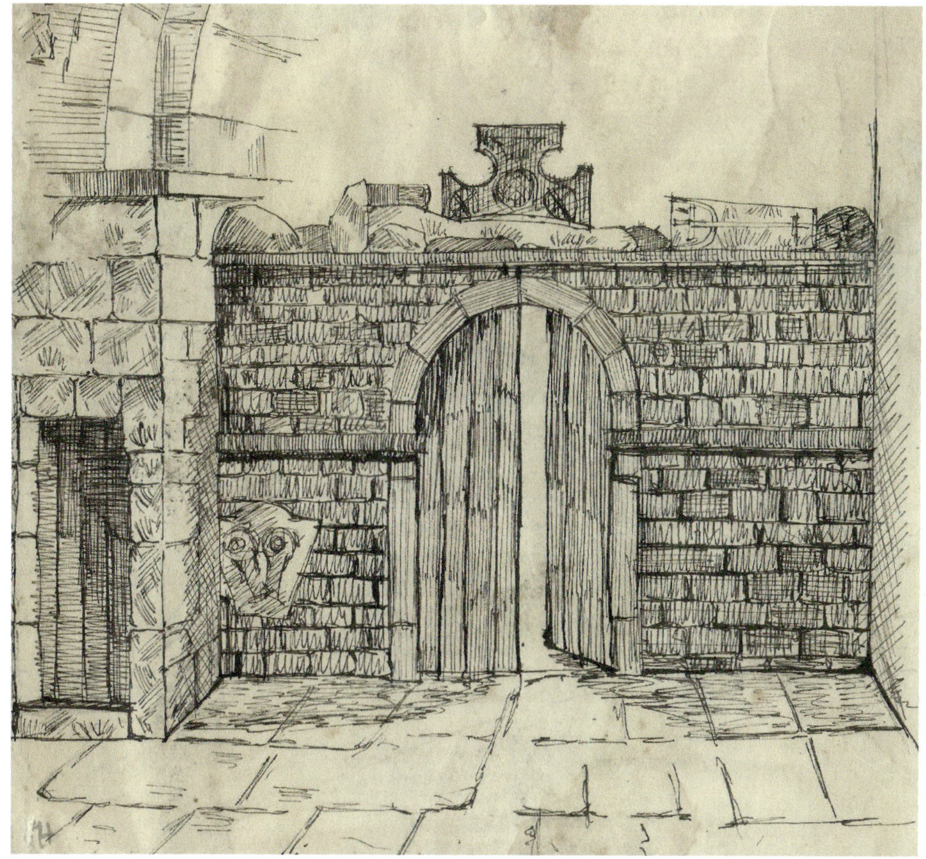

WOODHORN CHURCH

As a choirboy at St Bartholomew's, Newbiggin, we often used the Mother church,St Mary's at Woodhorn for special services. This drawing of the vestry was made on leaving school to start my short architectural career.

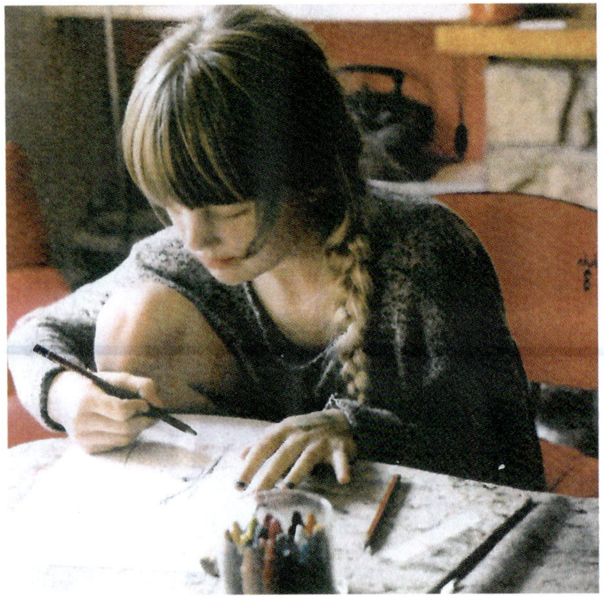

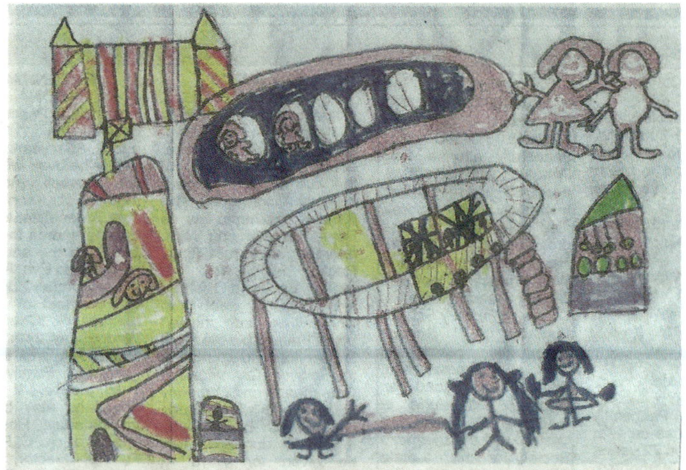

By Anna Highmoor, aged five, from Heaton Park View, Newcastle

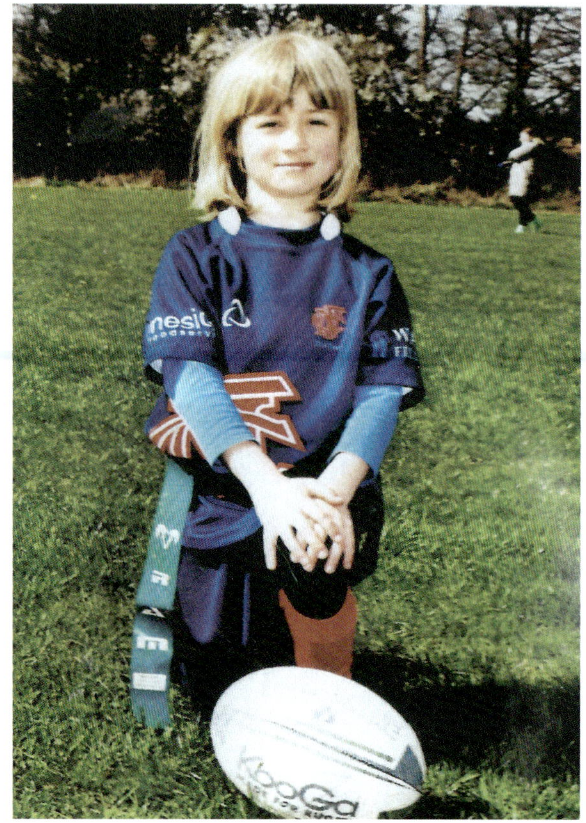

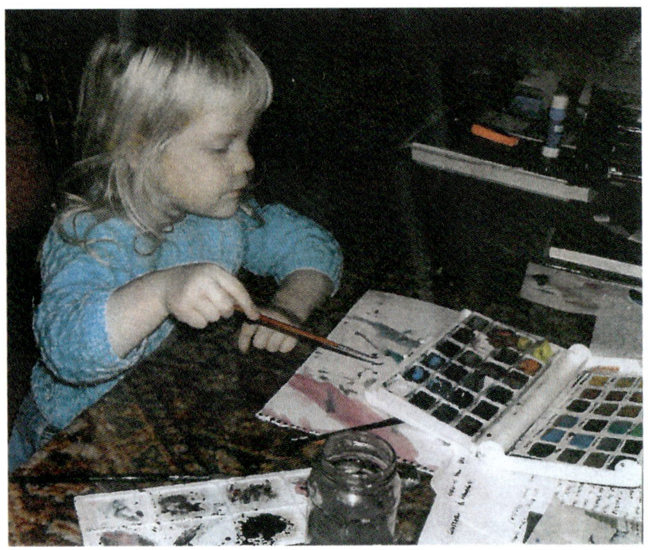

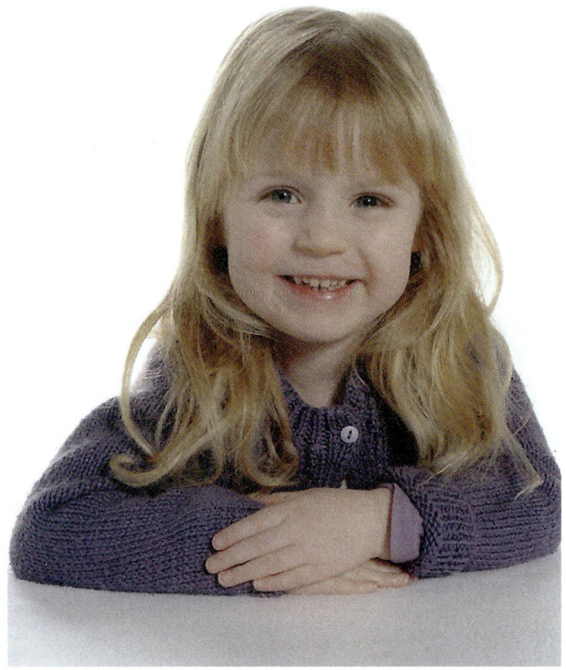

Of my grandchildren, the two girls show an early flair for drawing. Cerys (far left) seen here barely three, and recently aged eleven.

Anna (left) aged five also loves to draw and recently won a competition in the local newspaper.

Owen (above - aged seven) is a keen rugby player at Northern and has won lots of medals already.

A SENSE OF PLACE

There is very little, if any, landscape in its natural state left in Britain. Even in the wildest reaches of Northumberland, in those areas which have escaped what I call ''pollution by tourism', the landscape has been affected, shaped and formed by man's presence and activities. And there are many sites where there is evidence that Neolithic or early Bronze-age man added his mark to the landscape as a conscious creative act - in megaliths, circles or alignments of stones, and in the inscribed marks on the softer rocks of the region such as the fell sandstones. These configurations of symbols, including the so-called "cup and ring marks", are commonly termed rock art by archaeologists although there is little evidence to suppose that they are conceived as "art". The sitings in the landscape and their proximity to burial and other ritual sites however, seems to suggest that the carvings were certainly an integral and significant force. But, because the images were made by what many imagine to be preliterate people and were realised before spoken and written language had developed into the sophisticated means of communication we know today, it might be supposed that such symbolic associations should be thought of as crude or illogical. On the contrary, they may well be the clearest and most economical of all language forms, synthesising the subtleties of human thought and experience.

When, as an artist, one confronts such landscapes, one becomes aware, as **Paul Nash** was of his 'special places', that they appear to be charged with another force above the purely visual. Although empty of human figures his paintings seem to be nevertheless, saturated with human presence and meaning.

And while the Northumbrian locations, with their rough-cut mineral masses of crag and outcrop and the constant dialogue with the natural elements provided a rich source of inspiration in my work, I always felt that the landscape had more to reveal. My longstanding interest in, then realised experience of archaeology, has done much to heighten my knowledge and perceptions yet, in a curious way, has deepened the mystery.

A long career as a Senior Lecturer in Visual Communications has given me access, not just to a history of art, but to early symbols and alphabets and other systems of communication including phonetics and, of course, music. I do not use these however as a means of describing the landscape, but rather to **invoke** it, my works becoming inextricably linked with the feelings which certain pieces of music, or poetry suggest, whether spiritual or descriptive. The work illustrated here is only a small fragment from a body of paintings and drawings, each exploring some facet or other of my environment. Thus, in *Rock and Ritual* I have explored that same Northumbrian landscape in which I grew up and subsequently came to know as a climber, archaeologist and artist.

Although my ideas are largely realised through drawing, I have always enjoyed manipulating materials broadening my scope over the years to encompass media other than paint, such as rock-dust, glues, grounds, wax-resists, and so on. The resultant surfaces are subsequently stained and worked in order to achieve the textural verisimilitude which is, in part, central to my ideas.

In another project - *Echoes of Survival* - I express a concern that a number of artefacts and grave goods, once associated with ritual and possibly imbued with great meaning, are finding their way into museum showcases or storage cupboards away from their original context. Worse still, many have been, wantonly destroyed or vandalised.

Finally, I have always been struck by how much the artist is like the archaeologist in that both activities are concerned with turning up evidence and collecting information which speculates about the past and our relationship with it.

Gordon Highmoor

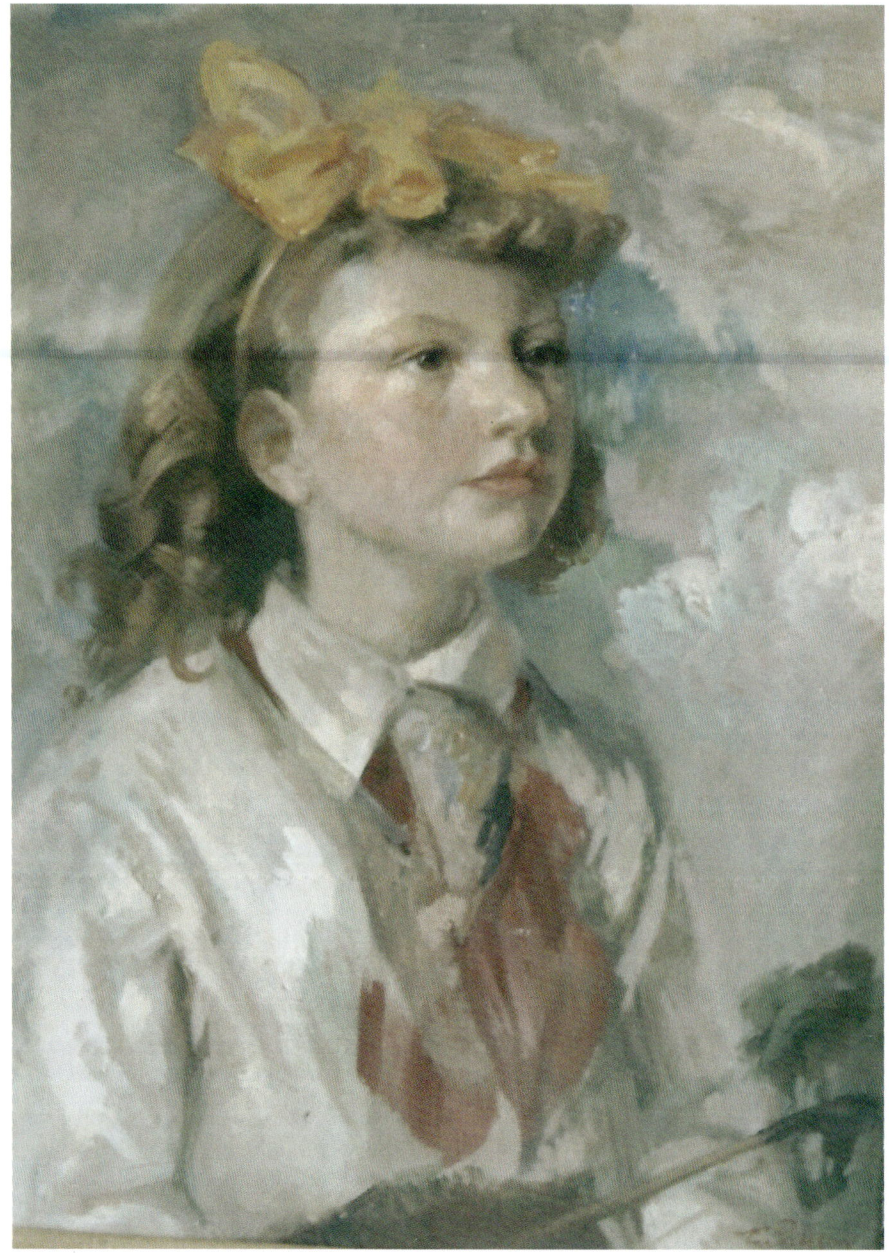

PAMELA (Oil)

A portrait painted in the the 1940s by Tom Patterson who taught painting at King's College (now Newcastle University) and who often used her, and her sister Barbara as child-models. His work was shown in the Royal Academy.

EARLY WORK

This catalogue of my work, is being produced at the request and nagging persistence of family, countless friends and students and for my grandchildren, at least one of whom thinks I am famous and make lots of money from my art. Alas fame and fortune have eluded me although I have always needed to draw and, as a child, I dreamed of being an artist, between bouts of wanting to be a footballer, a mountaineer, a fell-runner or a motor-cycle trials rider, careers which were denied to me by my parents, lack of opportunity or ambition. One thing for sure was that I would never follow the family pattern of working down the coal mines since an early visit with my father frightened the life out of me. I eventually attended a good grammar school although, among its failings, it had a lousy careers guidance programme and played rugby instead of football. On leaving I became apprenticed to a firm of architects in Newcastle where, besides allowing me the opportunity to draw, it opened my eyes to the far reaches of Northumberland where one of my tasks was to make improvements to farm workers cottages on some of the large estates. This was interesting enough but eventually my bugbear of mathematics caught up with me as increasingly we were obliged to work out quantities of building materials or to calculate the stress factors of concrete or steel. Fortunately National Service intervened and I joined the Royal Engineers, worked in an architectural drawing office, lived in Germany for a while and played football for the garrison XI. It also gave me the chance to take stock and, since there were a few art students in the barracks who boasted about their various art schools, this intrigued me somewhat. Then, as I remember, while on guard duty inside the vast BAOR Headquarters one night, I came across, in one of the offices, a notice-board on which were pinned some postcards and among them a Degas drawing. I was smitten. The card subsequently turned out to belong to Basil Beattie, then a clerk in the RASC, (who DID become famous as an artist) and on demob, I applied to and was accepted by the College of Art in Newcastle.

I suppose to someone whose background was a rather naive mixture of the Scouts, rock-climbing and football, and whose habitat was a small fishing/mining village on the wild Northumbrian coast, Art School in the early sixties must have seemed a fairly alien place. But even before the upheavals of the Coldstream Report and his subsequent investing of degree status to art as a subject, it was nevertheless a fairly well-organised and structured system with a clear demarcation of subject disciplines being evident. In the first two years for example, we did everything from painting, basic design, anatomy, life drawing, and sculpture, to History of Art and Architecture with options in Fabric Printing, Bookbinding and Pottery. In in the final two years we chose a specialist and a subsidiary subject in which to be examined along with the submission of a dissertation and carefully composed and mounted study sheets. The lecturing staff were all practising artists and taught from a position of experience, the discipline implicit in this making for a hard-working student body. There were also part-time lecturers employed for various subjects and I remember one final-year Architecture student from the University who was charged to teach History of Architecture and who used to arrive on a butcher's bike, a typical affectation of the period. Alas, he was neither very confident nor very good and,when he learned of my background, would place me at the front of the class in order to corroborate what he told us.

A subdivision into vocational and subject boundaries was also apparent in the various demeanour, dress and hair styles of the students, so you could tell at a glance what each was studying. The **Industrial Design** (mostly lads) who were destined for careers in Furniture, Product or Interior Design for example, seemed to favour college ties and blazers or sports jacket and flannels which complemented the shortish, neat hair styles that young professional designers seemed to wear at the time, while the **Commercial Artists** or **Graphic Designers** as they liked to be called, were more trendy, favouring button-down collars and pointed Italian shoes,and were usually to be seen carrying *"MJQ"* or *"Dave Brubeck"* LP covers under their arms. The **Fine Art** students, on the other hand, looked exactly like what my Dad feared I would turn into. No doubt feeling that they had a long tradition of scruffiness to uphold, thanks to the example of those bohemian, free-thinking British and "School of Paris" artists of earlier in the century such as Augustus John or Chaim Soutine and that ilk, they sported beards and wild hair (the boys that is, but not exclusively), patched and multi-coloured shirts and jeans. Somewhat mysteriously, this latter garb, even by the second or third day of a new term, became spattered with a rich multi-coloured patina of oil paint thus securing their status as true free-thinking creatives - "a load of Pollocks" as one wag put it! Some girls did paint but the prettier ones soon escaped into the **Fashion Department**. Needless to say, the majority of my football team, was recruited from amongst the Industrial Designers.

Today they might well be thought of as posers but actually they were all just pretty naive. Straight from school, an Art education for most of them was the equivalent of their National Service so to speak, and a valuable formative experience. Many were extremely talented and all very hardworking and earnest. A lot ended up in teaching since the job market was not all that exciting at the time and some drop-outs became famous pop singers. But looking back, I feel that it proved to be very useful, and, as I keep reminding myself when I regard the present generation, at least we could draw!!!

However, there was a major student revolt going on in other parts of the country mostly in protest at the impending degree situation with its attendant insistence on academic entry qualifications. This came to a head particularly at Hornsea School of Art where the students took over the building and staged a mass sit-in. There were a lot of posters produced together with a large consumption of drugs and alcohol, but this only served to alienate local authorities, the press and the general public. Perhaps it shows how out-of-touch we were up north, that, when a deputation from Hornsea came up to our student union to recruit support for their cause, they were poorly received. Inevitably the change did happen, and those small art schools which escaped the chop became, first Polytechnics, then Universities and I ended up myself working within the new 'system.'

For me art school was another world and, despite my father's misgivings about drug taking, long hair and *"giving up a good career as an architect"* it turned out to be what I had dreamed about. Perhaps as important as finding myself at last, while there I met Pamela, my wife-to-be, who was herself a talented artist and designer. I also found time to organise and run a college football team and we eventually joined a local league in which we made fairly undistinguished progress. My first influences as an art student were social realist painters such as **Breughel, Millet, Bastien Lepage, early van Gogh** and **Degas**. Subsequently, thanks to the marvellous Stone gallery of Mick Marshall, I came across the likes of **Josef Herman, Joan Eardley, Sheila Fell** and sundry **Glasgow Boys**. Since I was from fiercely working class stock myself and living in Newbiggin by the Sea with its proximity to the Ashington Pitmen Painters, this seemed to be the obvious direction to take and, for a while, I drew and painted my environment and its people. My years as an architectural draughtsman however had left me with a legacy of rather "tight" drawing that found an outlet more in illustration than in large, free painting. I had ideas of finishing my training in Edinburgh College of Art where, on a visit, I met Bill Gillies the principal and a major Scottish artist, but the County Council Education Department were not prone to giving student grants to *"study in a foreign country"*, and so at Newcastle I became an illustrator, my aspirations to become a painter being put, as it were, on the back burner.

My real sporting passion was for rock climbing and although it meant that I and my old Triumph motor bike got to see lots of remote Northumberland as well as Scotland and the Lake District, I had never thought of being a landscape painter. But, from scribbled drawings of fells and farms, of moors and outcrops, I began another social quest - that of depicting the harsh life of the hill farmer - and began to explore this in paint. By necessity these were essentially textural recreations of the landscape and in which I began to use a variety of media including rock dust, plaster, sand etc and colours from earth itself, bilberries, heather and the like in an attempt to create some sense of verisimilitude. My chosen landscape was, of course, one in which the weather plays a crucial role and it resulted in a series of works which explored the effects of rain, snow or wind. Most artists work from sketches and, by their observation and scrutiny of nature, develop a strong visual memory which informs any subsequent studio work, Sometimes, however, that memory needs to be jogged, and my own stimulus has been poetry and music.

As the only artist in the family, although I do count among my ancestors **Joseph Highmore (1692-1780)** who was a well known portrait and subject painter who rivalled his contemporary **William Hogarth** in the character and intimacy of his *"conversation pieces".* I do feel that I owe a great deal to my maternal grandfather James Flynn, an Irishman and World War 1 hero, who came to live here and who, like many of his people, told marvellous stories, wrote poetry and sang songs. I'm certain that it was he from whom I inherited my interest in literature and in verse. He taught me about the Yeats family, G.B.Shaw, J.M. Synge and others and, by the time I was five or so I could recite *The Lake Isle of Innisfree* and sing all the songs made famous by John McCormack the Irish tenor. Sadly he never saw my later work but I'm sure he would have encouraged me and approved of the direction it took.

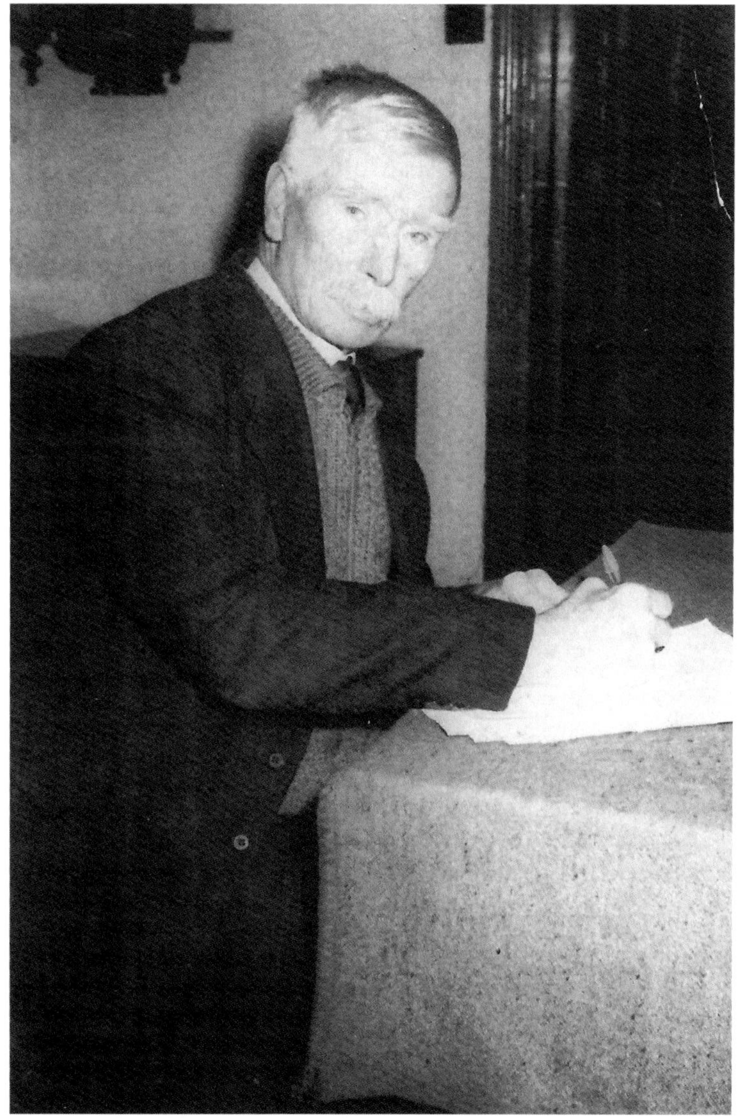

Granda Flynn writing his book of poetry 1963

MUSIC and LANDSCAPE

I have always been struck by how much landscape painting and some forms of music have in common. In Eric Fenby's memoir of **Frederick Delius** there is an account of the blind, paralysed composer dictating to his amanuensis, Fenby, the opening of his orchestral piece *A Song of Summer.....* Delius approaches his task just like any plein-air painter setting up his canvas. *"I want you to imagine"* he tells Fenby, *"that we are sitting on the cliffs in the heather overlooking the sea. The sustained chords in the high strings suggest a clear sky and the stillness and calmness of the scene."* To this he adds a phrase in the cellos and basses *"to suggest the gentle rise and fall of the waves"* and a single figure on solo flute which *"suggests a seagull gliding by."* Delius's love of landscape was no passive affair and until paralysed in late middle age he was a tremendous walker spending many summers in Norway walking in the mountains. His *Song of Summer* is a classic musical seascape similar to others in British music of that period, for example the opening of **Bax's** *Tintagel*, or of **Frank Bridge's** suite *The Sea* (where an oboe replaces Delius's flute). *The Sea* was the first orchestral piece that Benjamin Britten heard as a boy and, in his own words, he was *"knocked sideways by it."* Britten of course went on to produce a series of definitive English seascapes in music. His opera *Peter Grimes* set at Aldeburgh near where he lived for most of his life, evokes all the sullen calm of a grey winter dawn, the sparkling waves on a bright sunny day and the pent-up violence of the storm.

The evocation of landscape in music began properly when the orchestra had developed as an organism sufficiently precise enough to match the richly coloured palette of the Romantic painter. Thus landscape seems to be the province of the full symphony orchestra and landmark pieces such as Beethoven's *Pastoral Symphony* or Mendelssohn's *Fingal's Cave* both date from the period of the great landscape paintings of Constable and Turner. **Gustav Holst**, throughout most of his life, also made long-distance solitary walks in the countryside which gave him an intimate knowledge of its nature. This is evidenced in *Egdon Heath* which he wrote in 1927 and which expresses the essence of that mysterious and savage landscape. It was Thomas Hardy's description of the heath in the first chapter of his Return of the Native which inspired the piece as he wrote....*"It was a place perfectly accordant with man's nature - neither ghastly, hateful, nor ugly' neither commonplace, unmeaning nor tame: but like man, slighted and enduring."*

It is **Vaughan Williams** however who inspires my own late landscapes most, and in pieces such as T*he Lark Ascending*, *Variations on a Theme of Thomas Tallis* or the Third and Fifth symphonies we see a profound solitary communion with nature. The opening of the Fifth for example, might be **the** archetypal landscape in sound. I believe that Vaughan Williams's understanding of the British musical tradition and his love of his native landscape came together at a particular moment during the Second World War when everything he most cherished was under threat of destruction.

Ruskin famously wrote that the artist should *"go to nature in all singleness of heart and walk with her laboriously and trustingly having no other thoughts but how best to penetrate her meaning and remember her instruction."* One thing Ruskin did not want however, was photographic precision in the depiction of nature and, in his own drawings he usually left some part of what he was drawing either undrawn or underdrawn as If to indicate mood or atmospheric effects. It was a lesson lost on many of his followers including some pre-Raphaelites with their obsessive naturalism and who insisted on a leaf-by-leaf or a grass-by-grass empiricism.

I have always been intrigued by what he meant by *"penetrating its meaning."* In many artists this has manifested itself in either the scientific study of nature where the surfaces are pared away to reveal the silent, colourless, textureless, micro-physical world below, or abstract painters like **Ben Nicholson** or **David Blackburn** who seek, whether successfully or not, a distillation of appearances, rather than a quasi-scientific turning away from them altogether. Nicholson works with the colour we see, Blackburn with the line we see, to examine how far it may be abstracted from its original context without losing its meaning altogether. They are not attempting the paradoxical task of showing us the colourless or formless substratum which underlies the colours and forms of that which we, as humans, discern.

But, since Darwin, it is not so easy to see landscape as a coordinated and designed system. There has been a sea-change in landscape painting from Gainsborough and Constable to Paul Nash and Sutherland for example. All show nature as a habitat, however uncomfortable it is and however unfitting towards it we might on occasion feel. It is, in fact, difficult to see the point of landscape painting if such painting did not manifest something of our own affinity with nature, something of nature as our home. It can be argued that there is a failing of sensibility at a deep level; if we cannot rejoice in nature's beauty, harsh and pain-filled as it may be, after so many artists have demonstrated just how profound and multifarious that beauty is. Both Nash and Sutherland, for example are able to find a kind of beauty even in nature's less conventionally beautiful aspects.

Kathleen Paine, the writer on Blake, has said.... *"The work of the artist is not to reproduce what everybody sees, but to heal the soul, to remind us, as it were of our native country - the world of the spirit - and tell us that it is there all the time. Blake says of Wordsworth that what he thinks is in nature is not really in nature at all, it is in the imagination, that is what creates the landscape, not the natural features.. Blake also says that Nature has no outline, but imagination has. Nature has no tune but imagination has. Nature has no supernatural , imagination is eternity."* This is precisely what one finds, particularly in the early work of **Samuel Palmer**, but also in that of **David Jones** and **Stanley Spencer**. While all seem, in projecting an inner landscape, to take a certain amount from the outer landscape, it is the imagination which works the transformation.

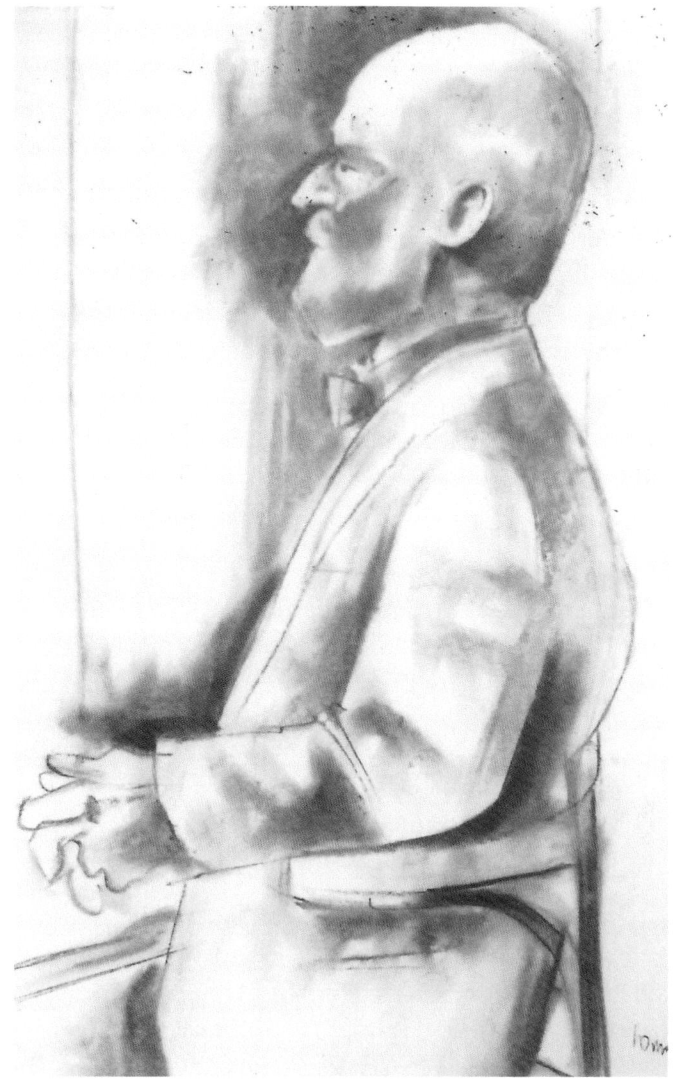

MAN IN PUB (Charcoal)

A typical quick sketch (in about five minutes) often used to make a more substantial painting later

THE “POWER” OF PLACES

I spent a great deal of time in my youth, walking the Northumbrian landscape perhaps looking for new crags to climb on, and being sufficiently intrigued by its geological structure, by its changing moods, by its colours and textures to feel that it could provide enough of a rich source of inspiration on which to base my painting.. But my increasing admiration for **Paul Nash (1889-1946)**. made me aware of what he called his *“special places”*, those areas that appear to be charged with another force above the purely visual. Although empty of human figures, his paintings seem to be, nevertheless, saturated with human presence and meaning. I always felt that my own landscape had something more to offer, something perhaps intangible that, although I felt it, I could not fathom. So in order to discover the key to Nash’s thinking I took a Diploma in Archaeology at Newcastle University after I had retired from full time lecturing as Head of Art in an FE College. Although, in hindsight, this realised experience has done much to heighten my knowledge and perceptions, in a curious way it has deepened the mystery.

In an extraordinary way Nash developed intensely personal relationships with particular places. The first of these was in Kensington Gardens where he played as a child. *“It was beyond the Round Pond going towards the Tea Gardens that I came upon my first authentic* ***place****... It was strangely, beautiful and excitingly unsafe.... Yet whatever happened to me there, throughout my life I was conscious always of the influence of the place....never in any sinister degree, rather with a force, gentle but insistent, charged with sweetness beyond physical experience, the promise of joy utterly unreal.”* The garden of the house at Iver Heath in Buckinghamshire which had been the family home since 1902, was another such place, and, in the summer of 1911, Nash began to explore it with a series of drawings. *“It seemed to respond”*, he wrote, *“in a dramatic way to the influence of light....the place took on a startling beauty, a beauty to my eyes wholly unreal. It was this ‘unreality’ or rather this reality of another aspect of the accepted world, this mystery of clarity that was at once so elusive and so positive,that I now began to pursue.”*

In the following year, Nash first drew Wittenham Clumps, perhaps the most intriguing and memorable of all his special places, the distant vision of which was to hold such a fascination for him in the last years of his life. The Nash family had been staying near Wallingford in Berkshire for shooting holidays each autumn since 1909 and the trees were within walking distance. Nash later wrote that the Clumps was... *“a landmark for miles around. An Ancient-British camp, it stood up with extraordinary prominence above the river at Shillingford. There were two hills, both dome-like and each planted with a thick clump of trees whose mass had a curiously symmetrical sculptured form. At the foot of these hills grew the dense wood of Wittenham, part of the early forest where the polecat still yelled in the night hours. Ever since I remember them the Clumps had meant something to me. I felt their importance before I knew their history. They eclipsed the impression of all the early landscapes I knew.... They were the pyramids of my small world.”*

Nash’s work, for me, is about his sensitivity to the feeling for ancestral echoes in the landscape, for the enduring quality of its outlines through times past, present and future. In 1911 he was to write about *“the grey hollow hills crowned by old trees, Pan-nish places down by the river.... full of strange enchantment.”* One day the following year, he set out to capture the spirit of the Clumps. *“I wanted an image which would express what they meant to me...one aspect which, had I the wit to perceive it, would convey the strange character of the place which, in its form, would contain its individual spirit.”*

The result of his day’s quest was most probably *The Wood on the Hill* (1912) for which he found the perfect viewpoint, allowing himself *“time to think and absorb first before beginning to interpret.”* Nash’s view, in fact, from one hill to the other, is almost reverential in its feeling of distance. The rising path through the corn stooks a field away, conveys the idea of ascent towards a summit, but access is barred by a closed gate at the bottom. Birds wheeling in the sky over the sombre trees add further to the mysterious attraction of the place; it demands to be approached but there is a hint of menace. Already the simple drawing suggests things behind and beyond its primary subject.

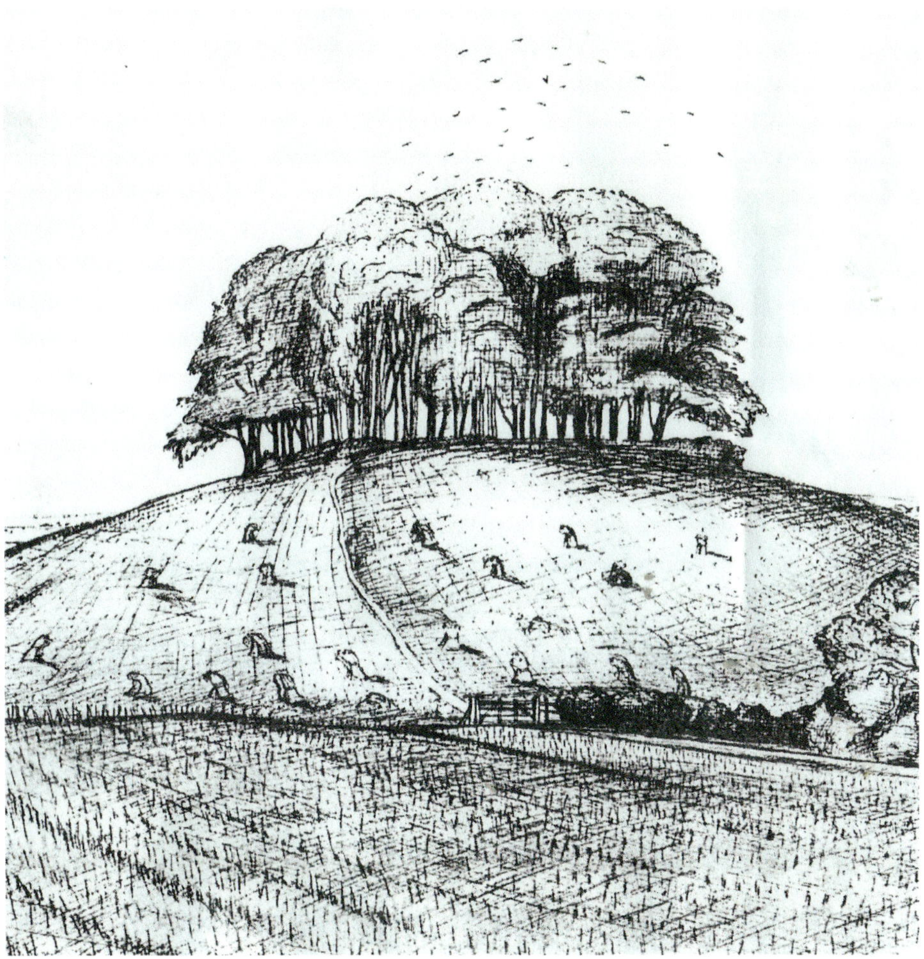

The Clumps appear again in two of the greatest paintings ever to be produced in this country - *Landscape of the Summer Solstice* (1943) and *Landscape of the Vernal Equinox* (1944) - and the last pictures he made before his death aged only 57. Roger Cardinal in his scholarly book *The Landscape Vision of Paul Nash* (Reaktion Books 1989) writes

... *"Nash's places are not mere locations, and would never have become his were he not somehow always making sure that he was himself present in them and through them. His landscape vision is a dialogue, a structured relationship, a creative mirroring: his exploration of the character of the* ***genius loci*** *is of a piece with his pursuit of insights into his own motives and yearnings. Nash's work teaches us that the witnessing self cannot but be a constitutive part of what is meant by the 'sense of place'... It is in this spirit that I have suggested that*

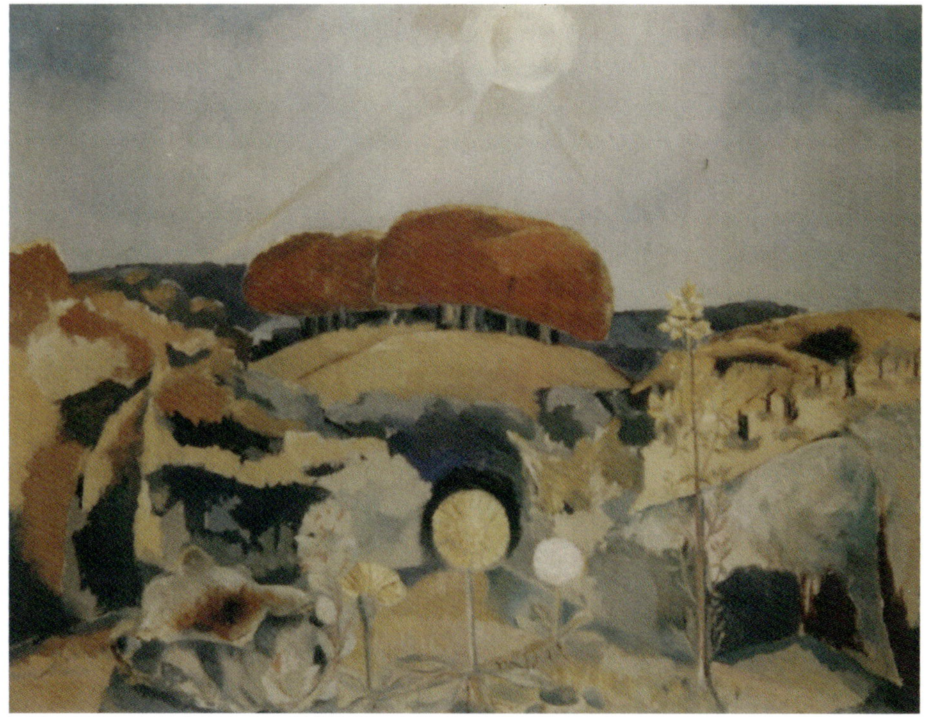

INSPIRED BY ARCHAEOLOGY

Two of **Paul Nash's** works mentioned in the text. Above (in colour) is his *Landscape of the Summer Solstice* (1943) and (left) the drawing *Wood of the Hill* of 1912, both of which refer to the Wittenham Clumps.

Nash's emptiest landscapes vibrate with implicit personality, that the scene is inseparable from the se-er. And we, for our part, whether as witnesses to Nash's pictures or to the actual places he loved, or indeed to any other pictures and places in the world, may similarly come to understand that we can only really grasp what is illuminated by our personal angle of vision."

In my own extremely humble way, I believe that I know of such landscapes in my own county of Northumberland which I have explored thoroughly over the years - from the so-called "Wild Hills of Wanney" to the area above Corby Crags on the Alnwick/Rothbury road and, primarily to Ros Castle and the marvellous Neolithic/Bronze Age landscape of Bewick Hill. I can only hope that my paintings, collographs and drawings echo even just a fraction of what Nash must have experienced and achieved.

ARCHAEOLOGY - ECHOES OF SURVIVAL

Archaeology is a science and, in my limited experience, many archaeologists seem to have little time for the conjectural analysis of lay persons or artists. Although it is changing and new approaches are being adopted I have, in my time, experienced some hostility from those who seems not to be able to approach their research in a really open minded way. In one project I have expressed a concern that a great many artefacts, often grave-goods and thus associated with ritual and possibly imbued with great meaning, are finding their way into museum showcases away from their original context. In extreme cases there have been what I consider to be, acts of desecration and vandalism.

In most good museums, those with a sense of responsibility, the flint arrowheads, shards of beaker pottery, or fragments of metal tools, might serve to educate the public about the history and customs of our ancestors. But how much better to experience these relics in situ and to leave the majority of them where they were once, perhaps lovingly, placed, rather than to store those who don't make it to the glass cases, in cardboard boxes in dusty back rooms.

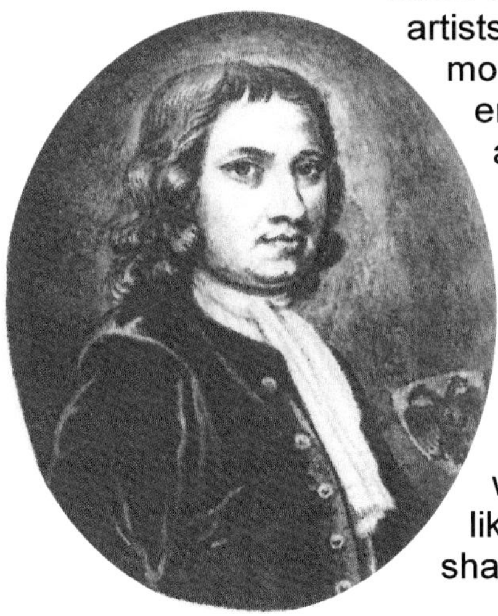

There have been, however, many antiquarian artists who specialised in depicting megalithic monuments through drawings and engravings before photography had advanced to the highly technical process it is today. These are often soul-less interpretations, often wildly inaccurate and possibly nothing to do with "art". Yet the work of **William Stuckley (1687-1765)** should not be associated with such criticism. Although his genius has never been justly acknowledged it was a particularly English genius and, like William Cobbett, a century later, he shared a gift for discerning layers of history behind the contemporary appearance of the countryside. The first book of his tours *Itinerarium Curiosum* published in 1725, was a fine folio volume wonderfully illustrated with his engraved drawings. As mere records of ancient monuments these have never been surpassed, and they show the ancient sites in relation to their local countryside, providing glimpses of old England before the great changes which were wrought by the enclosures of its commons. His topographical eye was later to perceive sacred symbols laid out over large areas of landscape by the ancient Druids even though, throughout his earlier career, he had no particular notion of Druids, and his drawings were made direct from nature, unconditioned by his own or other people's theories. His notes too were factual records of such monuments as came to his notice. Later in life he was to become a clergyman and his whole life became a kind of mission, evidently some kind of born-again conversion which altered the direction of his career. Although many of his contemporaries referred to this as 'fanciful' the mystical feeling for landscape declared itself even in his detailed plans and drawings. On his antiquarian tours he took no books and consulted no authorities, preferring to draw his own conclusions from ancient sites as he found them. There were indeed very few relevant books available in his time and none at all with the number or quality of the illustrations which he included in his own.

Few, if any, of his contemporaries approached megalithic illustration with the same kind of insight and outstanding examples are fairly rare. The Scottish painter **William Nesfield** however, made a painting in 1828 of the *Circle of Stones at Tormore, Isle of Arran* in which the haunted atmosphere of the old stones is enhanced by weird light from a thundery sky - something which other artists had "noticed" at megalithic sites. Here I am thinking of both **J.M.W.Turner's (1775-1851)** and **John Constable's (1776-1837)** 1836 rendering of Stonehenge, and later that of **J.W. Inchbold** (1869) of the same subject. Even **Thomas Girtin's (1775-1802)** watercolour of 1794 has shown the stones under storm clouds and lightning. Most awesome of all

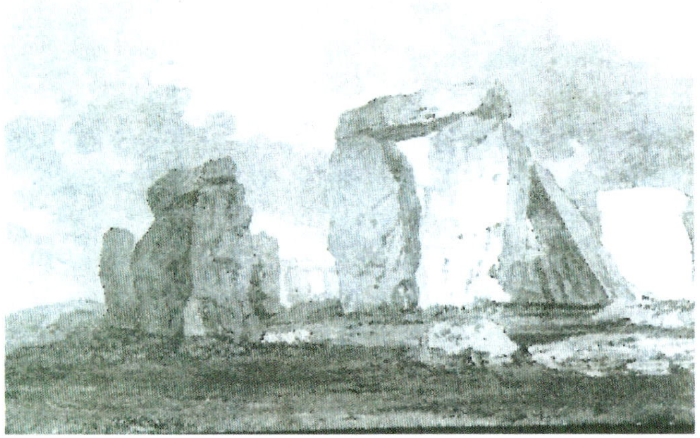

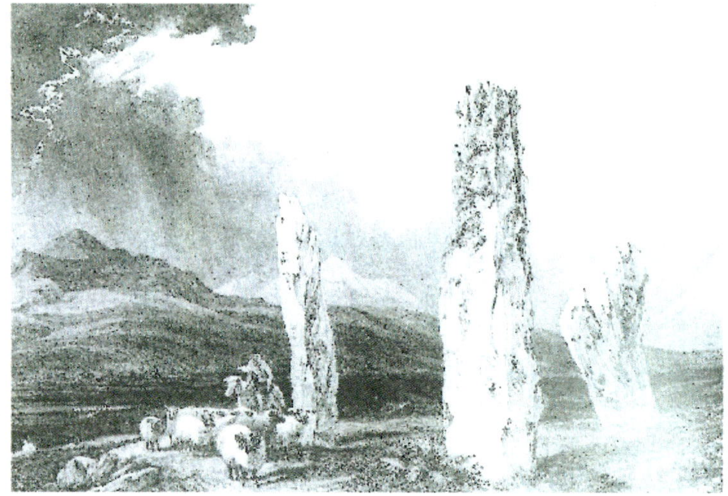

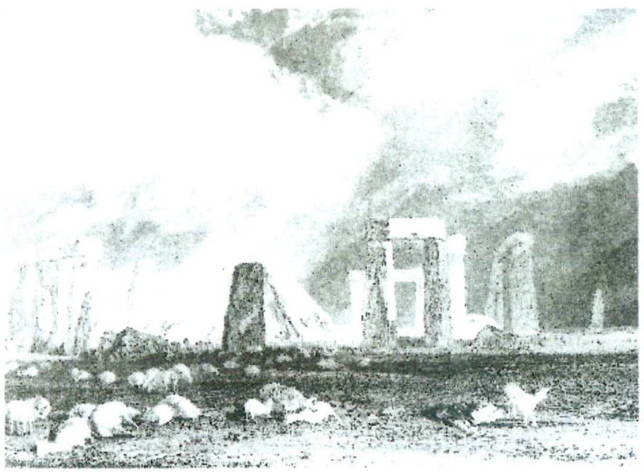

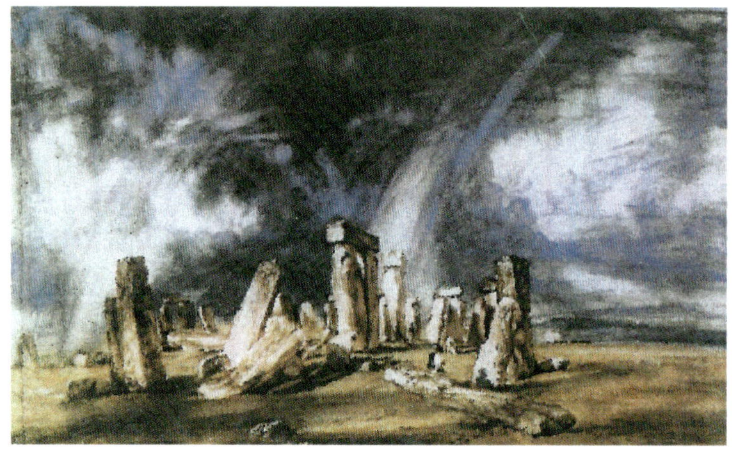

INSPIRED BY ARCHAEOLOGY

As mentioned in the text, Thomas Girtin's watercolour of *Stonehenge with Stormy Sky* (top) painted in 1794, and (bottom) J.M.W. Turner's dramatic view of *Stonehenge* in an engraving after his watercolour of 1828 in which a shepherd and most of his flock seem to have been struck by the violence of an electric storm.

The Scottish painter **William Nestfield's** *Circle of Stones at Todmore, Isle of Arran* (circa 1828) in which the haunted atmosphere of the old stones is enchanted by the weird light from a thundery sky, a phenomenon constantly referred to by artists at megalithic sites. **John Constable's** atmospheric view of Stonehenge with double rainbow of 1836 (bottom)

megalithic images however are those created by **Caspar David Friedrich (1774-1840)** whose *Dolmen or Giant's Grave in the Snow* (1807) captured the intense, otherworldly atmosphere surrounding the ancient sites in the north of Germany. Here the solid permanence of the stones, venerable sanctuaries in the days of the Nordic sagas, contrasts with the shivering transience of their surrounding trees and landscape. There are many of Friedrich's paintings which achieve the same quality especially his forest scenes such as *The Chasseur in the Woods* (1813), *The Cross in the Mountains* (1812) or *Rocky Ravine* (1822).

The first of the modern painters of ancient sites such as **John Piper (1903-92)** who, in making many works of Welsh dolmens, disputed the exclusive rights of archaeologists to interpret megalithic monuments. In 1949 he drew and took photographs at Stonehenge and wrote an excellent article about it in the *Architectural Review* (vol 106), at a time when the reign of the anti-Druid professors was at its height. Piper found that the writer of the official guidebook had devoted most of his space to denunciations of 'wild and unfounded' theories about Druids, human sacrifice and so on, and this inadequate account, as unworthy of the public's interest as of the site itself, moved Piper to make articulate protest. He recalled how Stuckley had *"tumbled over himself with imaginative and delightful assertions"* or of how John Aubrey before him was thrilled, during his lonely rides across the plain, by the strong exhalations of humanity and worship that came from both Stonehenge and Avebury. *"Today"* said Piper, *"if we refer to the sacred atmosphere round the old stones or speculate about the people who raised them - then we are drunk and disorderly."* Yet many of the painters, and most of the best ones, who have worked at Stonehenge have been inspired to depict an aspect of the site which the professors have almost entirely ignored, and which Piper emphasised in his article. The common reference in many of these artists' work is to the magical or elemental quality of Stonehenge in its peculiar landscape and most of them have indicated their individual perceptions of this quality by framing their Stonehenge views in tempestuous clouds, rainbows or lightning flashes.

Critics of this theory might suggest that, when he began work on his Stonehenge watercolour (qv), Constable was in a state of depression, stricken by the recent death of his wife and by financial and other set backs. But this is not true of his contemporary Turner who painted two highly atmospheric views of the stones at sunrise and sunset, followed by his extraordinary scene of an elemental upheaval around Stonehenge, so violent that the shepherd in the foreground together with most of his flock, seems to have been struck dead by the fury of it.

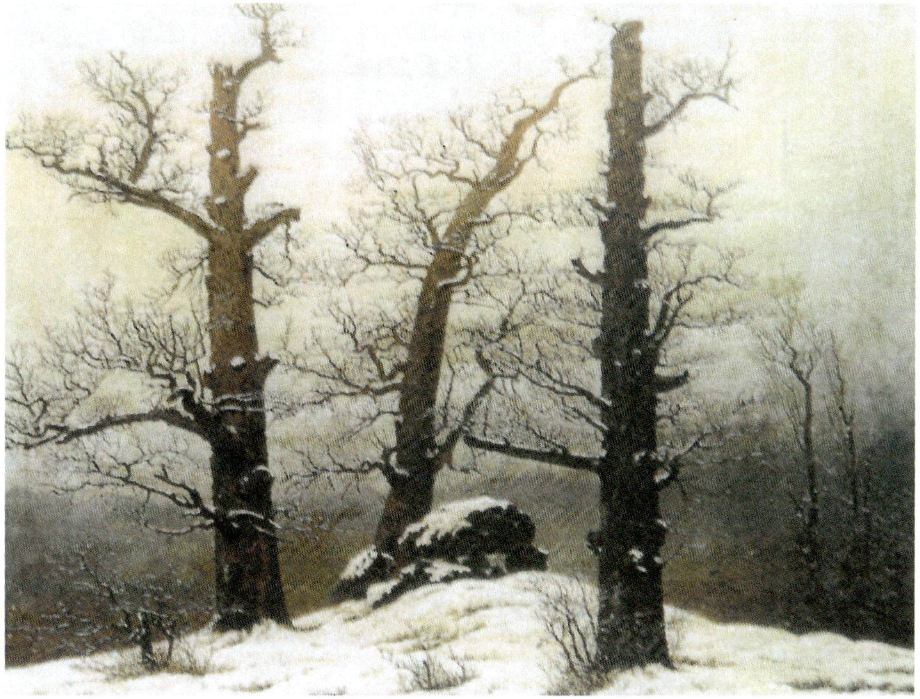

INSPIRED BY ARCHAEOLOGY

The oil painting *Dolmen in the snow* by the German **Caspar David Friedrich** in 1807 painted on one of his many excursions to prehistoric burial sites

In this context, I have also wondered about the work of the French Realist painter **Jean François Millet (1814-75)** who, lacking the advanced social attitudes of his contemporaries, is unquestionably sympathetic to the strivings of the peasants he knew and loved and who he depicted in a dignified, even noble manner. In paintings such as *The Gleaners* (1848) or *Man with the Hoe* (1862) he has imbued them with a monumentality which may have been inspired by ideas of standing stones being people who had been turned to stone for some misdemeanour or other, such as for working in the fields on the Sabbath.

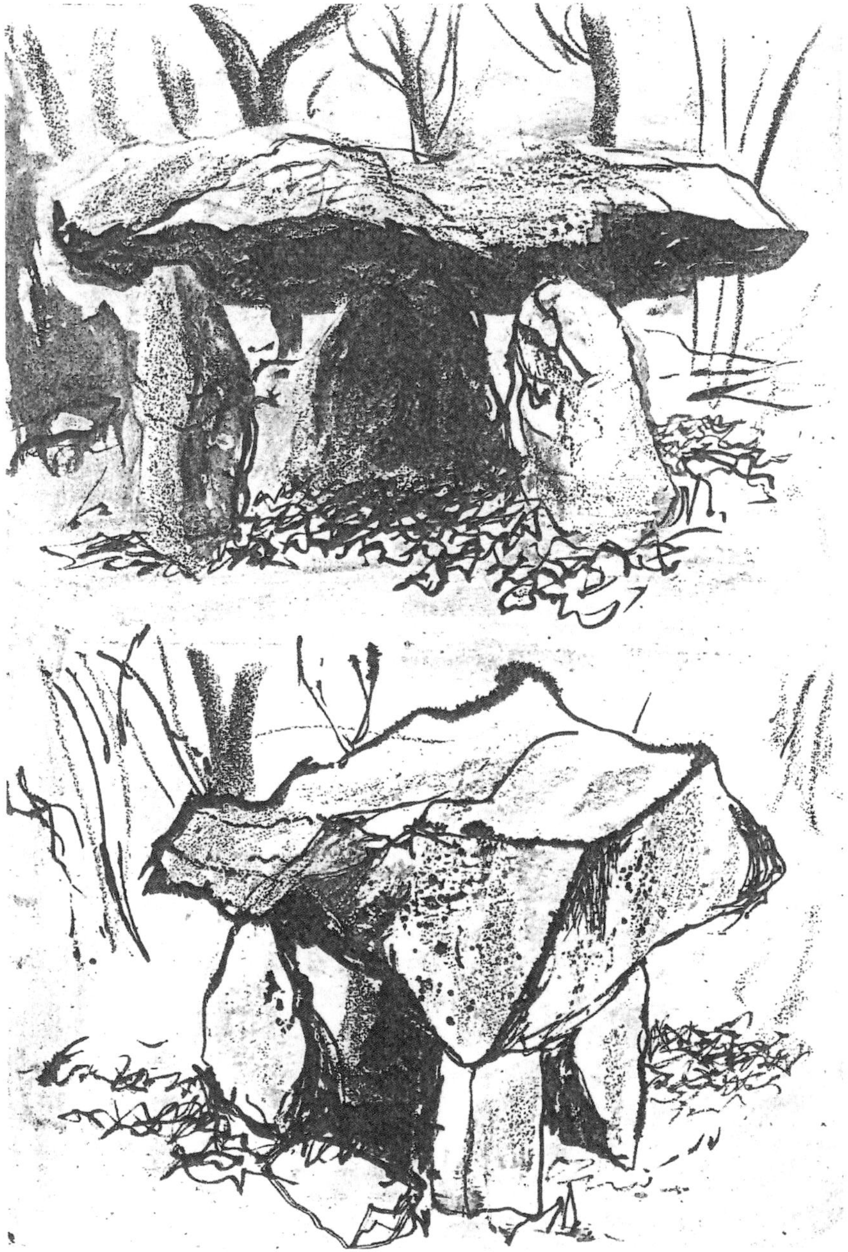

INSPIRED BY ARCHAEOLOGY

Sketches of a *Welsh Dolmen near Login, Pembrokeshire,* made in the 1970s, by **John Piper**, one of the first of the modern painters of ancient sites.

MY OWN WORK and INFLUENCES

There was a time, up to the early 1970s I suppose, when the legacy of the Euston Road School and the teaching of Coldstream and others was still being felt in Art Schools. Of course many people were critical of its worship of Post Impressionism and especially the obsession with Cezanne, but there was a creative freedom implicit within the discipline which meant that students learned from carefully gained skills and attitudes, where anti-aesthetic frippery and, dare I say, plagiarism were frowned upon, and by the students as well as by the staff. I don't wish to debate here where it went wrong, if indeed one believes that it did go wrong, but there certainly was a great sea-change in the 1980s and 1990s leading up to the get-rich-quick age of the YBA's. Blame the *"Basic Course"* of Thubron and Pasmore if you will, the coming of computers which allowed labour saving short cuts, or just, what many feel, that art as we knew it, had run its course.

I was lucky enough to be trained in an ethos of finding figurative solutions to problems, basically through drawing and my first and major task, as I have mentioned, was to shake free of the shackles of tight, almost mechanical draughtsmanship, the legacy of my architectural background. I slowly came to realise that those artists who had a real empathy with their subject, and within that were prepared to try new ideas and solutions, were more likely to create compelling images. The inspiration and physical satisfaction which came with the discovery of "landscape" coupled with the excitement of experimenting with new mediums and methods was something I came to know.

It was still very common in my day, to see students keeping sketch/notebooks and drawing out of doors in all sorts of odd places - in back streets, markets, allotments with pigeon lofts, railway sidings and pit yards, and making vigorous, if sometimes naive statements - what today's jargon refers to as "a learning-curve." Learning by looking, recognising mistakes and re-considering them, all the time pushing oneself and aiming high. Who are today's heroes I wonder? I could still list mine if pressed. In fact I once compiled a list in order to do an art lecture based on the Desert Island Discs radio programme and found that there were too many to make a short list, even when the criteria were limited to honesty and integrity.

Not only has art changed but so has the range of materials now available - an explosion caused by the rise of amateur painters and their attendant television programmes, clubs, courses and magazines. I'm not criticising this for there is an earnestness about most of these people which I admire. I have in fact worked in a number of locations in England and Scotland teaching summer schools or workshops, and have gained much from them. I feel that it is one of the great satisfactions of teaching art - that we learn so much from our students.

When I was a student myself, my preferred medium was gouache, largely because of its low cost and availability. I remember how we used to buy pots of cheap poster colours, one step up from powder paint!, usually vermillion, ultramarine or prussian-blue and yellow ochre, and share a large tin of emulsion paint. This resulted in a fairly limited colour range (it was the north-east after all) and led to a rather chalky appearance, but expressionism through impasto paint were seldom necessary because the strong drawing held it all together and meant that you could use fairly fluid techniques. Paper was usually cheap white cartridge which was, at that time, not acid-free, resulting in "foxing", brown spots which appeared months after the work was completed. One could get over this by using coloured sugar paper, although it tended to grow brittle with age, or by glueing several sheets of newsprint or wrapping paper together to give a more robust support. Brushes were the best that we could afford on our meagre grants although fortunately a kind of nylon/hair mix became available around that time which meant that one didn't have to splash out on Kolinsky sable or other extravagant hairs.

These mediums and attendant techniques served until the kind of work I felt disposed to do in order to illustrate a particular theme dictated otherwise. For example, a specific exploration of clouds and skies, began one wet day when we were rained-off climbing in the Wanneys and, while sheltering under a boulder, I began to observe the sky more closely. Later, at home, I came across a poem *"Drifting"* by **Margaret Gillies** (qv) which perfectly matched the atmosphere I wished to evoke, and I found a piece of music in which the voices echoed sounds rather than using words in the conventional sense. It was Irish, (a folk group called Clannad) which would have pleased grandpa Flynn. The medium also had to compliment the feeling so it had to be watercolour, something which I hadn't seriously attempted before although I admired the great watercolourists such as **Cotman, Girtin, Cox**, or the Scot **Arthur Melville**. The project therefore, wasn't completed without a great number of small studies and false starts, a process which I began to use a great deal.

Another "project" was built around a poem, *"Moors Threnody"* by **Vernon Scannell** (qv) in which he describes a landscape which was not unlike the Wanneys. I made these works in impasto oils and described the crags and moors of the area in which, as Scanned writes - *"no living creature moves, only the sky's slow turbulence,"* and this, i suppose, was the starting point for my landscape period. But the biggest (and ongoing) series of paintings and drawings was more concerned with *"echoes in the landscape"*and the reason I got interested in archaeology in the first place. I wanted the works to question not only the visual appearance of my places and their resonances, but to hint at **who** had lived there in prehistory, and **how** they lived, worshipped, hunted, farmed, made art and music. I also found that the medium of pastel was flexible enough to allow me to work quickly in order to establish my ideas without having to wait days for the paint to dry. We are fortunate in Northumberland to have, almost hidden away in the wilds, a cottage industry - Unison pastels - who make the widest selection of tones and hues you could imagine. Colour of course , is hugely important and I began to be influenced by the great 'colourists', the greatest of whom I believe was **Paul Gaugin (1848-1903)** especially in his later period in Atuana in the Marquesas Islands where he died. **Ivon Hitchens' (1893-1979)** paintings of the river and woods at his retreat, *Greenleaves* near Trewick Mill are another inspiration. The way he managed to capture only the essential mood and colour harmonies of the place with a complete lack of concern for topographical accuracy, provide, for me, a constant stimulus. In an art world whose taste is governed by people like Tracy Emin and Damien Hirst, it is refreshing to find unsung artists of real calibre and integrity. A few living artists who I admire for diverse reasons are **David Tress, Len Tabner, David Blackburn, David Prentice, Michael Porter**, and the Scots **Barbara Rae, Duncan Shanks, Frances Walker** and **Victoria Crowe**.

DRAWINGS

One can easily become so engrossed in "subject" that sometimes one loses track of arguably the most important aspect of one's art - that of drawing. Drawing has traditionally been associated with spontaneity but it is also the means by which an artist can rediscover the structure of a composition and I can't help thinking about the dictum of one of the greatest of English artists **David Bomberg (1880-1957)** about striving to capture the *"spirit in the mass."* Sometimes the activity in the drawings is not so much to do with collecting information as with moving it on, translating it. Sometimes lines come and go, are stated, removed, then re-stated. At times one has to be ruthless, not to flinch at destroying and re-drawing. Sometimes extra sheets of paper are added as part of the process as the drawing grows, and sometimes sections of paper may be patched in as the image continues to evolve.

In my large drawings I prefer to use charcoal rather than graphite or ink because I find it makes for stronger tonal contrast - both black and white are more intense - yet at the same time there is a softer bluer quality to the blacks. The logistics of working large out of doors tend to be trickier than using a sketchbook. Carrying the materials, the board and the paper can be problematic, as can the weather. Some artists can work in the wet but I can't, not with charcoal anyway. I like to kneel in the heather with the board flat, paper held down with rocks. Some find charcoal too thick or too clumsy but it's not. It can be shaped with a scalpel or thin shards snapped off to provide fine lines. If I need colour then I'll use the surrounding earth or berries, grasses etc. It's surprising how many variations one can find on the moors. I once conducted an experiment with my Ford Castle summer school students, when I wouldn't allow them to use manufactured colours and we found a surprisingly wide range when we really began to look - an ironstone-stained stream near Berwick, some sulphur oozing from a fissure at Cocklawburn beach, to some old, dead tree bark. Other tints came from mushrooms, bilberries and blackberries, various mosses and ferns - it seemed unlimited.

As impecunious students we experimented with various ways of making marks by using reeds, grasses, bits of sharpened stick, twigs, sponges and the like. To hell with sophistication, set against this charcoal feels like a refinement!!!

I can't work from photographs and in any case, one misses the point of drawing, that it is an engagement with the subject itself. I keep sketchbooks of course, lots of them, and I refer to them all the time. They're not full of pretty little drawings, but, like diaries or notebooks, they're reminders to myself about what I saw, felt, experienced. I am reminded of the process used by one of the most gifted artists ever to grace Scotland, **Joan Eardley (1921-63)**, who, having discovered Catterline on the north-east coast near Stonehaven, moved there to live and work. Her first impression was of the weather and she worked outside making charcoal and chalk drawings capturing the effects of rain and storm. In the extraordinary pages of her sketchbooks are to be found, arguably, the greatest concentrated group of landscape drawings done in Scotland since the War. From near-abstract seascapes to views of the windswept shore, her drawings conjure up the same animation of the forces of nature that the great **William McTaggart (1835- 1910)** had found in his pencil drawings of Macrahanish the previous century. The sketchbooks of **John Piper (1903-92)** (qv) too, echo his response to the landscape of Snowdonia, North Wales to where he had moved in 1944 to recover from the trauma of the bombing of his beloved Bath and Coventry. Although he had known the place as a child he was not prepared for the ruggedness, or for the heroic scale of the landscape. As an artist he could draw it, paint it and study it, but as a man he felt both dwarfed and humbled by the towering peaks and ridges. His sketchbooks and resultant drawings evoke some of the fear that this landscape induced and seem to suggest a man powerless in an alien place. They feature the black Welsh hills and valleys, shafted with light and shadows and are made in a range of media such as pen and ink, watercolour and gouache which he combined with pastel, using candle wax or crayons to create resists.

Indeed, it is difficult to see where sketchbook and "finished" drawings begin and end. What fascinates me as much are his detailed notebook/sketch- book entries which capture his thoughts and add to the rich store of knowledge. He seemed to have enjoyed rough weather almost as much as Turner had done. In an entry inspired by the summit of the Glyders, for example, he noted.... *"mist blowing across all day; visibility about 15-20 yards only. Curious sensation in the presence of gigantic boulders, coffin-shaped slabs, pale trunk-shaped rocks, disappearing into grey invisibility even at close range. Yet the affectionate nature of the mountain is not changed by the acute loneliness and closed-in feeling induced by the mist; rather the atmosphere of an affectionate cemetery"*

Although sketchbooks are private and precious things they tell us more about an artist than finished and framed work on the wall of a gallery can ever hope to do. Indeed no gallery would attempt or perhaps even know how to explain what an artist has witnessed or experienced in the making of the work. I remember how incensed **Will McLean** the Scottish painter was in response to some American who wanted to buy his sketchbooks. And I echo his sentiments by saying that mine are also my legacy to my children and grandchildren.

JOAN EARDLEY

Black Sky with Sun breaking through to Blue Sea

One of the many drawings Eardley made as a response to the wild north-east coast of Scotland at Catterline in the late 1950s. They capture the elemental, almost spiritual, nature of the weather rather than responding to the mere physical or geological properties of the landscape.

ROCK and RITUAL

Man, with his symbol-making propensities, often endowed objects with great psychological significance and expressed them in both his religion and in his visual art.

This is particularly true of stone, and we suspect that even unhewn stones must have had a highly symbolic meaning for primitive societies. Rough, natural stones for example, were often believed to be the dwelling places of spirits or gods, and their use in burials as markers or objects of religious veneration makes them a potent, if primitive, kind of sculpture. This may well have been man's first attempt to invest stone with more expressive power than chance or nature could give it.

In many early stone sanctuaries, the deity is represented, not by a single stone or menhir, but by a great many unhewn stones often arranged in distinct patterns. This can be seen in the geometrical stone alignments in Brittany or the stone circles of Stonehenge. Arrangements of natural, rough stones as expressions of spirituality also occur in the rock gardens of Zen Buddhism while the holiest sanctuary in the Islamic world is the **Ka'aba**, the black stone in Mecca, to which all pious Moslems hope to make their pilgrimage. Christian examples also occur in *1 Corinthians x:4*, where Christ was called the *"spiritual rock from which the water of life springs."* And in *Genesis 35*, Jacob's revelation caused him to set up a stone which he anointed and called **Beth-el**.

Medieval alchemists who searched for the secret of matter, hoping to find evidence of a divine activity, believed that the secret was embodied in their famous *"philosophers stone."* This alchemical stone, **the Lapis**, symbolised something that could never be lost nor dissolved, something external that has been compared to the mystical experience of God within one's own soul.

Whether the great menhirs or stone circles of pre-history represented sites of religious ritual, warrior tombs, astronomical laboratories, or petrified human forms (as in the case of Northumberland's Duddo Stones) there is no doubting their sheer visual presence. Despite this, many poets have remarked upon the striking contrast between the solid physical appearance of megalithic monuments and their silence about their own meaning. And Dr Johnson, who said in 1773, after visiting a stone circle near Inverness, *"to go and see one Druidical temple is only to see that it is nothing, for there is neither art nor power in it, and seeing one is quite enough"* was being both historically incorrect (the Druids came long after these stone monuments were set up) as well as absurdly dogmatic. There is indeed, a history of artists and poets for whom the fascination with stone has resulted in whole bodies of work, ranging from William Stuckley in the 18th century, through **William Blake, Henry O'Neill, Richard Tongue, John Constable, John Inchbold, Paul Nash, Caspar David Friedrich, Samuel Palmer, Paul Devereux, John Piper**, and many others, while poets range from Wordswoth to Ted Hughes.

ROCK ART

Many natural rock formations and megalithic stones in Northumberland, as well as in Scotland and Ireland, Durham, Cumbria, Yorkshire, Europe, Malta, the Sahara and even California, are inscribed with "cup and ring" and other abstract symbols whose meaning has, so far, defied interpretation. Despite this, many archaeologists and others, have called the marks **rock art** as if there is some definitive proof that they were made as "art". Alas, there is none and I have railed for years at this rather trite and over-convenient nomenclature The archaeologist, poet and historian, Stan Beckensall, whose integrity and knowledge of this phenomenon I greatly respect, has agreed on their "religious" significance however, and puts their date as late Neolithic or Bronze Age (about 2000/3000 BC) He also believes in the importance of a *"power of place"* in their siting within the landscape. As will be seen, these sites, especially our Northumbrian ones, feature strongly in my work.

By 4000BC Neolithic societies were organised into strong communities with powerful leaders to plan and direct communal projects, and it is probable that these societies became stratified , perhaps with priests or Shamen as well as chiefs and craftsmen. So the rituals of summer and winter became more formalised. Within this we can imagine that they necessitated the laying out of accurate alignments, possibly to mark the times of important gatherings. Not every orientation was astronomical so that entrances faced the direction of the rising or setting of the sun or moon. The Milfield henges near Duddo, had their entrances arranged so that they offered differing views of the horizon sometimes towards a prominent hill, while others had tall outlying stones. It is worth considering that, if prehistoric astronomy did exist, what was it used for? Were there astronomer/priests, scientifically studying the heavens, or were the alignments for other purposes, for the dead, or for the Spirits of the other world?

Current thinking seems to suggest that stone circles are lunar based, but the moon is complex. Its risings and settings move swiftly from one extreme to the other within a fortnight, waxing and waning from full moon to crescent to invisibility when it is "new".

The retired professor of Engineering **Alexander Thom** whose book *Megalithic Sites in Britain* (1967) caused the greatest disturbance to established patterns of archaeological thought, has suggested that prehistoric people divided the year into 16 equal periods which might be a slight over-refinement of a simpler calendar. In Thom's chart, 8 of the declinations correspond very closely to those of Iron Age feast days 3,000 years later. Still later, Christianity adopted and adapted these when the Church was struggling to overcome heathen customs. It is also interesting to see how many alignments in the early stone circles correspond to the times of the Celtic festivals of **Beltane, Lughansa, Samain** and **Imbolc**. Unfortunately, despite my own fascination with it, little is known of Duddo despite its impressive setting with the Eildon Hills to the NNW and Yeavering to the SSE. Neither has the suggestion of an outer circle or outliers, although suspected, been corroborated although there is a central pit. An unusual feature is that the stones in the Duddo circle, which is sited on a knoll above the river Tweed, do not stand circumferentially as is customary, but are at eccentric angles to the perimeter of the ring. The name Duddo, which in 1208, according to Ekwall, was *Dudehou* the Old English for **Dudda's Hoh** (a projecting ridge or by a hill).

Another favourite site, and the subject of much of my work, is **Roughting Linn** (NT 983376) like a huge whaleback of sand-stone covered with varied motifs from large concentric circles around cups to other rather delicate flower-like designs, inverted U-shapes and a unique 'radiate'. Perhaps because of its proximity to the road it may have been in danger of being quarried away at one time and, indeed, large chunks are missing. A later Iron Age promontory enclosure stands nearby above a valley and a waterfall. The name Roughting means *'bellowing like a bull'*, while Linn is a pond. Further up the escarpment is **Goatscrag Hill** which lies on a track over Broomridge to Ford Moss where there are remains of an old colliery village, the area having been mined for coal since Elizabethan times. There are quite a few low-profile boulders on Broomridge which contain a series of "cup and ring" markings while Goatscrag itself has revealed signs of prehistoric burials and flint tools under the overhanging rock, and there are animal carvings of an unknown date, on the vertical face of the crag. The area has been extensively excavated and recorded (see *Arch. Ael.* Vol 4) and more recently by Stan Beckensall (see *Prehistoric Rock Motifs of Northumberland* and other books).

ALEXANDER THOM'S MEGALITHIC MONTHS

			AZIMUTHS		FESTIVALS	
Epoch	*"month"*	*declination*	*sunrise*	*sunset*	*prehistoric*	*Christian*
2	8 May	+16.6	60	300	Beltane	Whitsun?
4	21 June	+23.9	45	315	Midsummer Solstice	
6	9 August	+16.7	60	300	Lughansa	Lammas Harvest Festival
8	23 September	+0.4	90	270	Autumn Equinox	
10	6 November	-16.3	119	241	Samain	All Souls All Saints Martinmas
12	21 December	-23.9	135	225	Midwinter Solstice	Christmas
14	5 February	-16.2	119	241	Imbolc	St Brigid Candlemas
16	23 March	+0.4	90	270	Vernal Equinox	

PAGES TORN FROM THE BOOK OF LIFE....

Genre painting, or that which depicted the lives of ordinary people, rightly began as an independent subject in 17th century Holland. It was broadly-based, sometimes moralistic and at other times, satirical, and practised by such masters as **Vermeer, Hals** and **Jan Steen** as well as **Breughel** and **Brouwer** in the Netherlands, **Velazquez** and **Goya** in Spain and **Hogarth** and **Luke Fildes** in England. In France the great Genre painters were, first **Chardin** and **Daumier**, then the movement of Realism under **Courbet** and the Barbizon painters such as **Millet, Bastien Lepage, Rousseau** and others. Later, I was to discover the work of the Camden Town painters under **Sickert** and the 1960s Kitchen Sink paintings of **Bratby** and **Middleditch.**

While our new art school was being prepared we were "farmed out" to the upper floor of a local school and an early project concerned the relationship between the shapes of children and various linear structures such as swings, cloak-room furniture, hop-scotch patterns and the like. Interestingly, these were the paintings which L.S. Lowry admired on a visit to our exhibition and he told me that I'd "go far". Well, I did eventually move from Newbiggin to Jesmond!!!

As a young man from an essentially working-class background I was gradually drawn towards a kind of social realism but, lacking any strong political or spiritual voice, my work was more observational and nostalgic. And by the time that Thatcher had decimated north-eastern communities, I felt that, to paint the lives of the 'working man', was a little patronising, although one or two pieces depicting derelict pit heads and ship yards, sea-coal gatherers, local football, pub interiors and the like, occupied my attention. I was aware of criticisms, from my father mostly, that I was being hypocritical and, as an outsider so to speak, my work lacked a certain "truth". Coming into contact with a few of the Ashington Pitmen Painters made me realise that my approach was, by comparison, rather shallow and ingenuous and, in any case, I had by then, discovered the landscape.

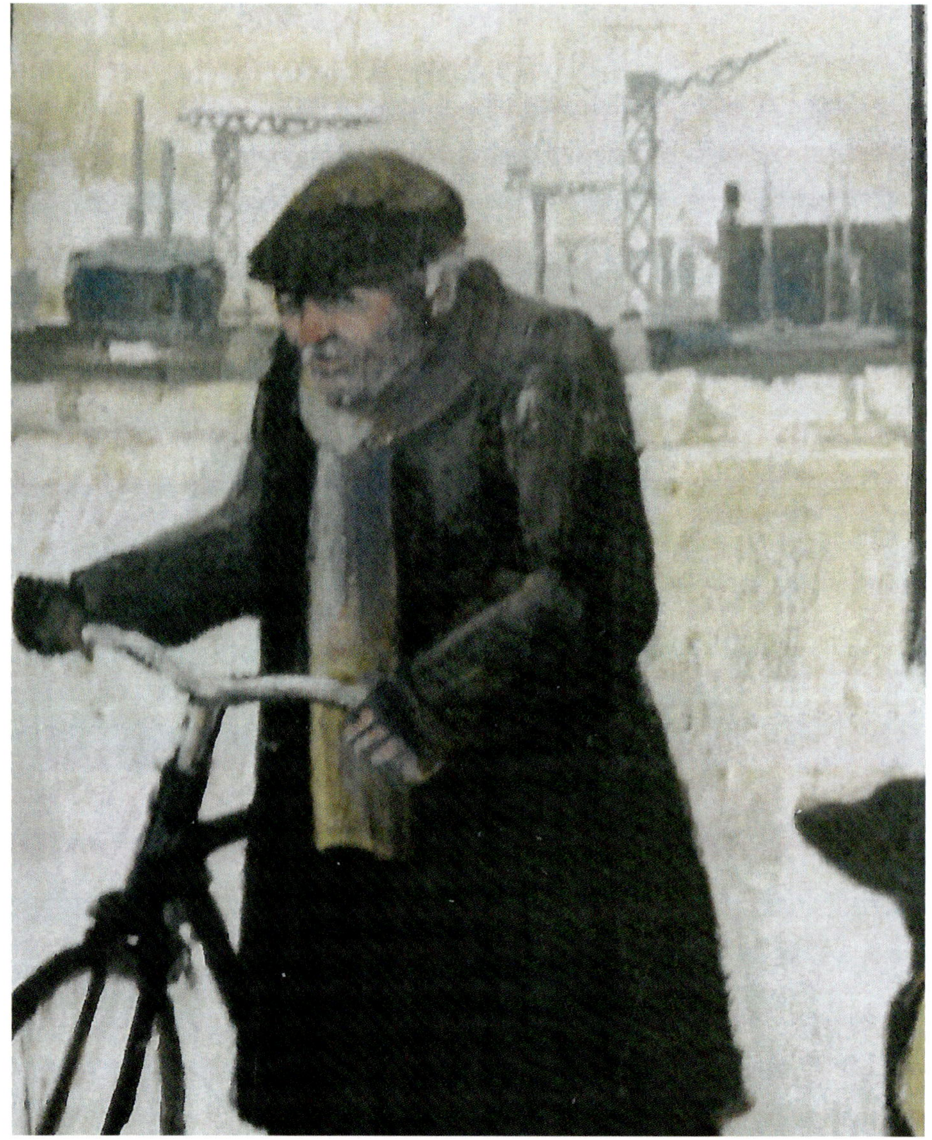

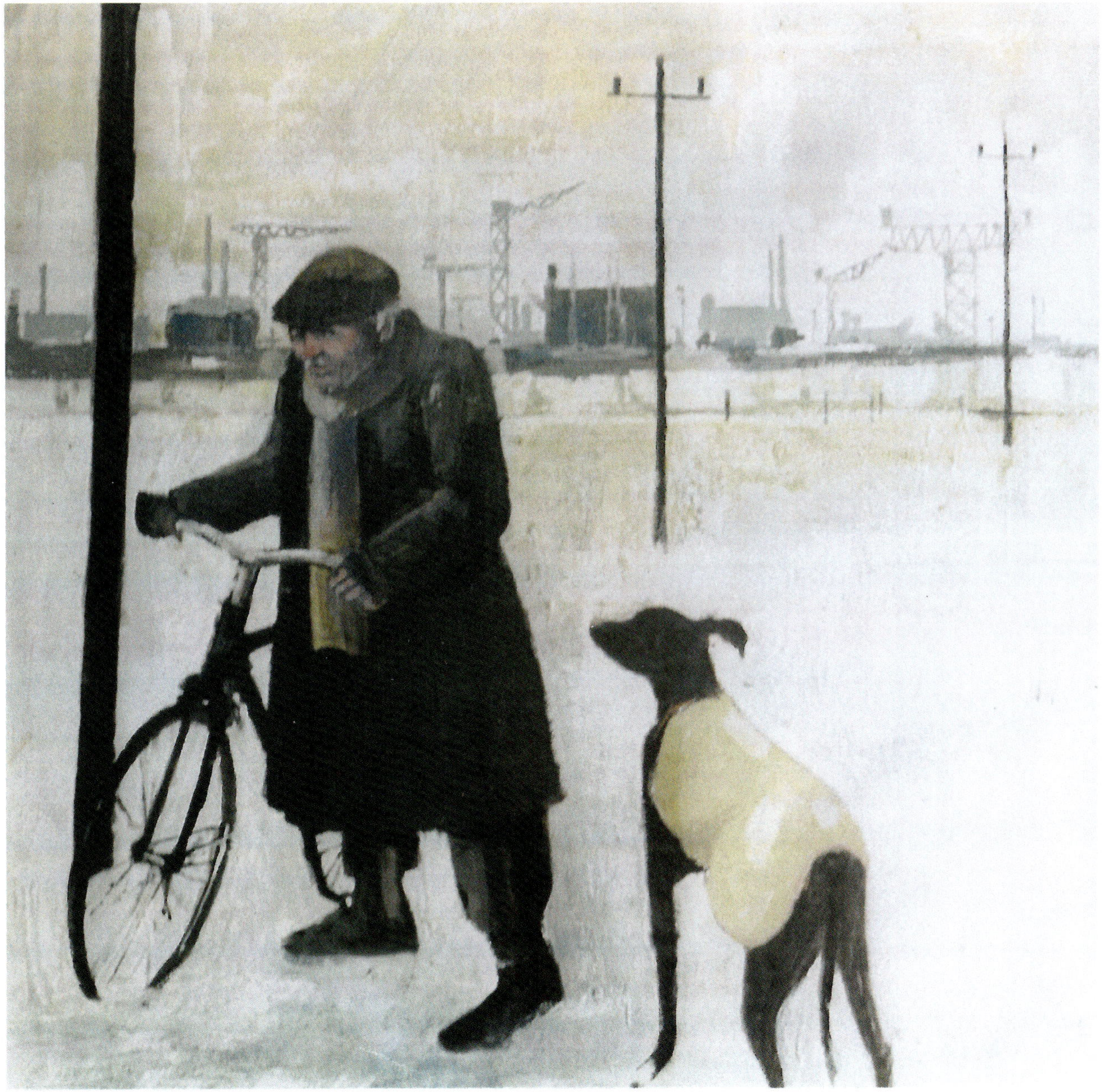

SEA COAL (Gouache)

As the pits closed, many redundant miners were obliged to pick washed-up sea coal from the beaches for their domestic fuel. This would be bagged and carried home through the frame of an old bike, while some turned it into a business using carts and ponies. Here I wanted to show the irony of the new power station going up at Cambois, where a new industry was replacing one which had thrived in the area for years. What was worse was that, although there were still millions of tons of coal in the ground, the government were prepared to sacrifice, not only coal mining, but the communities themselves.

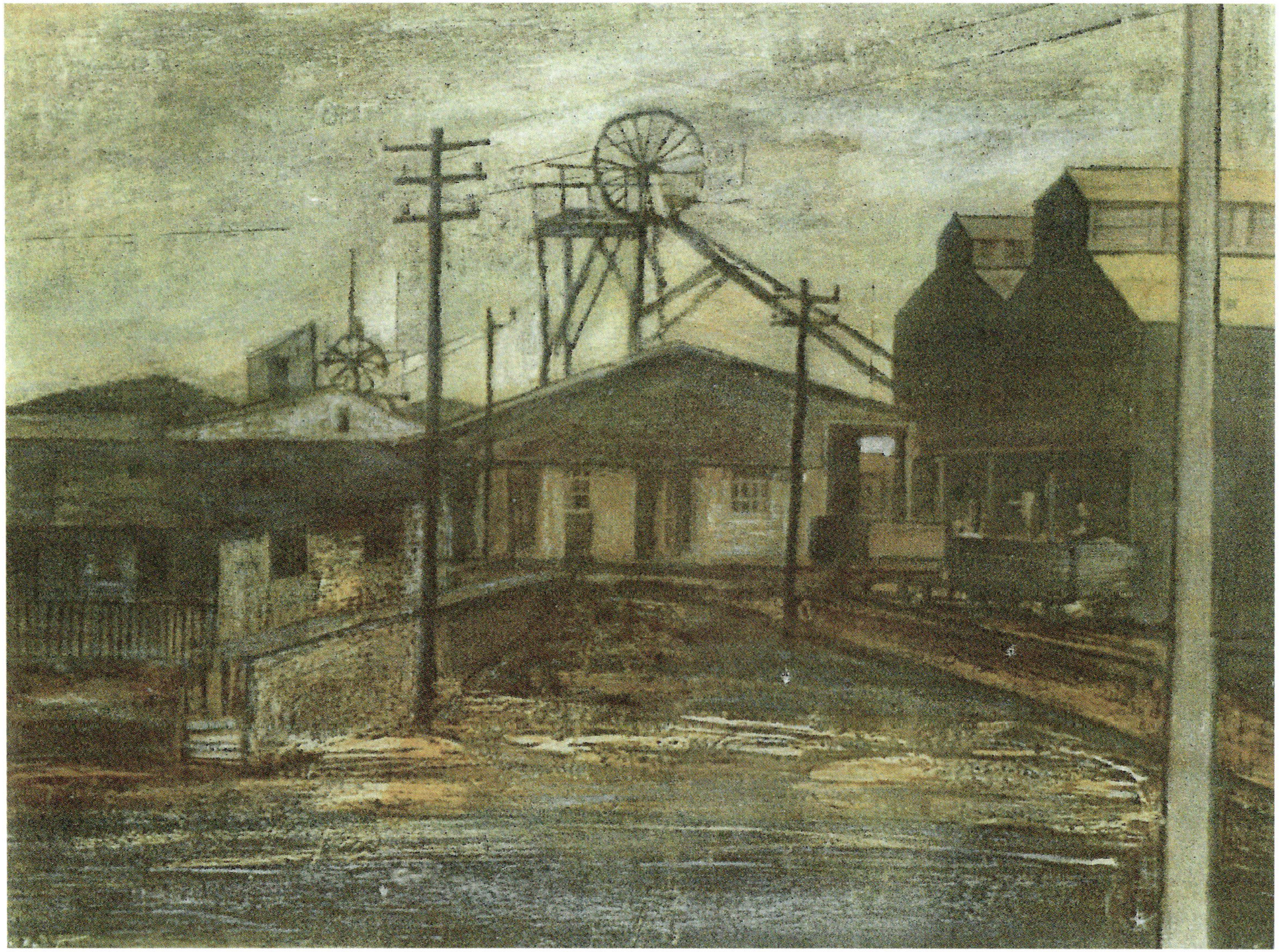

THE PIT (Gouache)

One part of Newbiggin was dominated by the colliery, sunk in 1908 and closed in the 1960s along with many others in the NE coalfield. My father was a coalcutter working in seams many miles out under the sea and consequently often chest deep in water. It was a hard life for little reward and accidents from stone falls were frequent as was the ever - present threat from coal dust on the lungs.

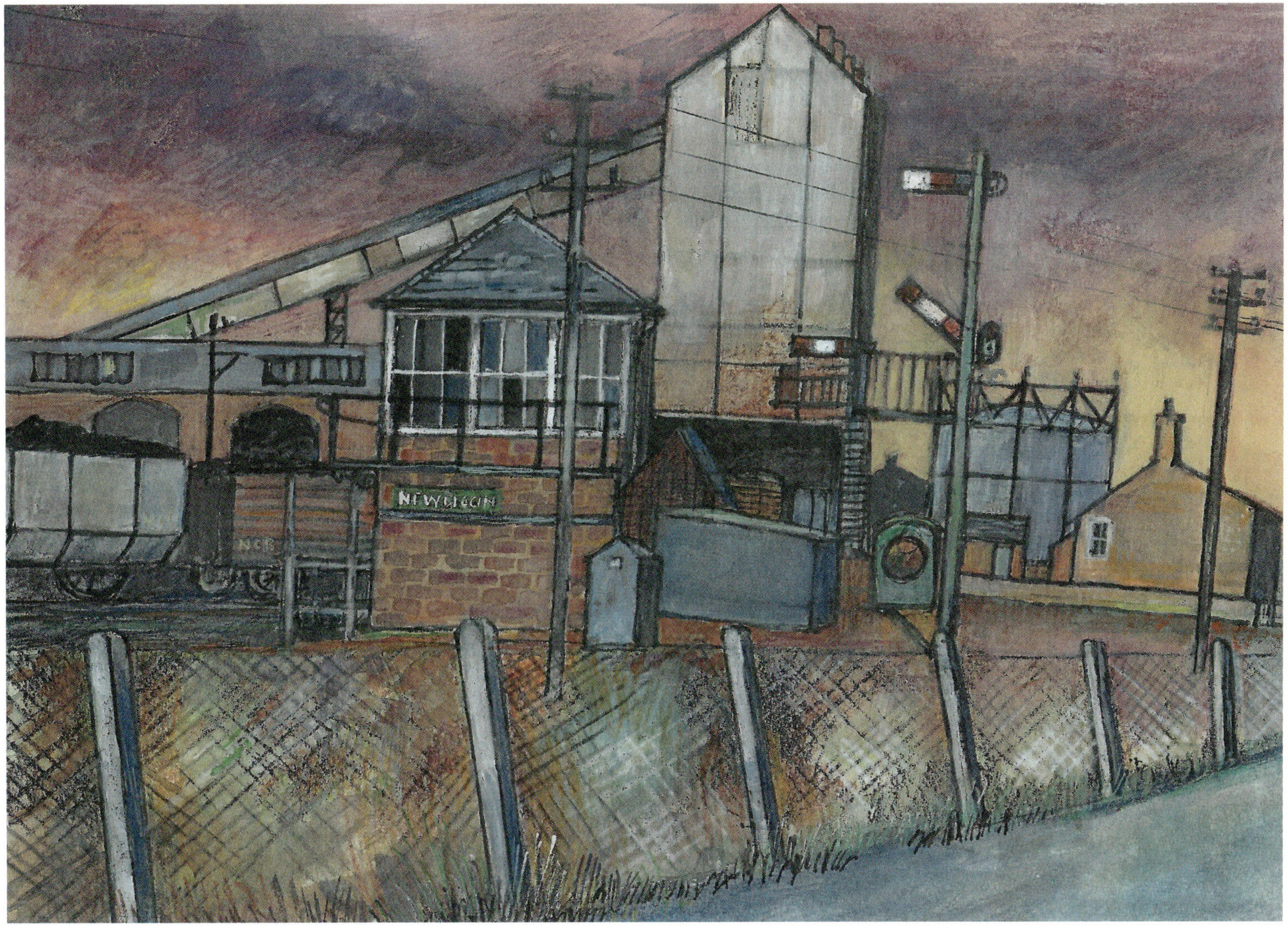

THE PIT (Gouache)

By 1910 Newbiggin colliery had screens to wash the coal, pit-head baths and, in 1929, was described as *"an up-to-date concern, being one of the first collieries to be completely electrified and equipped with high- class modem machinery"*

Next to this were the colliery houses where most of the miners and their families lived,

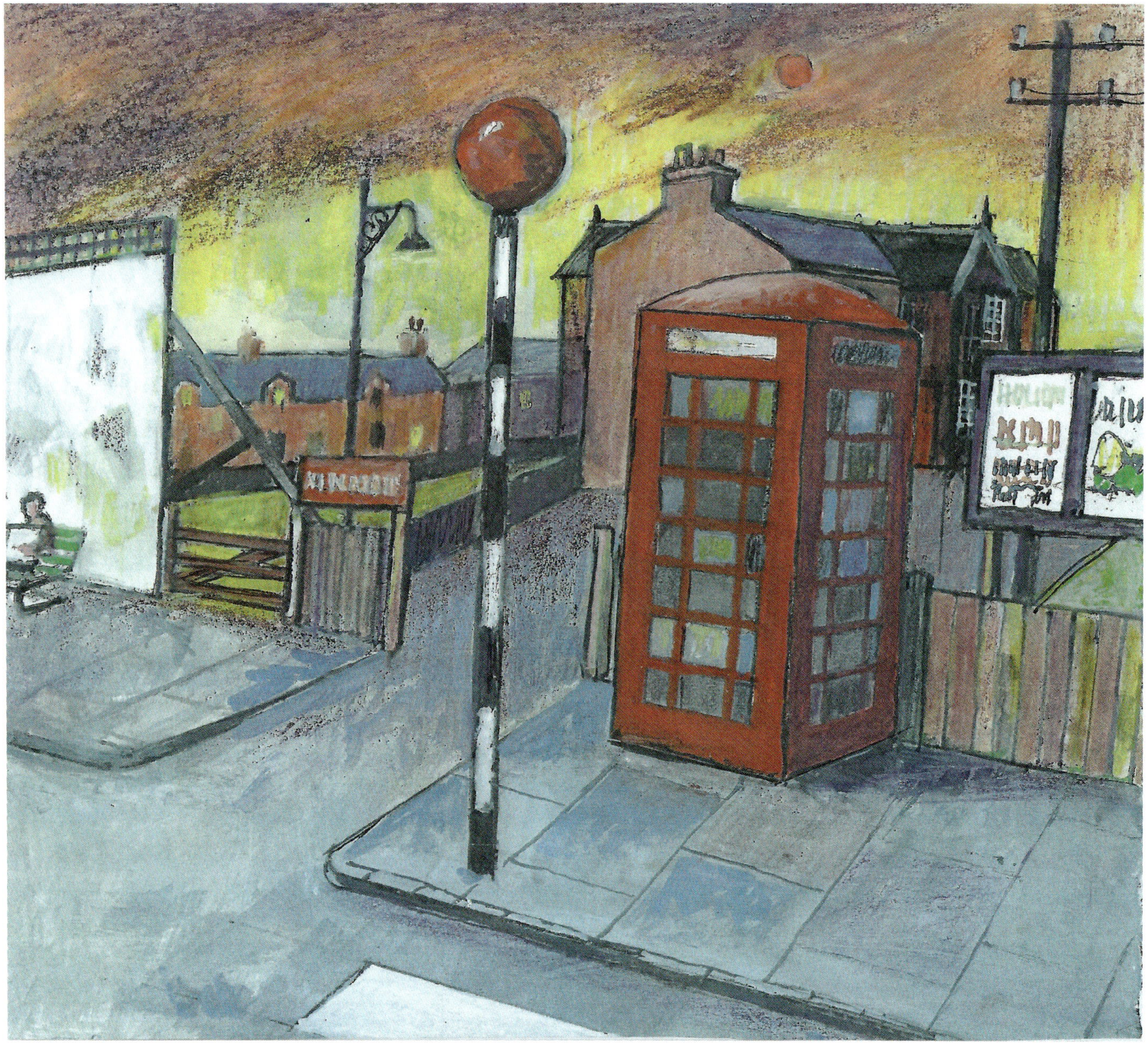

THE STATION (Gouache)

Although well used by schoolchildren, commuters and holiday-makers alike, The Newbiggin/Newcastle line was axed in the 1960s along with many such lines in the area as part of what we can only assume was the Tories' misguided grand plan. The so-called "Beeching Axe" was something which we have had cause to regret ever since.

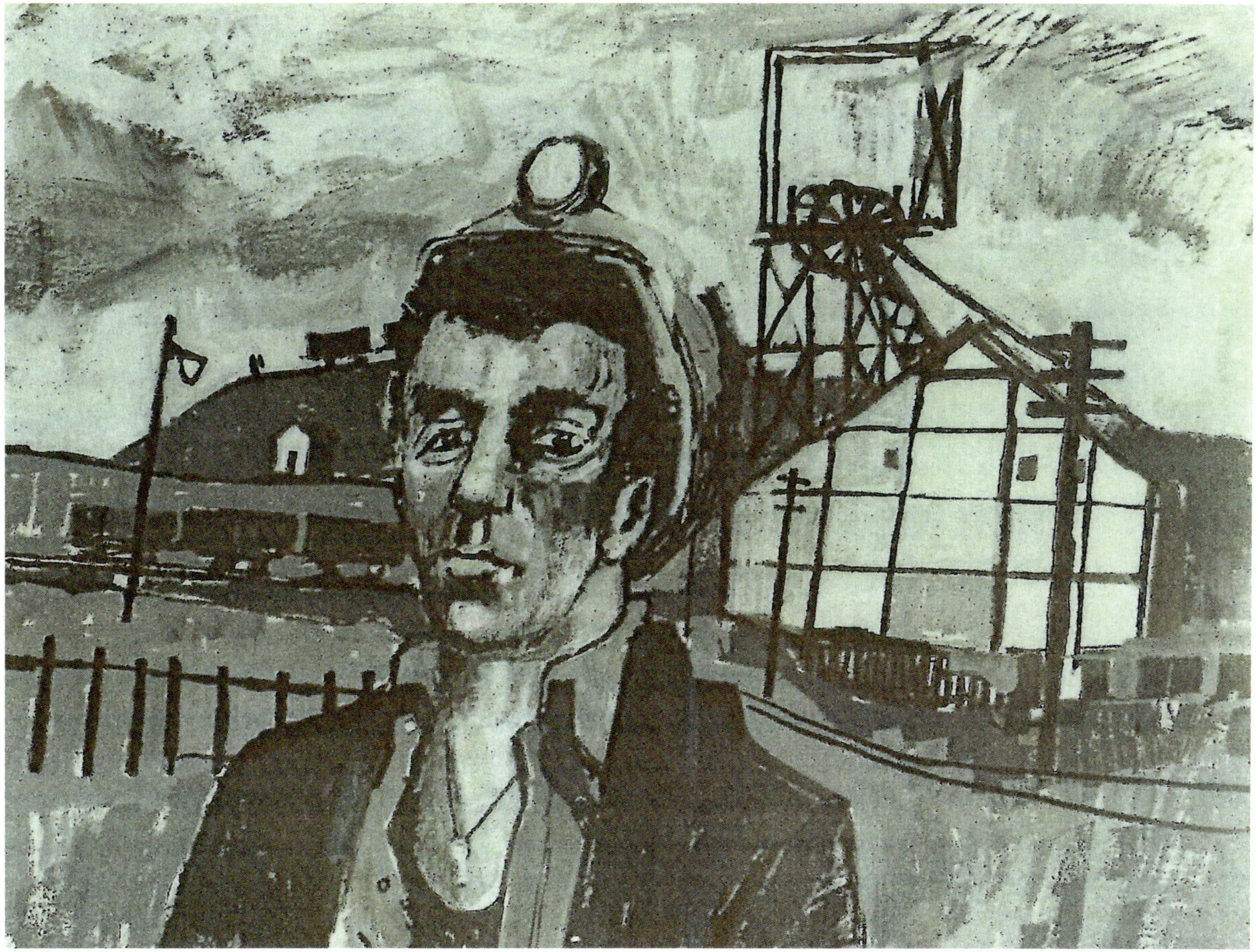

THE PIT (Gouache)

An early comission to design the cover for an NCB publication although it was never used in this form, the committee preferring a more 'photographic' rendering

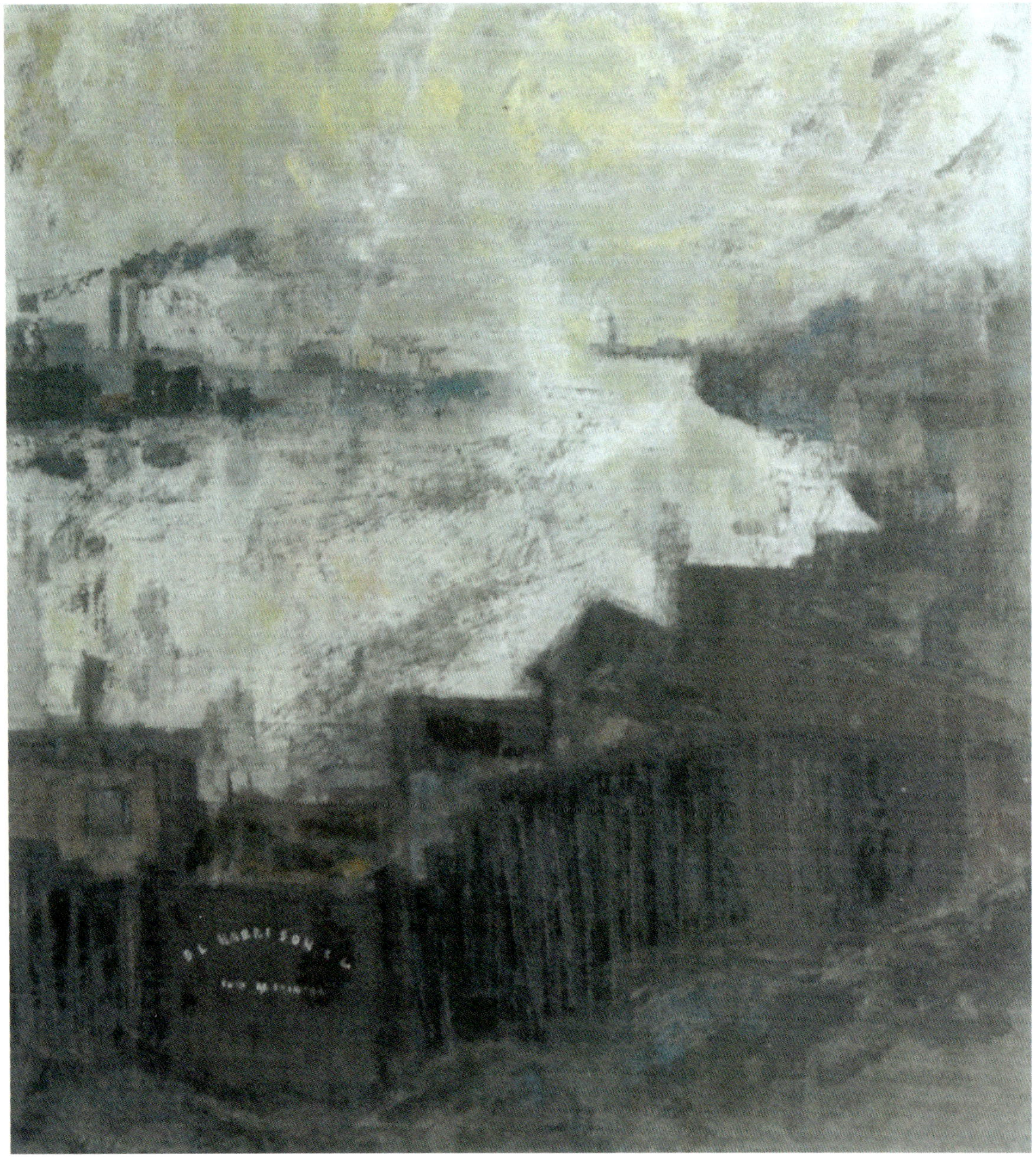

THE TYNE (Gouache)

Part of the project depicting the demise of the North East's industries and one of the few mildly "political" statements I allowed myself to make. This painting deals with shipbuilding along the river, once the pride of Britain, and now a series of empty yards and a redundant workforce of highly skilled men.

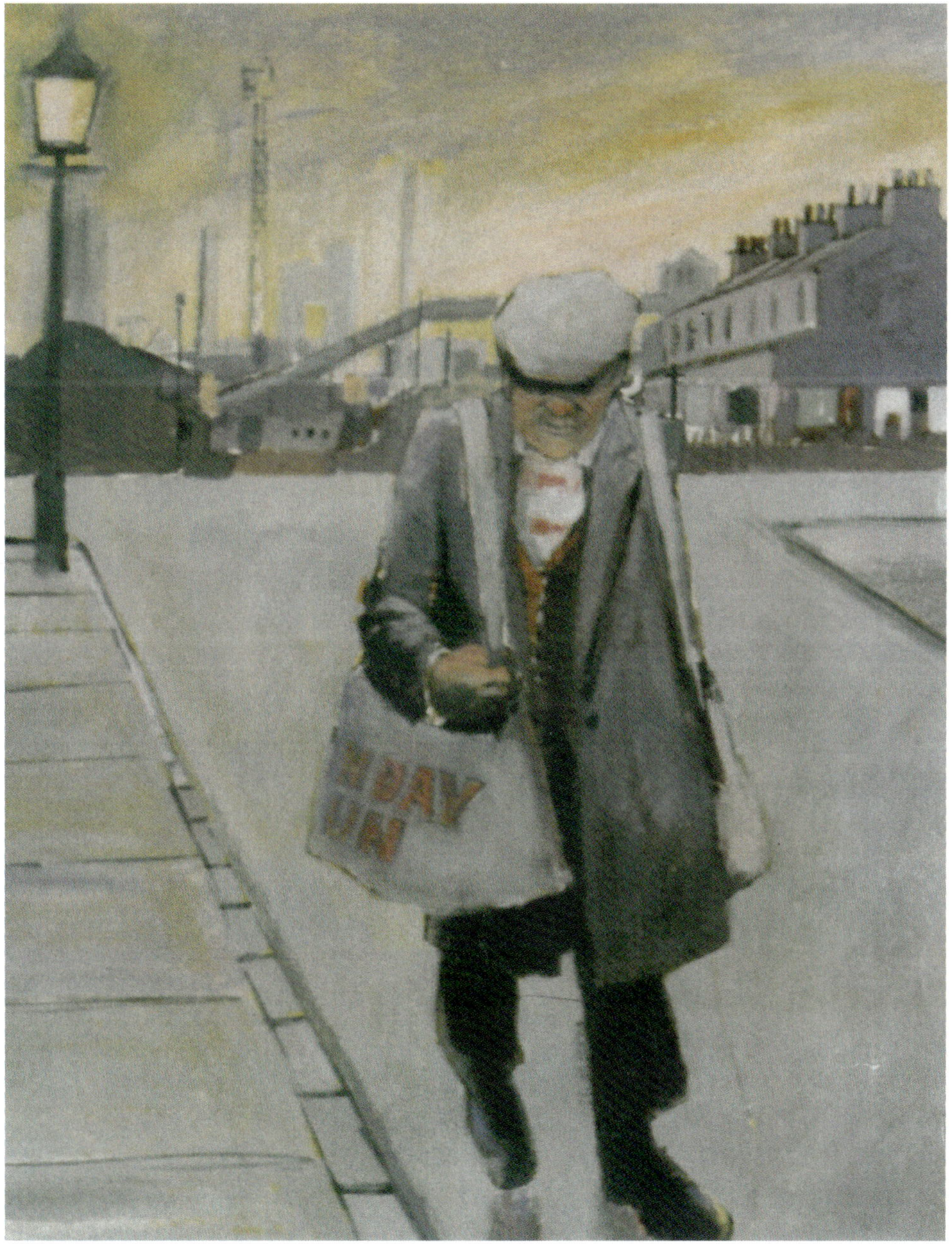

THE PAPER-SELLER (Gouache)

One of the many "characters" who worked in the north-east in the 1950s. I remember this man's garbled shouting of the names of his various papers (notably the Saturday results "Pink") on street corners. What sounded like "Urinal" turned out to be "Final".

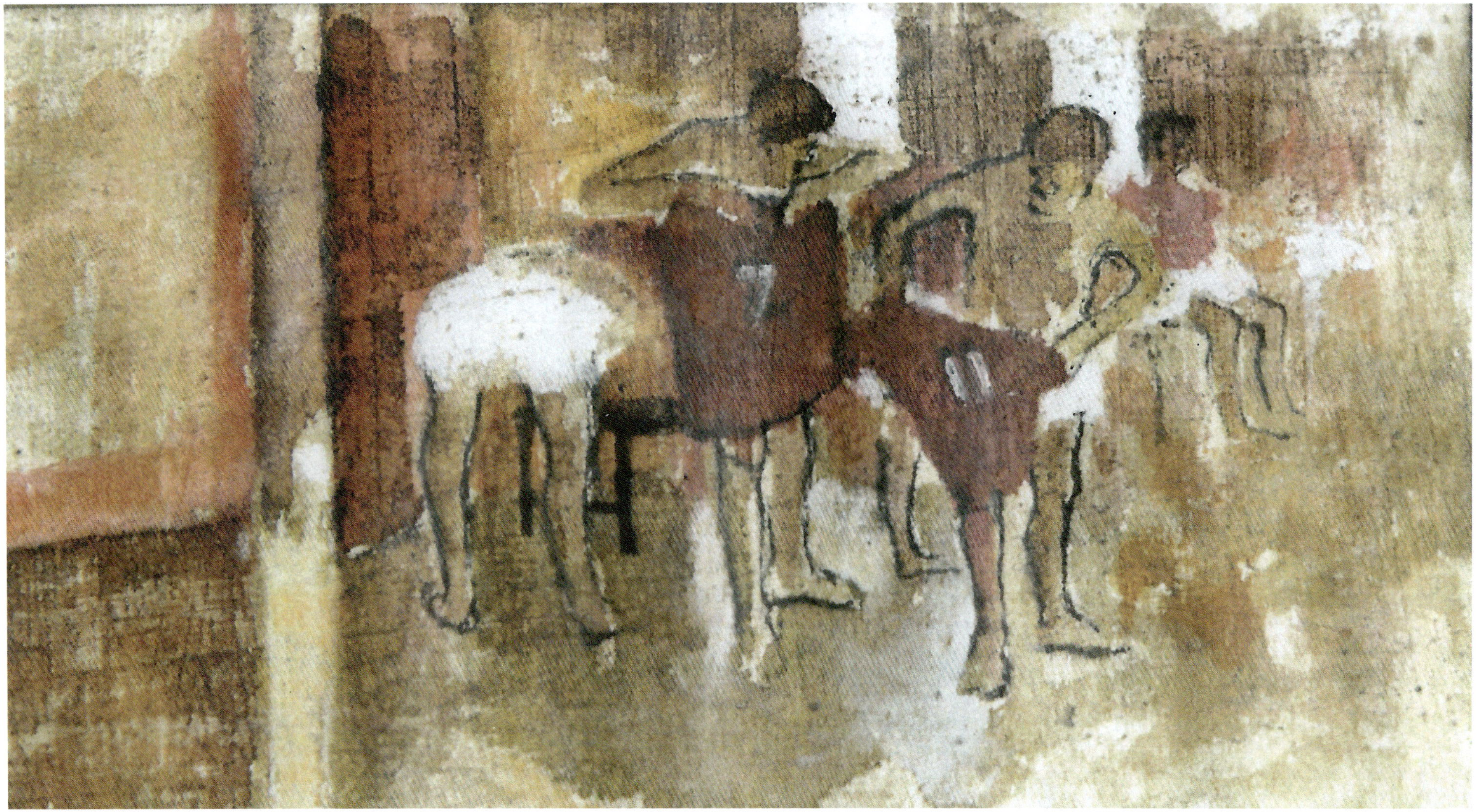

FOOTBALL (Inks)

My admiration for Degas began as a student and coincided with my running of the College football team, resulting in a series of works which paraphrase his ballet studies.

Many opponents reckoned we played like ballet dancers!!!

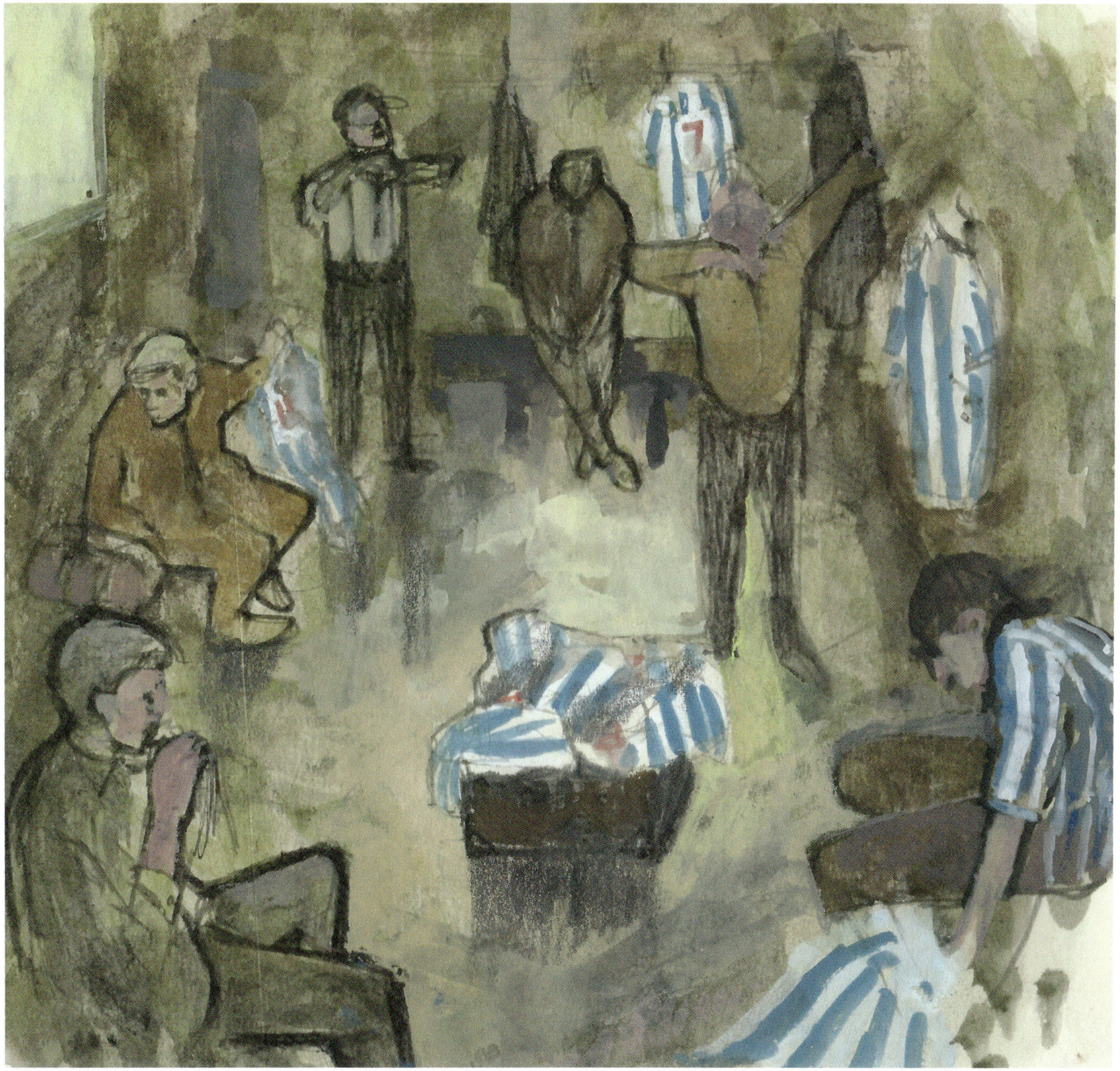

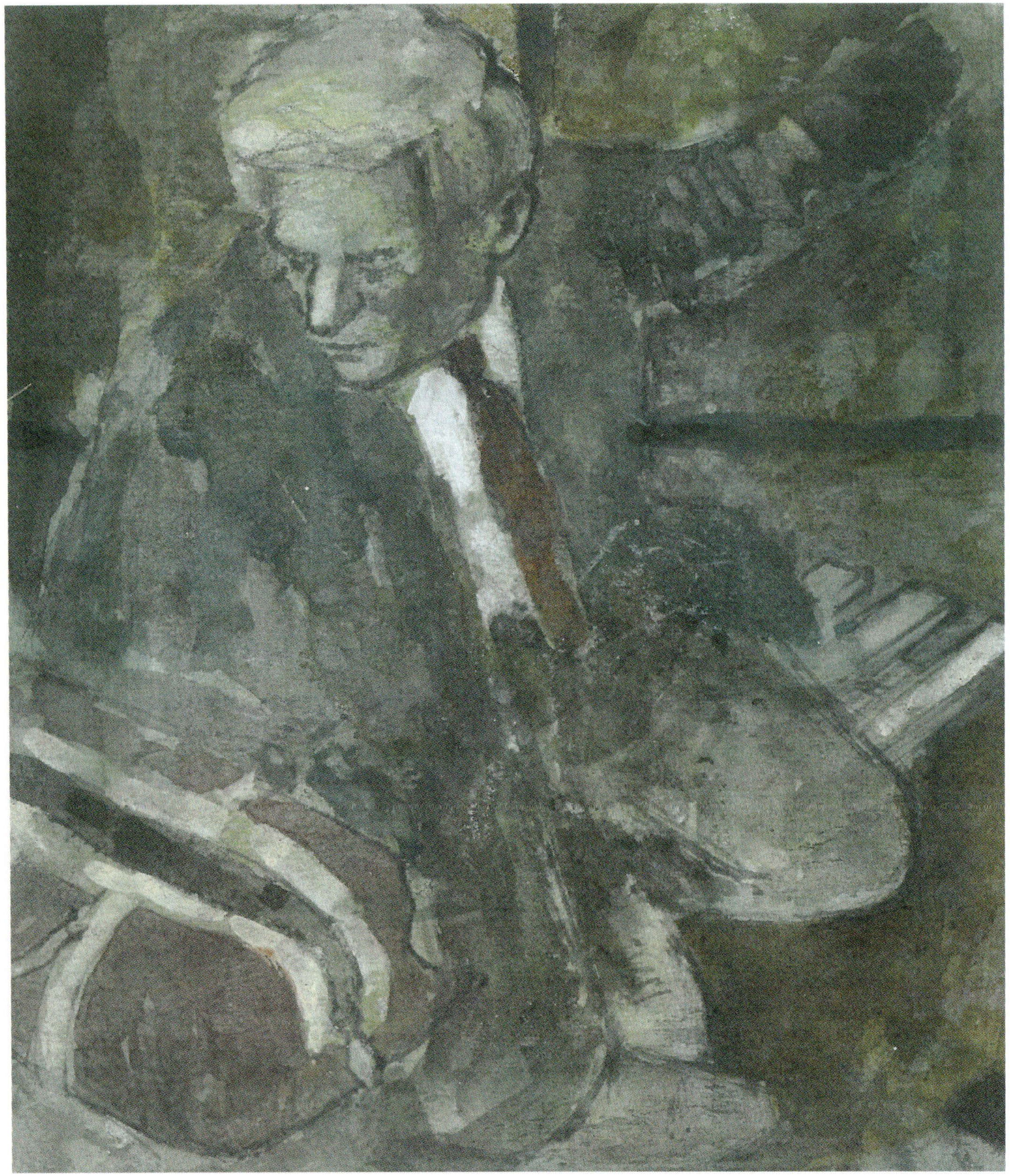

FOOTBALL (inks)

Possibly a self-portrait - the only one I ever made.

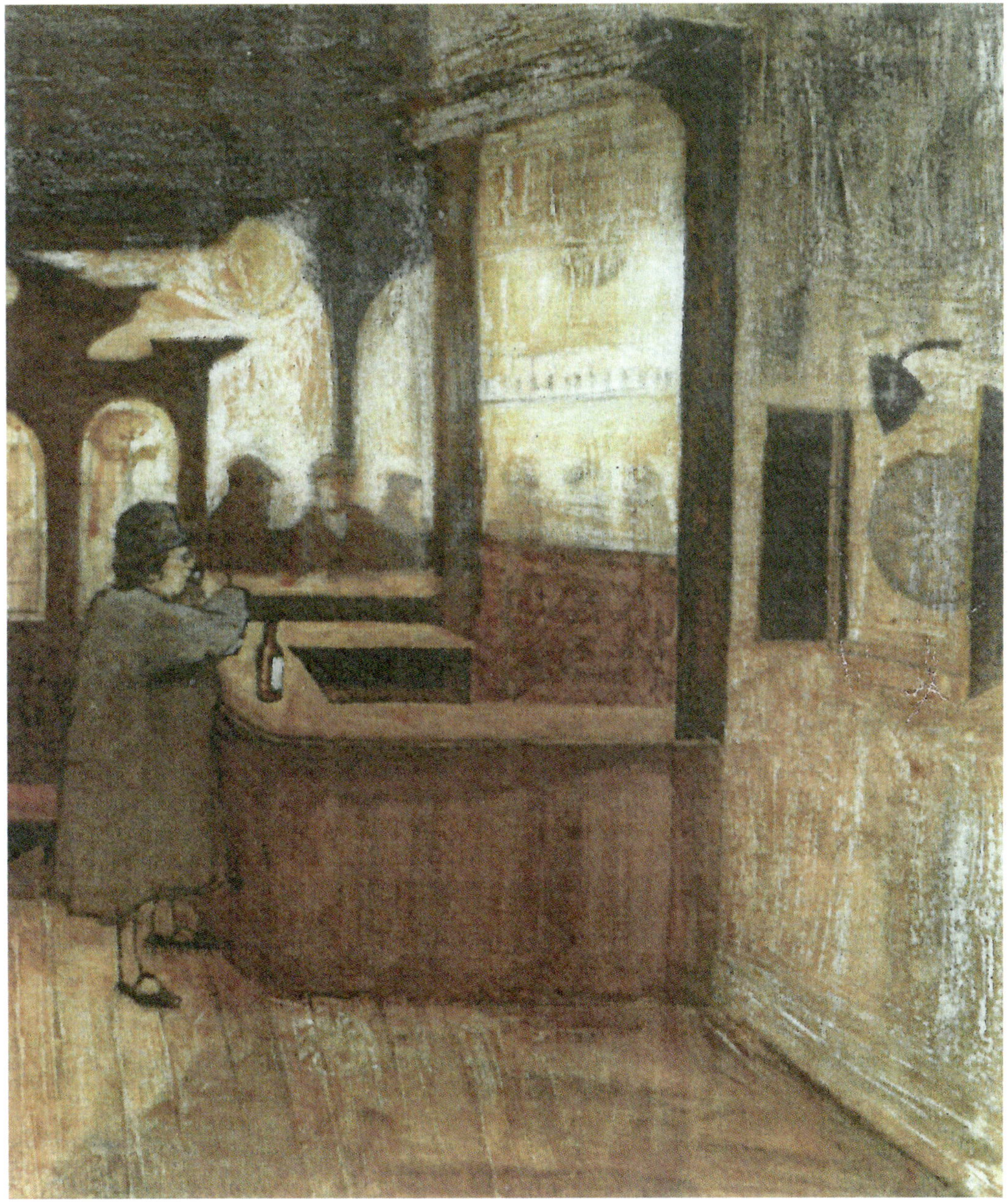

THE LOCAL PUB (Gouache)

Although not a drinker, I was fascinated by the interiors of various public houses - their decor, bar tops, stained-glass and warm colours - as much as in the local people who frequented them. With only a few exceptions, many of them were delighted to be sketched although they drew the line at posing which meant working from quick drawings.

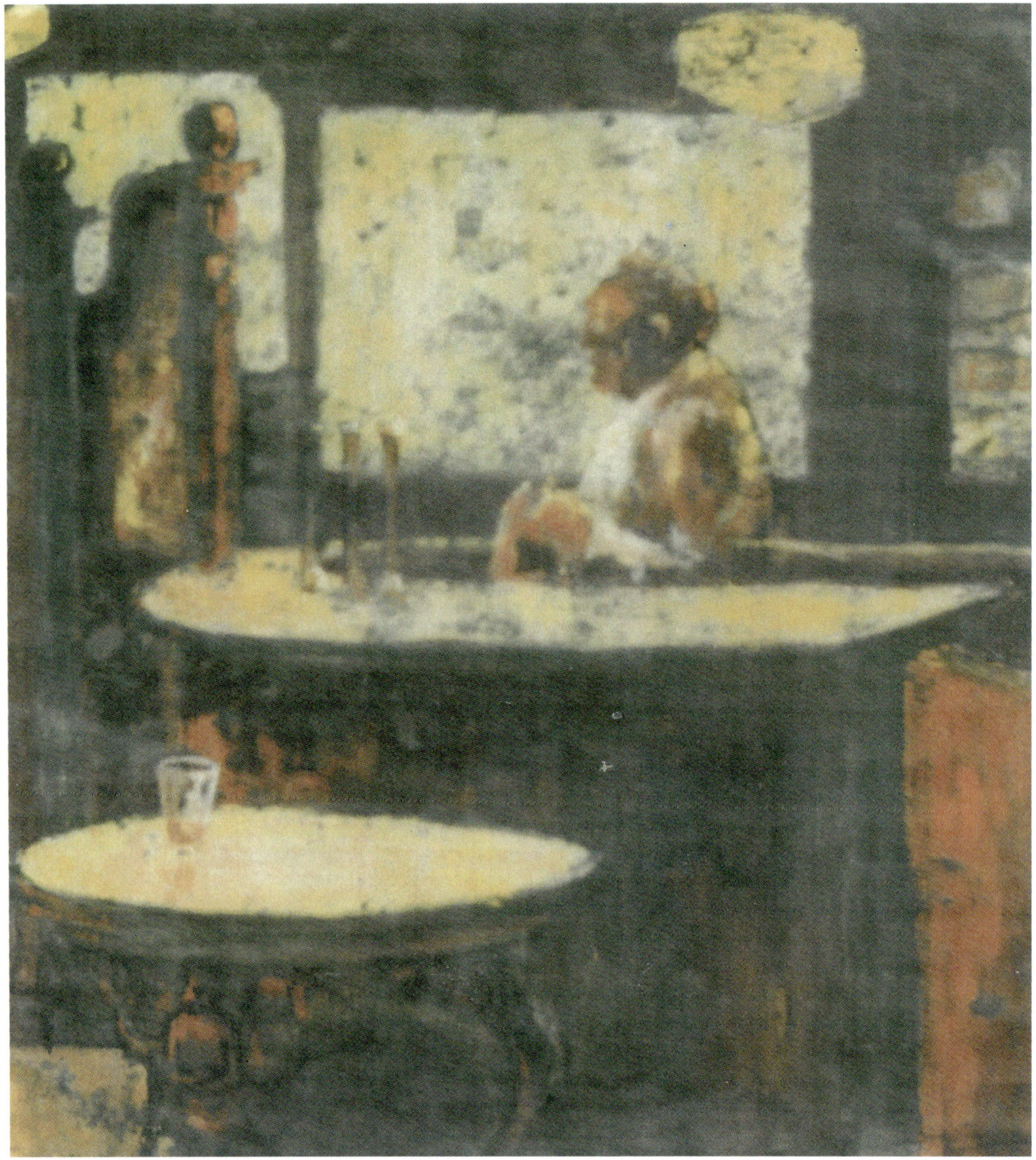

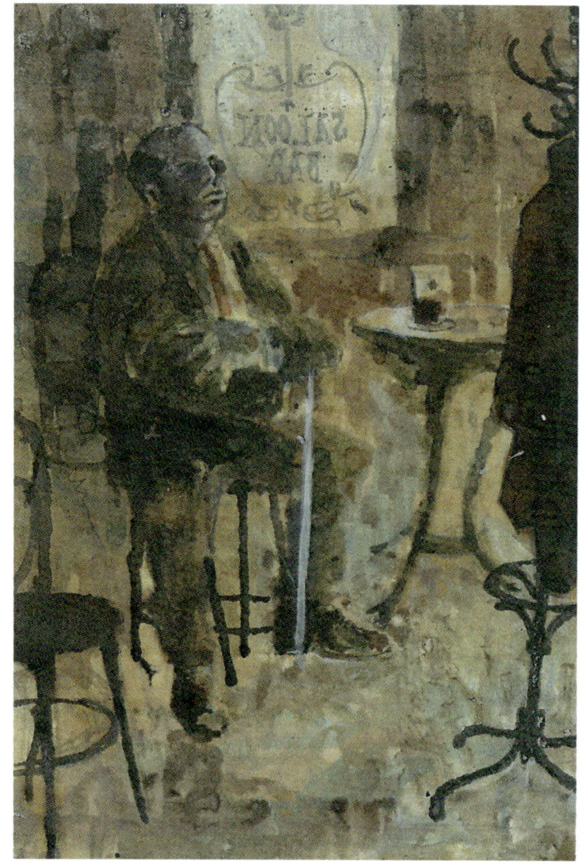

PRELIMINARY SKETCHES

Most paintings begin with drawings then, possibly, watercolour sketches where compositional and colour details are finalised

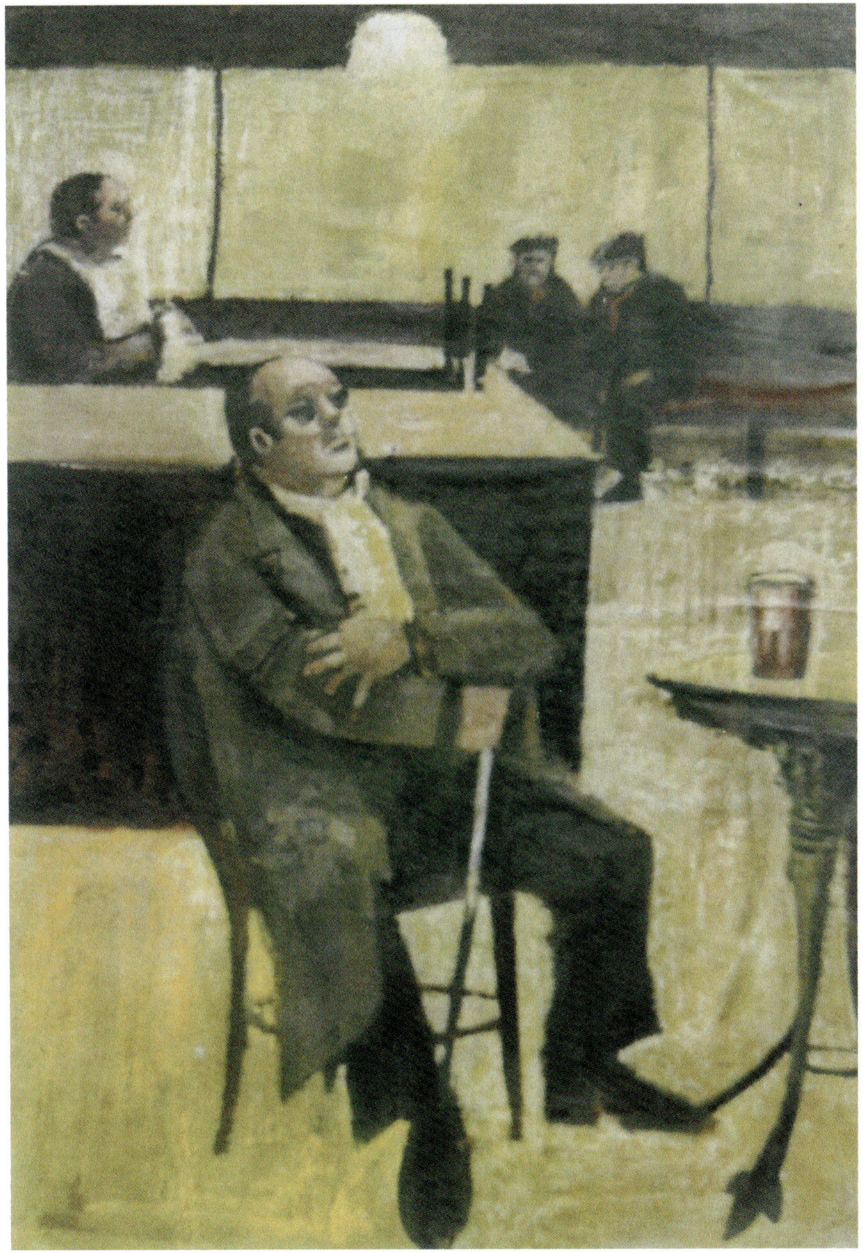

THE LOCAL PUB (Gouache)

One evening, in the Coble Inn, we met a blind piano-tuner who turned out to have an extensive knowledge of jazz pianists. It was a riveting session and added much to one of our "cultural" interests at the time. He was also aware that I was surreptitiously drawing him and seemed mildly flattered.

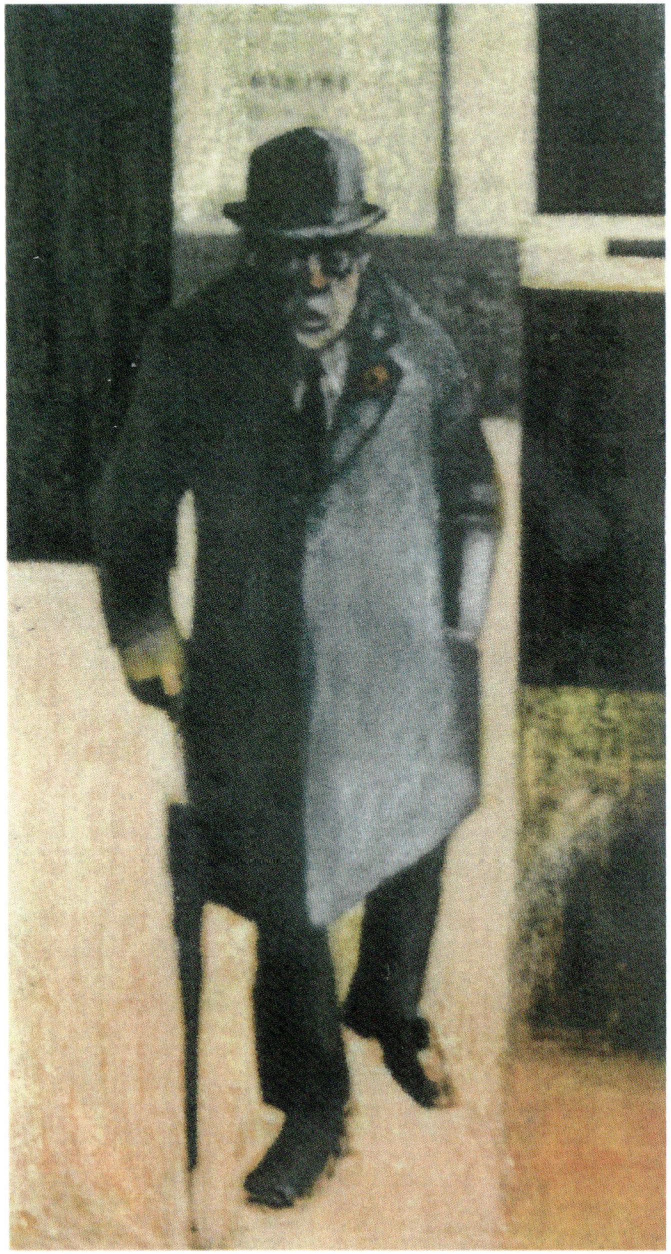

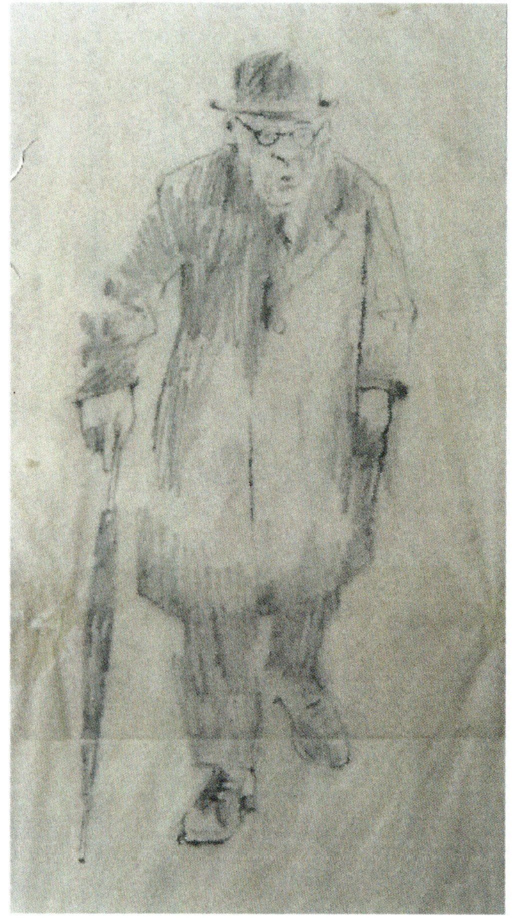

THE LOCAL PUB

(Gouache)

Tommy Forster ran the local Post Office and I had done one or two posters for him. I liked the juxtaposition of his red nose and his poppy as he came into The Ship after an Armistice Parade, but I only had some grease-proof paper with me so the painting was made later from a quick drawing.

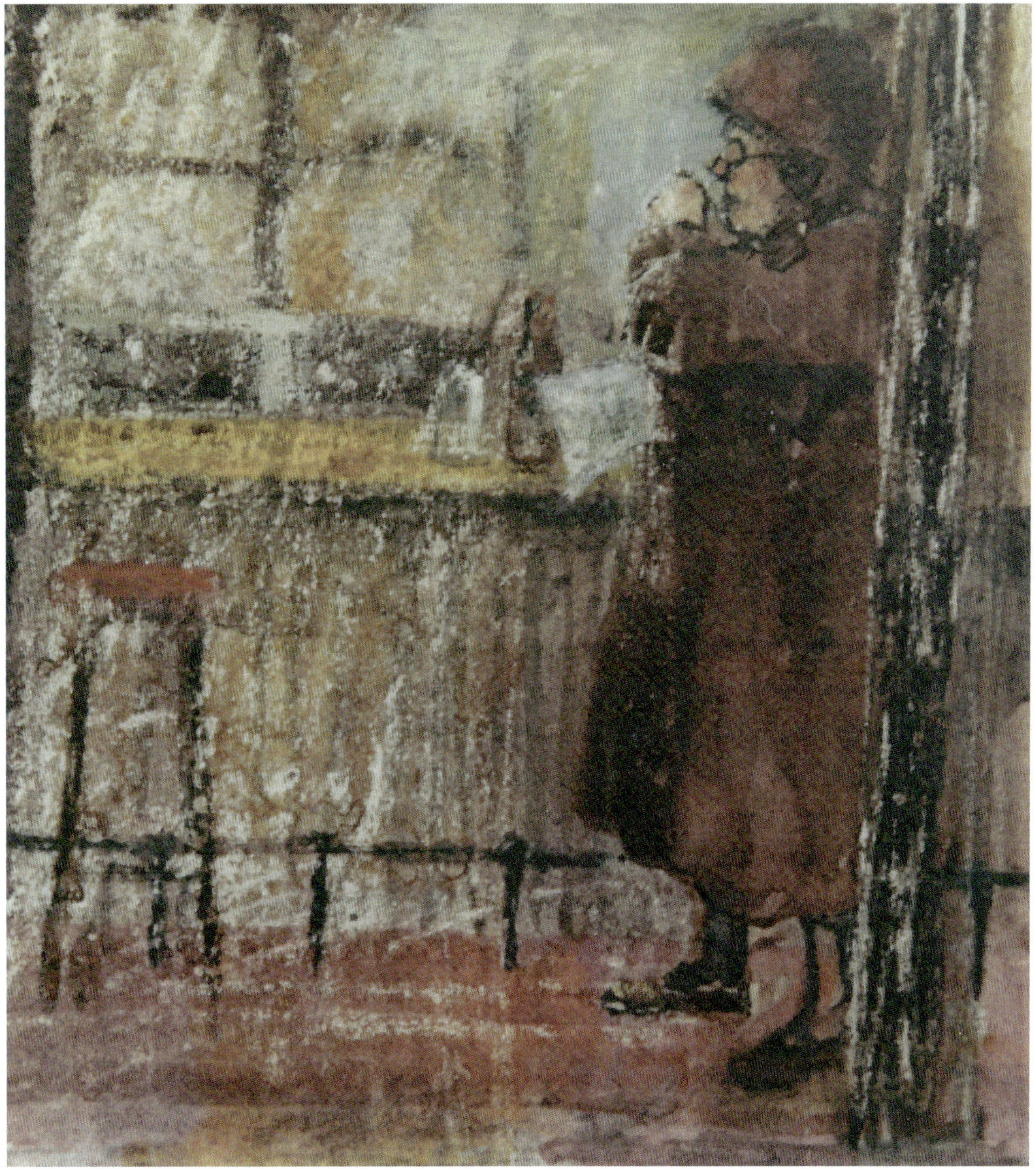

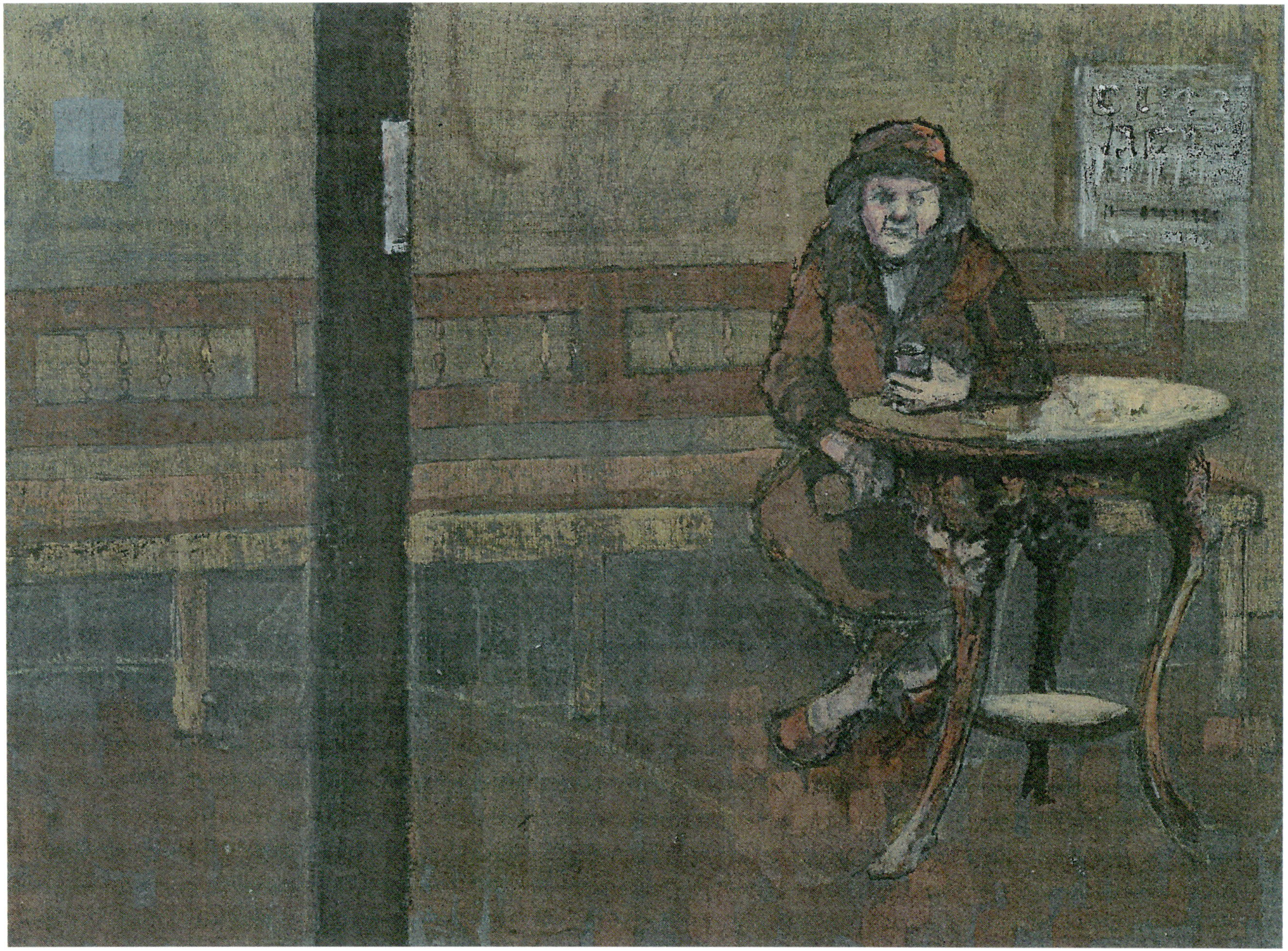

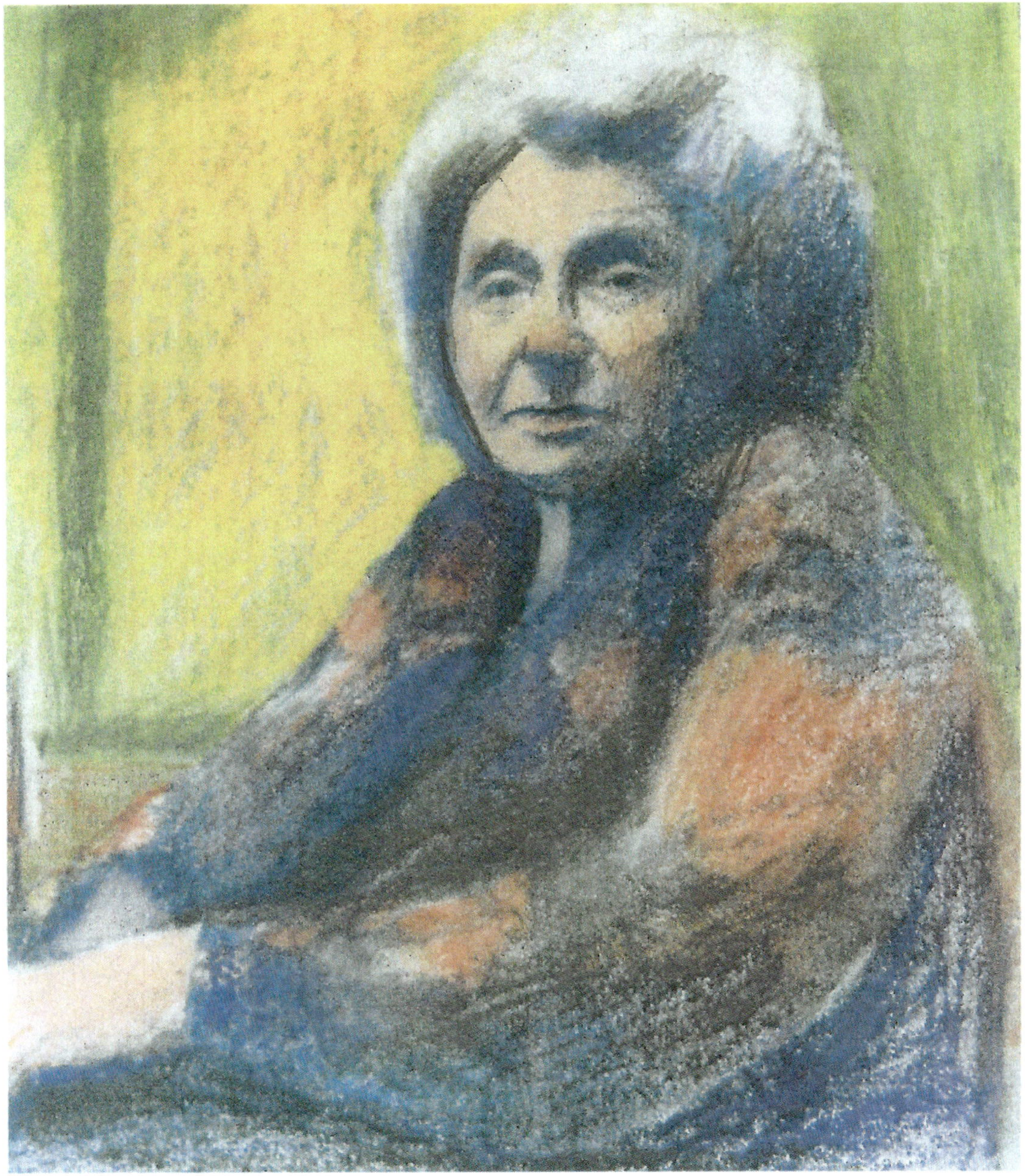

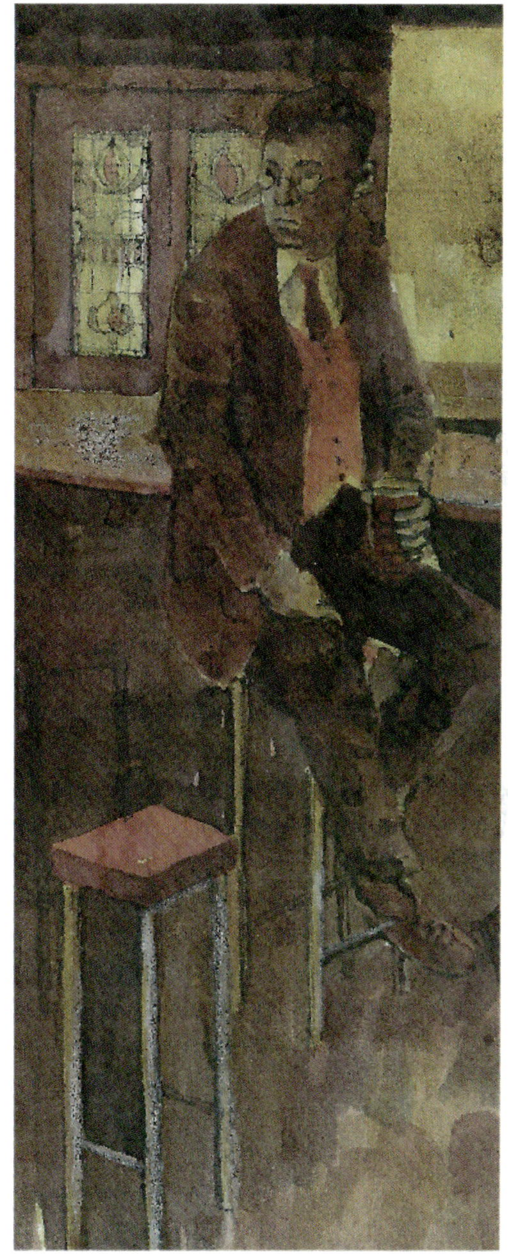

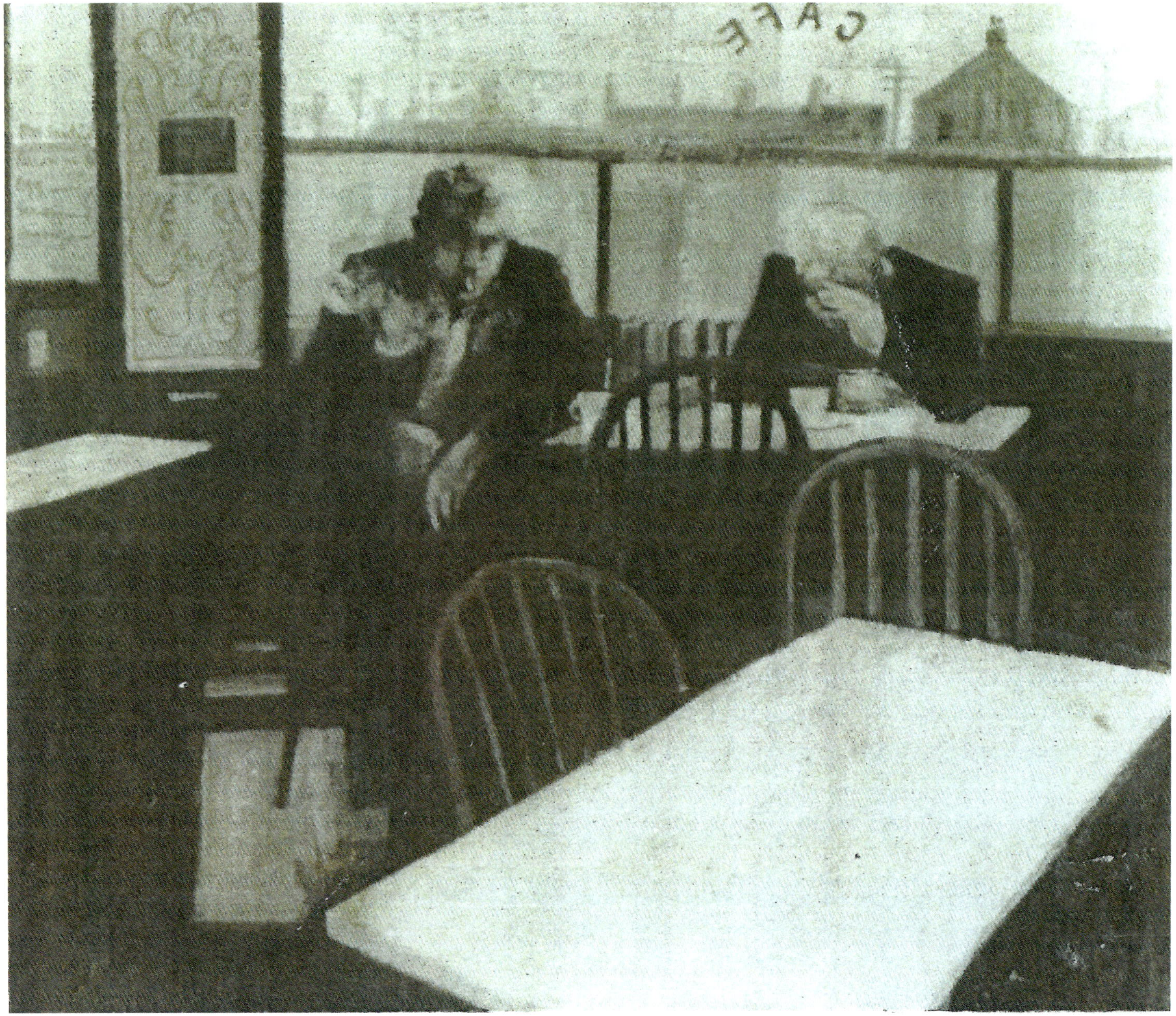

CAFE INTERIOR (Gouache)

Normally the patrons of such establishments were happy enough to sit with their mug of tea and the newspaper racing forecast, lost in their own world. Actually here I was initially more interested in the Degas-like patterns of chairs and other linear features and perhaps should have ignored the men, for one of them became quite belligerent and I was forced to beat a hasty retreat.

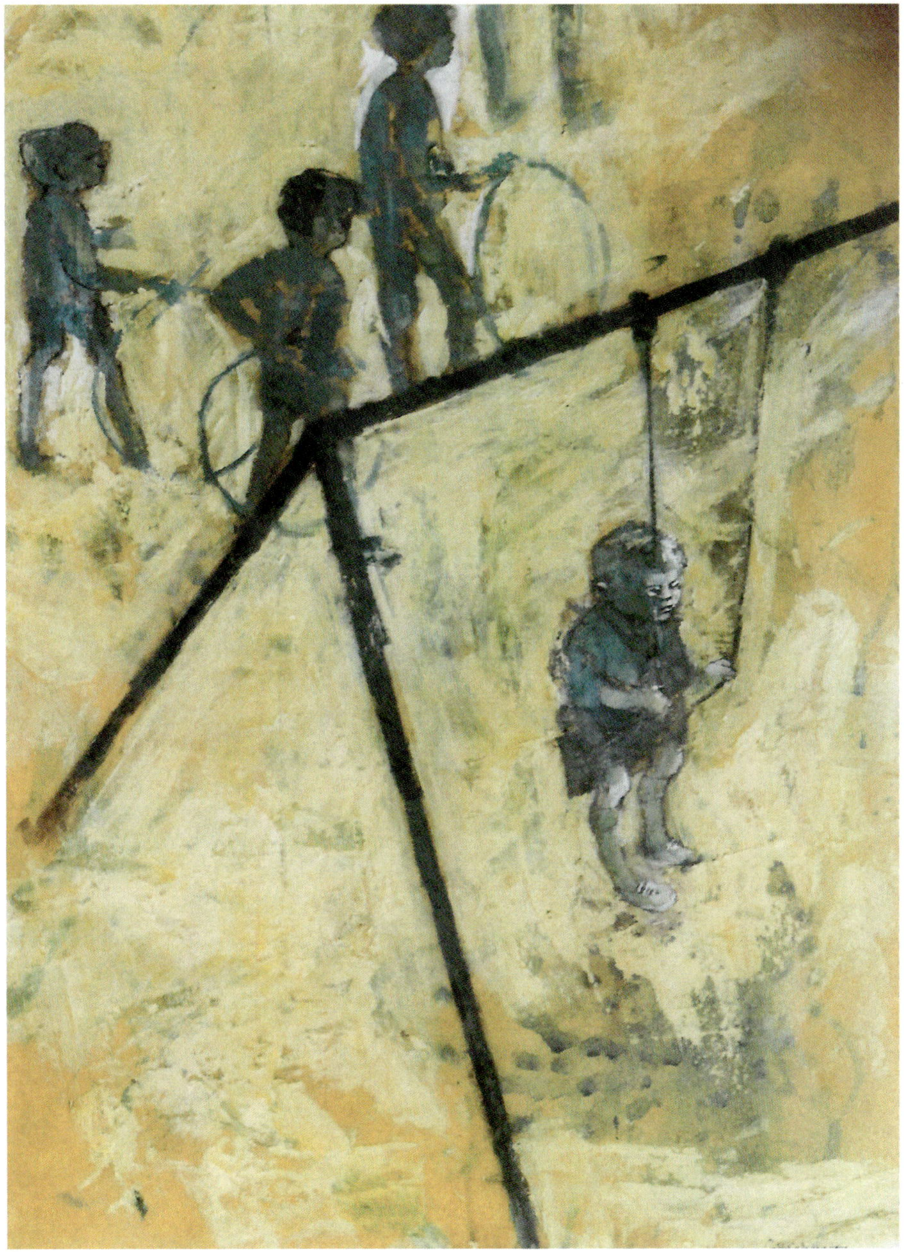

CHILDREN PLAYING (Oils)

An early theme was that of the relationship between the shapes of children playing and various linear structures such as hop-scotch patterns, swings, bicycles or cloak-room furniture. Here my young brother and his friends proved to be involuntary models.

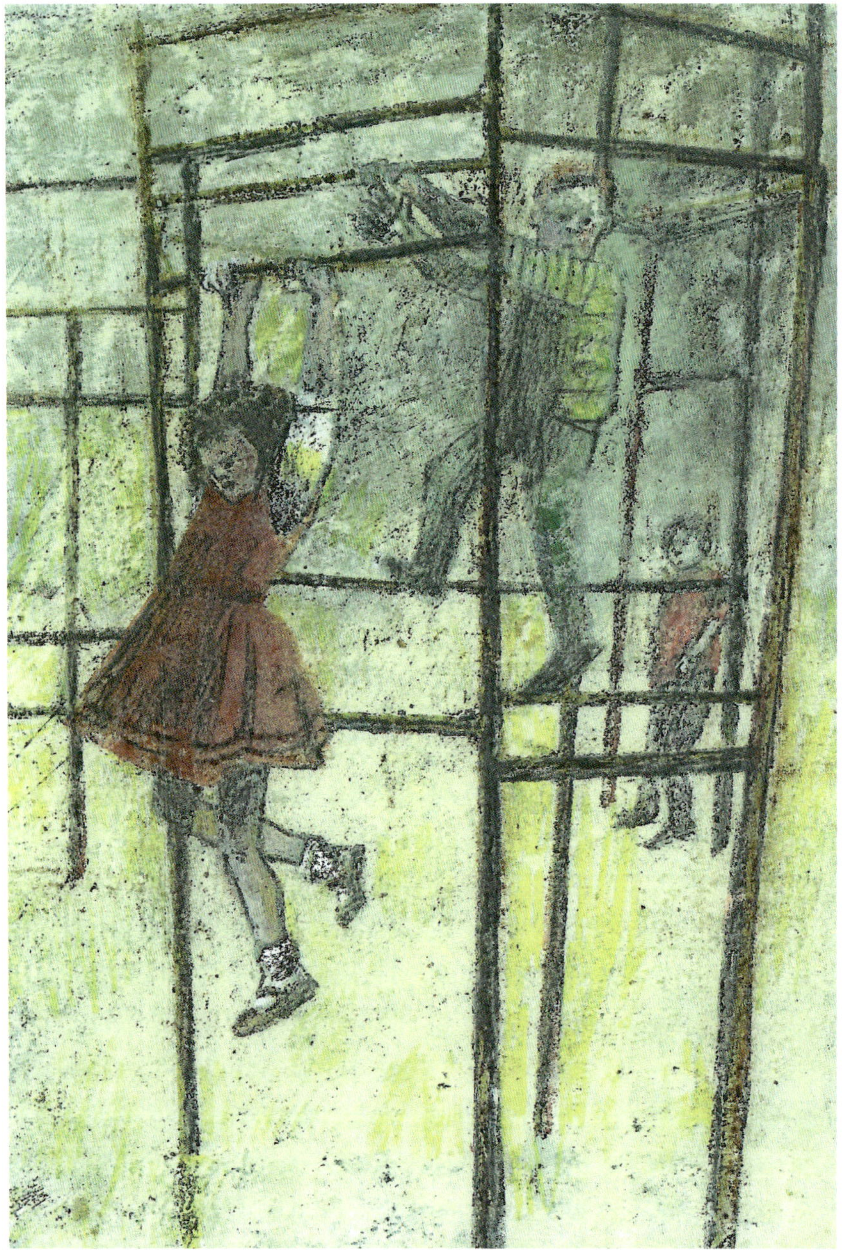

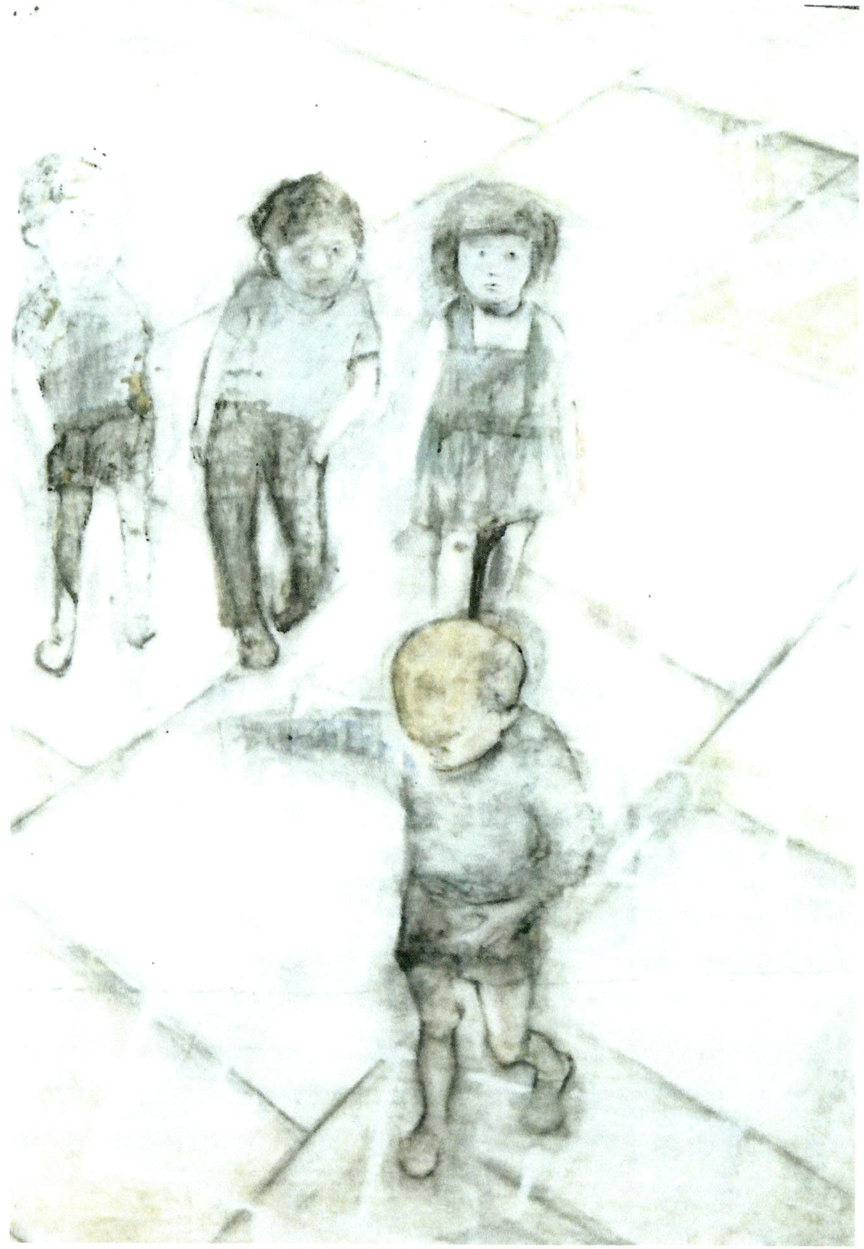

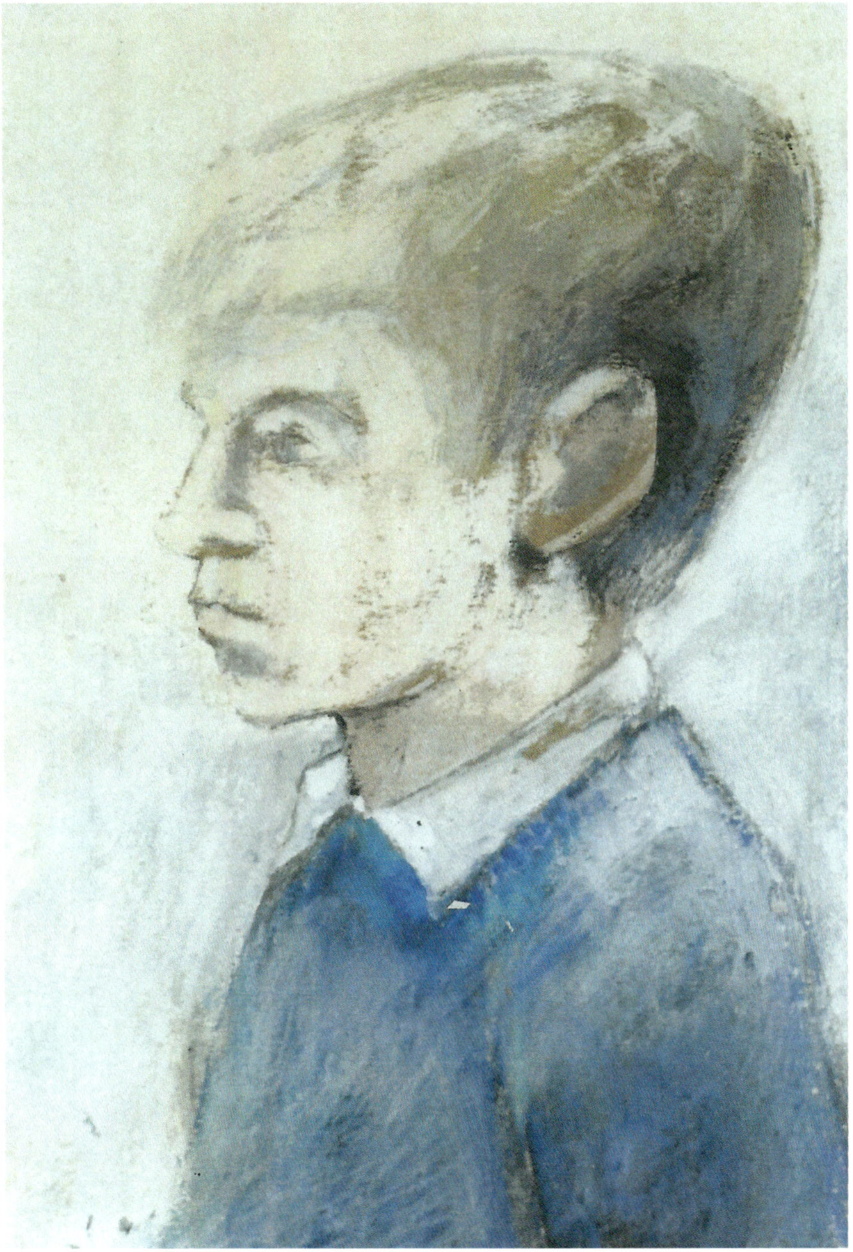

ROBIN

(Gouache)

My young brother was a reluctant model and it was difficult to get him to sit without resorting to bribery. This was one occasion when he did pose, but only for a few minutes.

He also appears (with his equally reluctant pals) in some of the group paintings.

ONLY THE SKIES' SLOW TURBULENCE.....

Motor-cycling home from a weekend's climbing, I would often stop and make drawings and notes of lone crofts or small groups of cottages nestled in the rugged hills. I had, of course, made contact with many of these fellsides in my erstwhile architectural career after leaving school when I made surveys hereabouts. The harshness of the terrain and the thin, acid soil, suggested that those who lived here must have made a tenuous living, and I have tried to echo this by making a series of essentially textural paintings in which the impasto is created by additions to the paint of glues, resins, plaster, rock-dust, wax and the like. Initially a lack of colour helped to emphasise the bleakness of the landscape, but the same landscapes, in summer, are quite different and this is reflected by the introduction of yellows and greens. Even so, they fail to disguise the ruggedness and loneliness of the habitat.

Eventually, however, the series began to move towards abstraction, emphasising pattern and structure, at the same time losing the sense that I had first wished to invoke, and so it was abandoned.

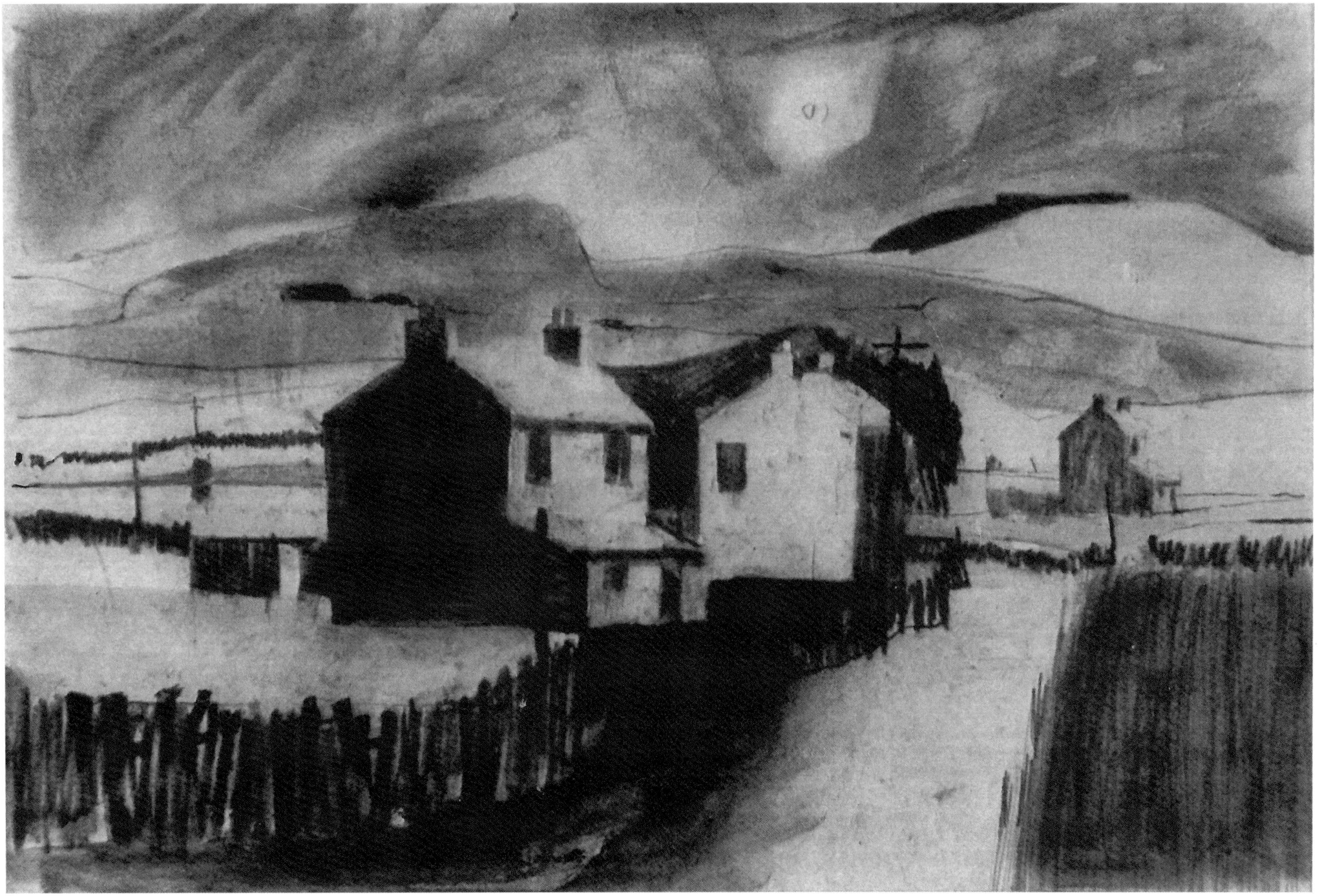

MAN'S PRESENCE (Charcoal)

A sketch, done at the roadside, which inspired the subsequent series of paintings.

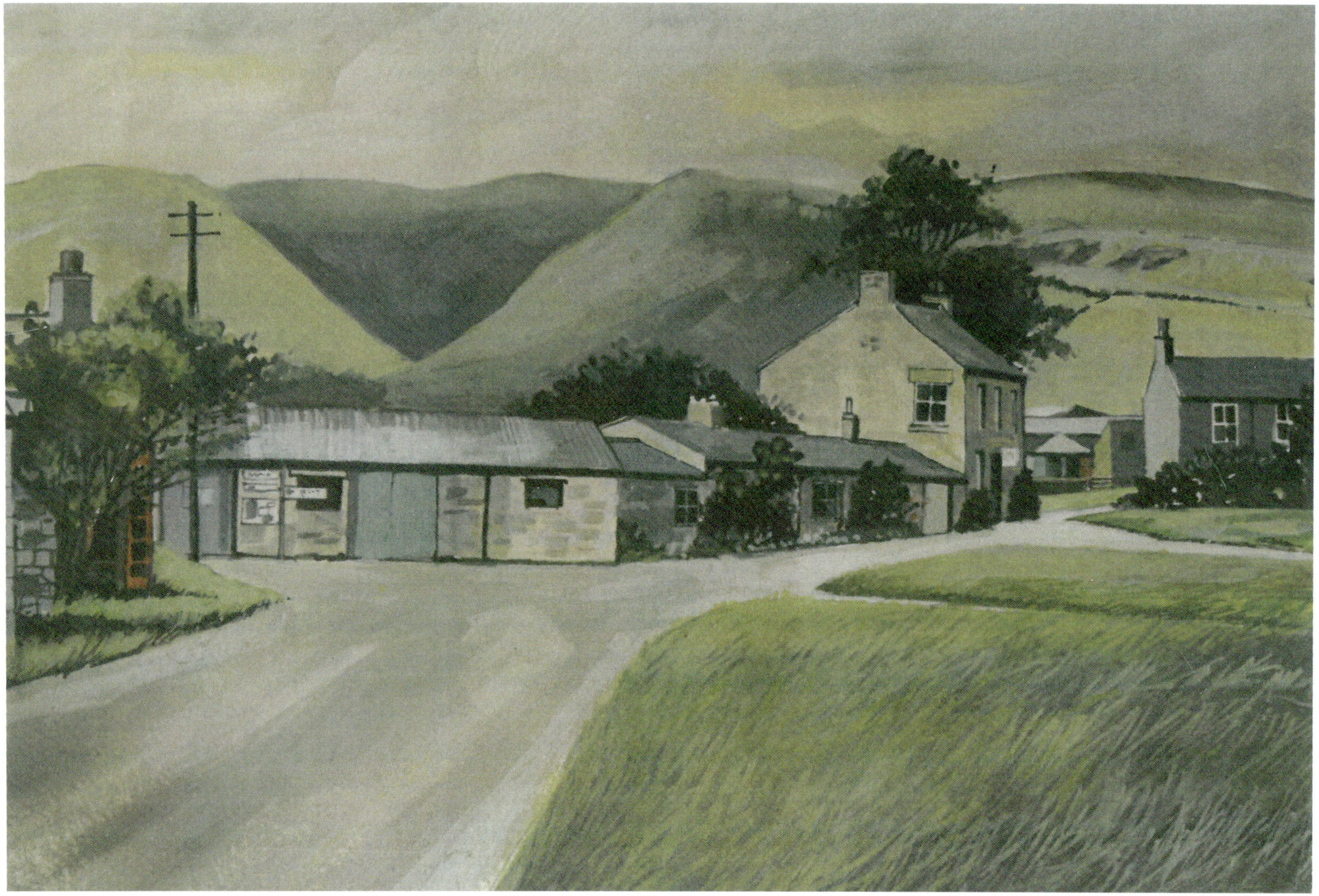

MAN'S PRESENCE (Gouache)

The first works were essentially figurative and used descriptive colour before moving into a more abstract rendering.

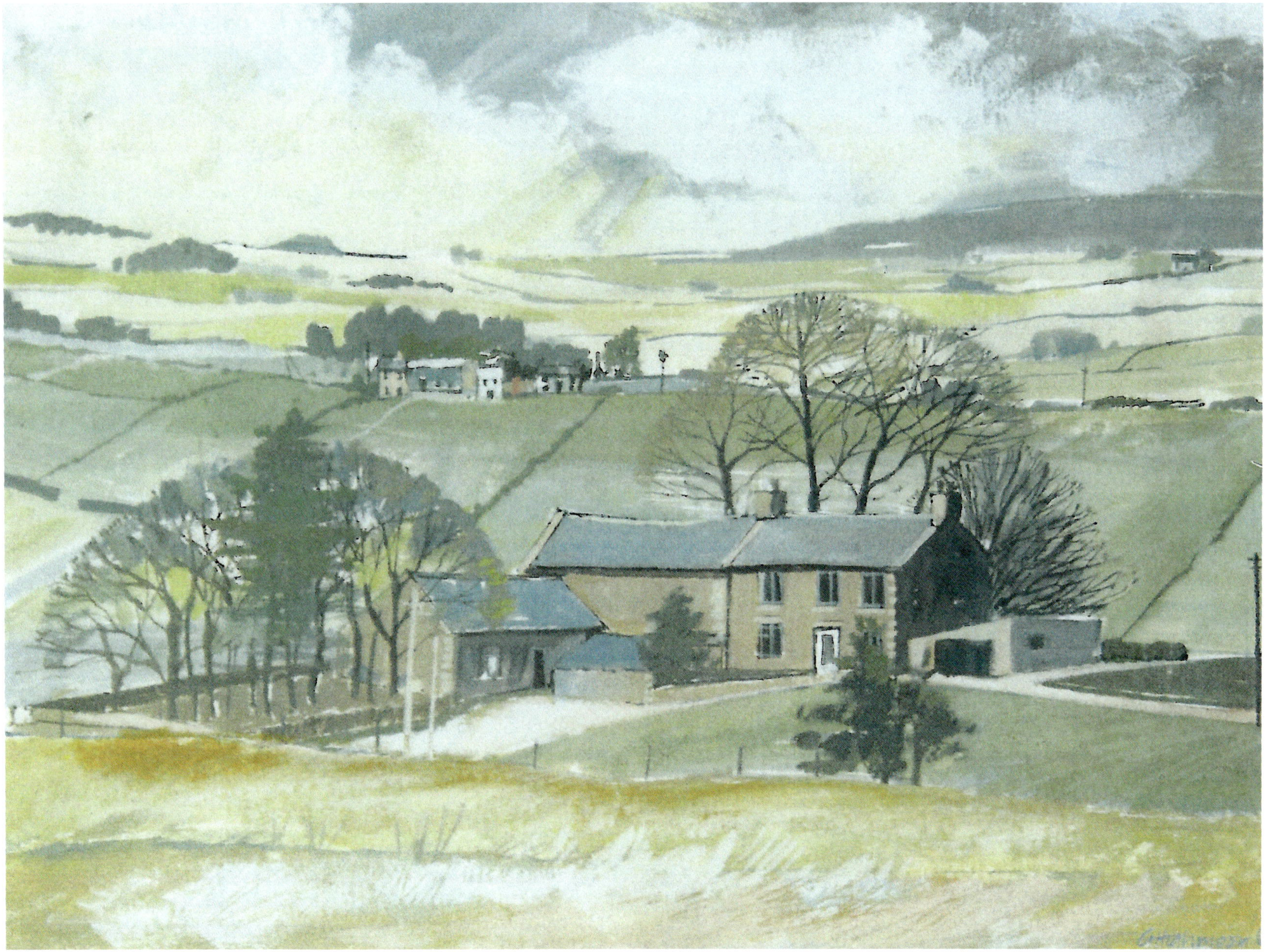

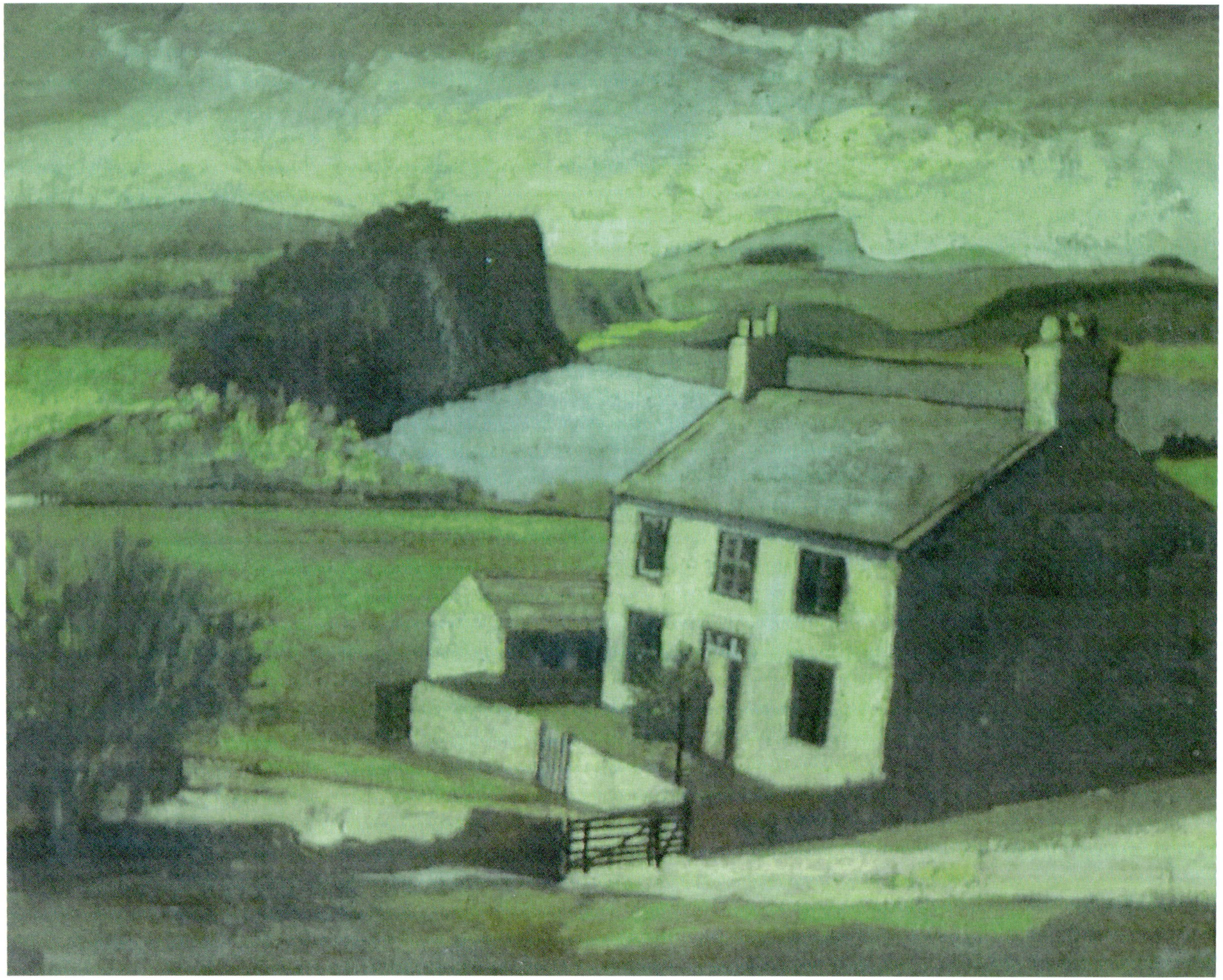

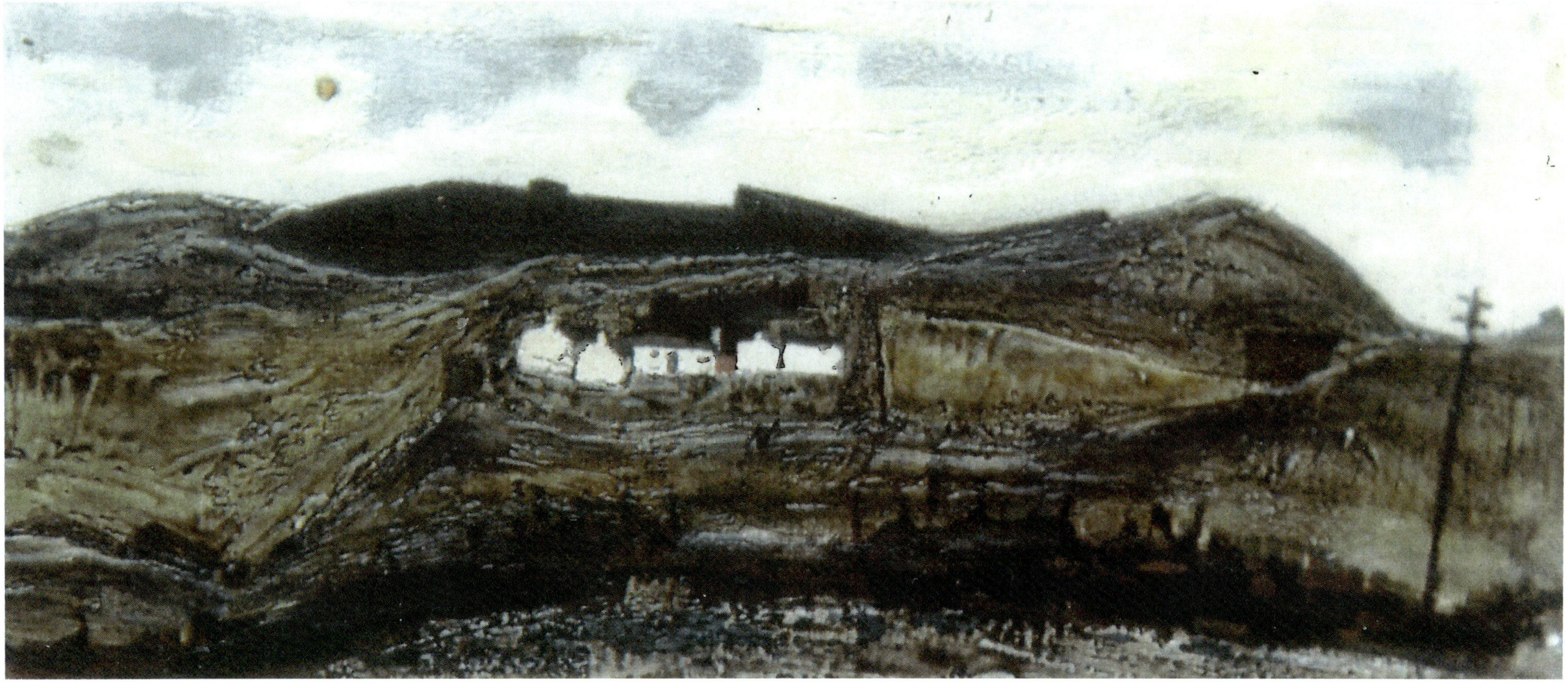

MAN'S PRESENCE (Mixed media)

This project began with drawings inspired by the lonely dwellings nestling amid the rugged fellsides in central Northumberland.

The resultant paintings use various mediums, including additions of glues,resins, stains etc., in an attempt to make textural statements about an essentially inhospitable landscape in which man and sheep lead a tenuous existence.

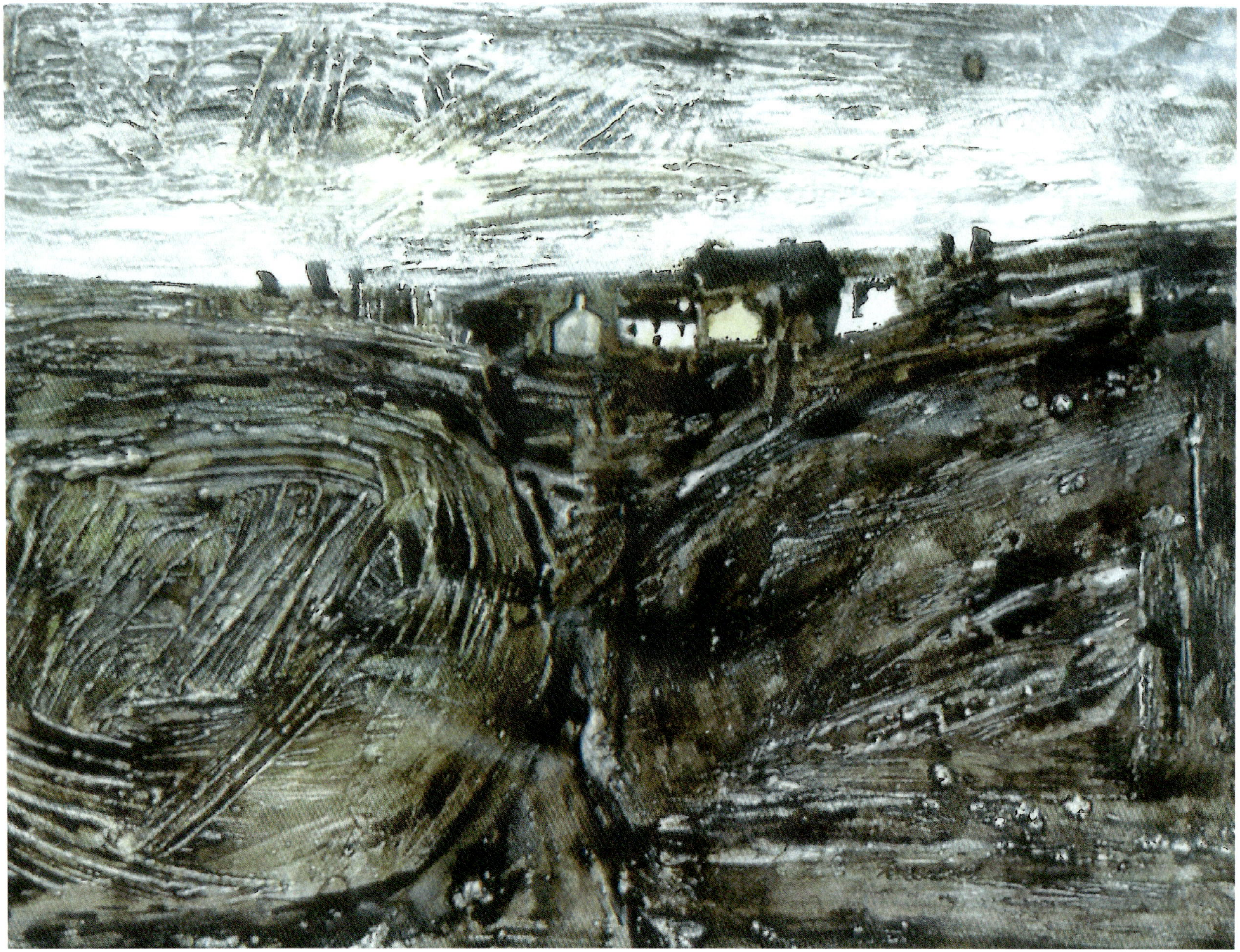

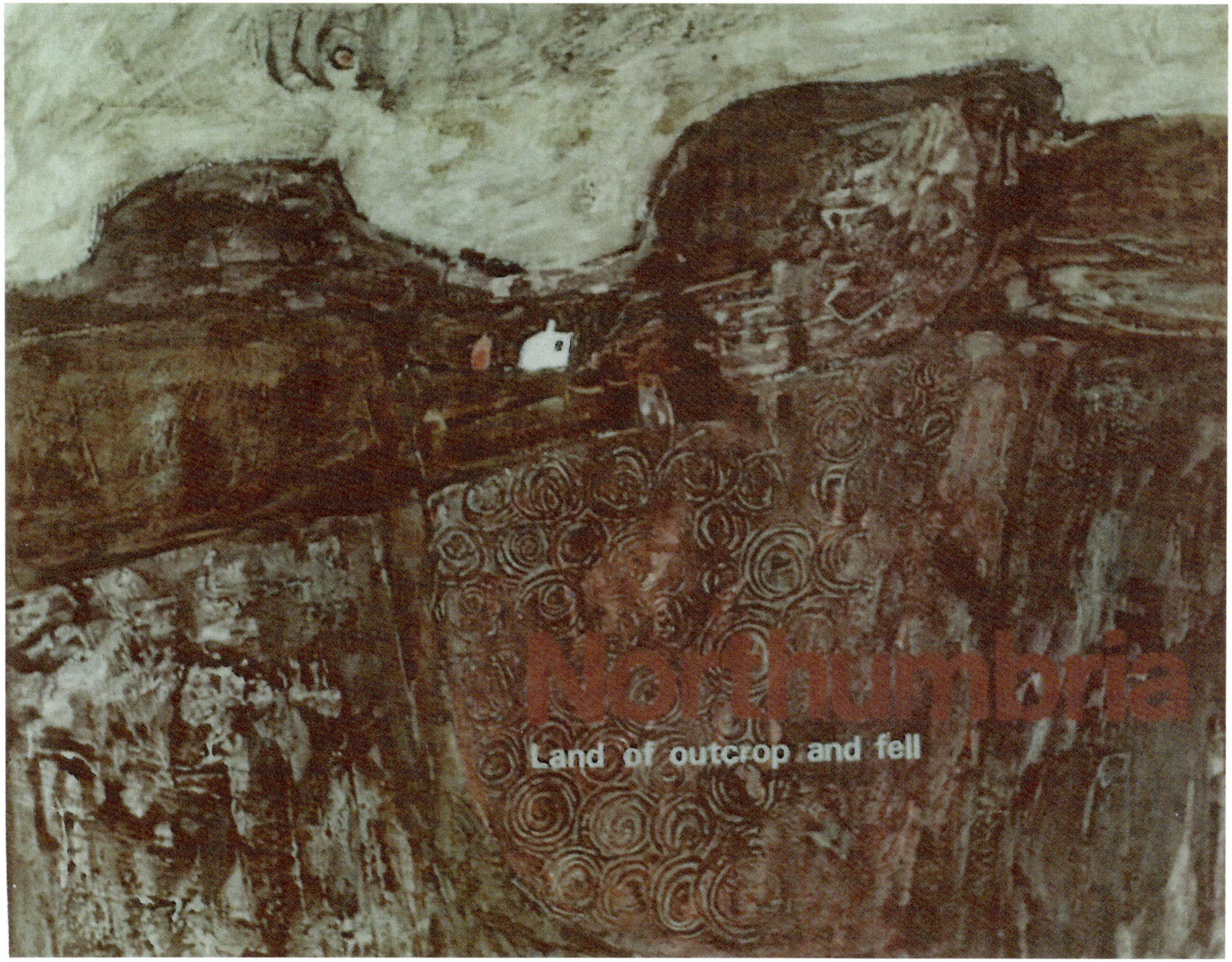

MAN'S PRESENCE (Gouache)

One of a series used as a book cover.

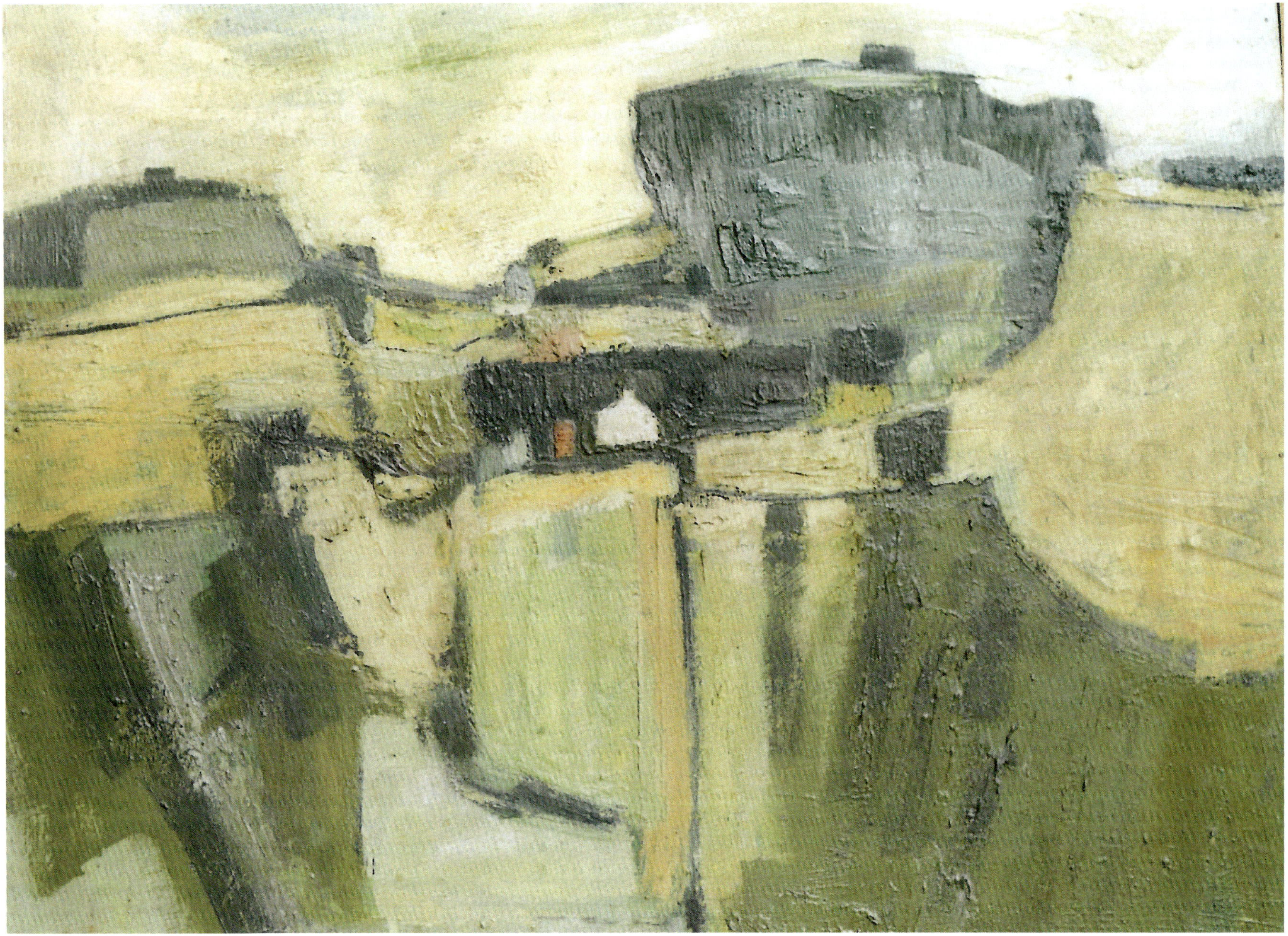

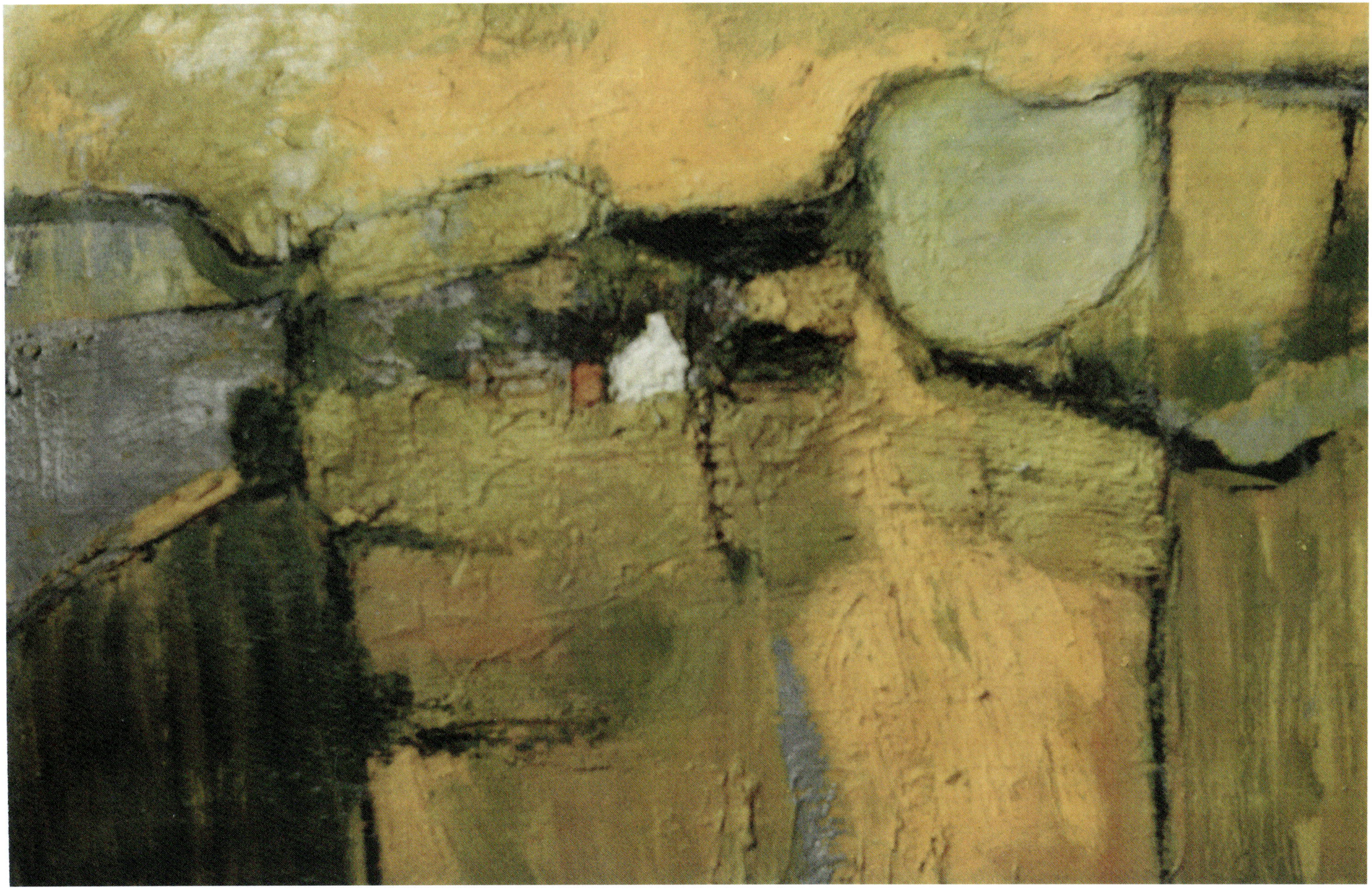

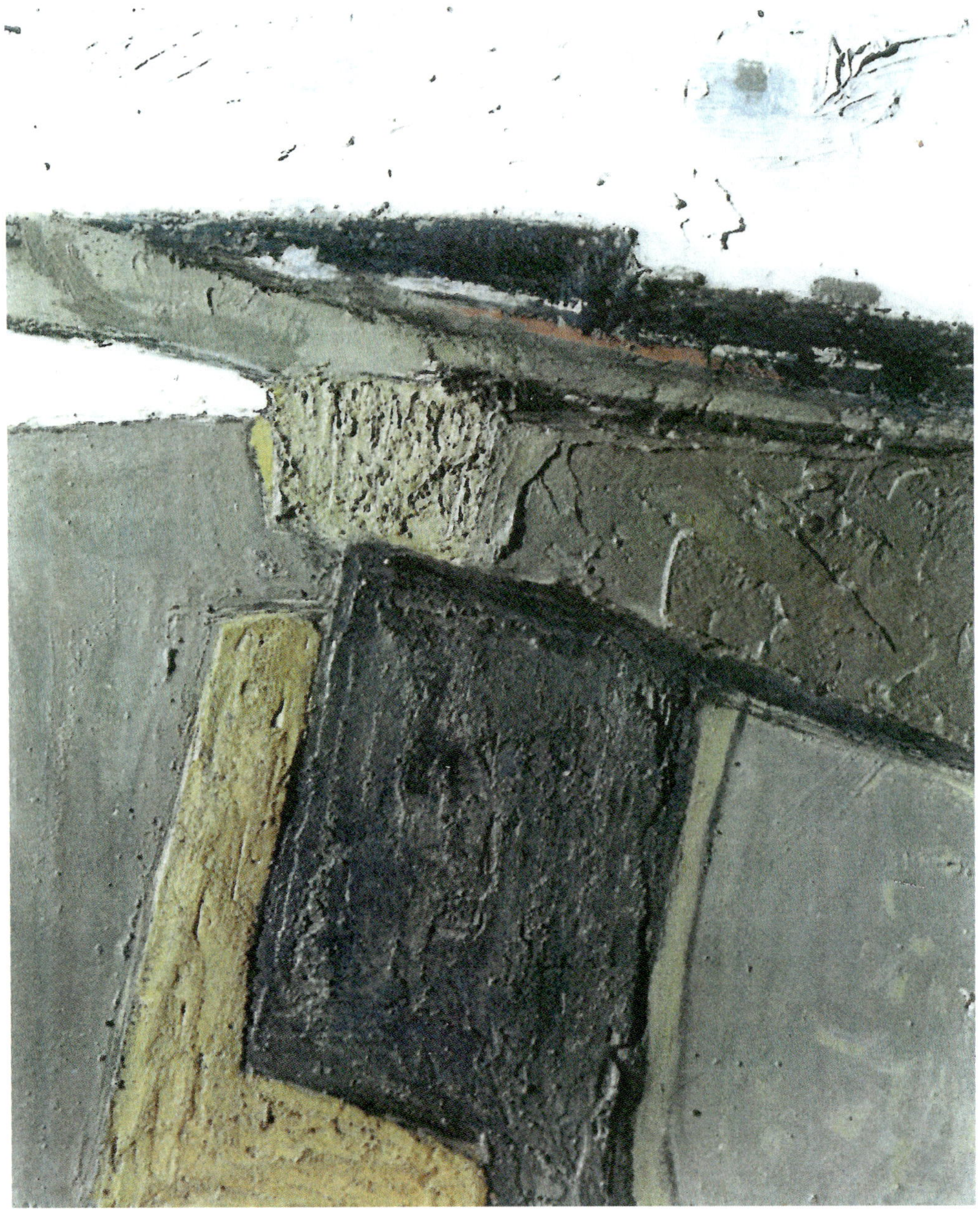

ABSTRACTION (Mixed media)

It was perhaps inevitable with all the patterns of dry stone walls, tracks, hollow-ways, enclosures etc, in the landscape, that my work should begin to go abstract.

I was still too preoccupied with mood and atmosphere however to let this happen and I never felt that the abstractions worked as well as the figurative statements.

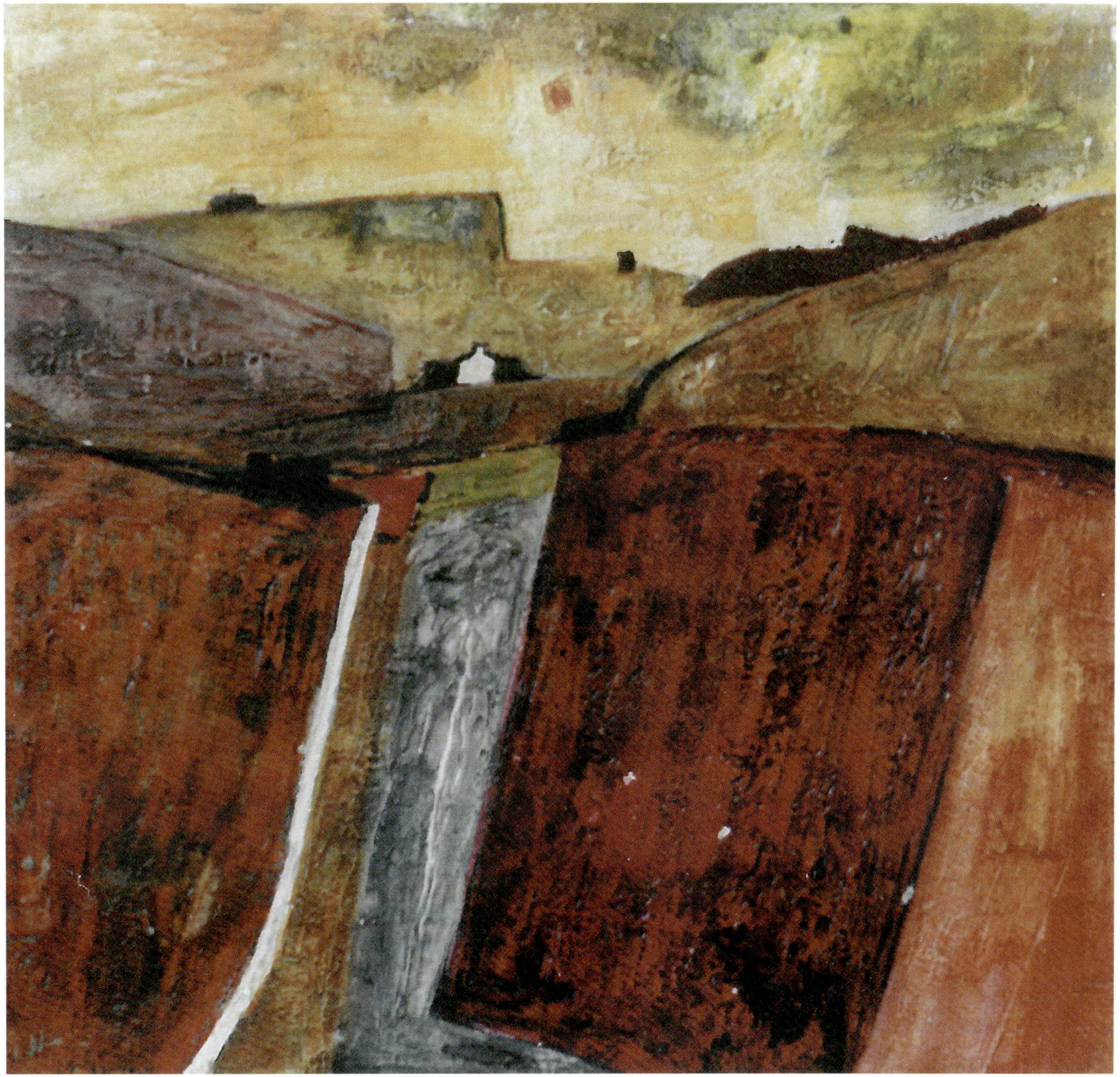

OUTCROP STONE IS MISERLY......

From the fell sandstones to the granites and andesite lavas of the Cheviots or the dolorite slabs of the Whin Sill, crags are visually fascinating. They punctuate the landscape edges against the sky, while close-to, the textures and colours are infinitely variable.

The activity of rock-climbing in Northumberland and in other similar areas of Britain, grew out of a need to practice movement on rock faces that would prepare Victorian mountaineers for their ascents in the Alps and elsewhere. By the end of the 19th century however, it had developed into a sport in its own right, first by scaling the weakness such as gullies and cracks and then the featureless walls and overhangs. Part of the joy in outcrop climbing must have been in the situations of these crags, the fact that most of them were situated in outstandingly beautiful and tranquil areas. The physical problem-solving together with the intellectual, chess-like manoeuvres, made it a sport enjoyed , in the first instance, by men such as doctors, writers, lawyers, teachers and the clergy, then, as it grew, by miners, engineers, builders and the like, men whose strength and ambitions helped to develop the sport at a great rate.

A key figure in the pioneering days of climbing in Northumberland was the writer and explorer **Geoffrey Winthrop Young** who, in about 1900, together with important local landowners, men such as **Sir Charles Parsons, Professor G.M.Trevelyan** and **Sir Charles Trevelyan**, made climbs on the Wanney crags and recorded their attempts in the old visitors" book which was then kept in the *Armstrong Arms, Ridsdale.*

In the foreword to the fist guide book, *Some Northumbrian Rock Climbs*, published in 1950, Young was to write....*"There is no nobler county than Northumberland, as it rolls processionally northwards to the Border in great waves of coloured and historic moorland, cresting upon the skyline into sudden and surprising crags, which crown for us the magnificent walking with admirable rock climbs. May the growing tide of northern climbers flow onward as great-heartedly."*

High o'er wild Wanny's lofty crest,
Where the raven cleaves the cloud,
An' gorcocks beck around Aid Crag,
Sae crousely and sae proud.
Gurlin' through the glens o' Reed
Wi' a weird and eerie strum,
When around yon auld cot
The winter winds they'd come

JAMES ARMSTRONG of RIDSDALE Wild Hills o' Wannys

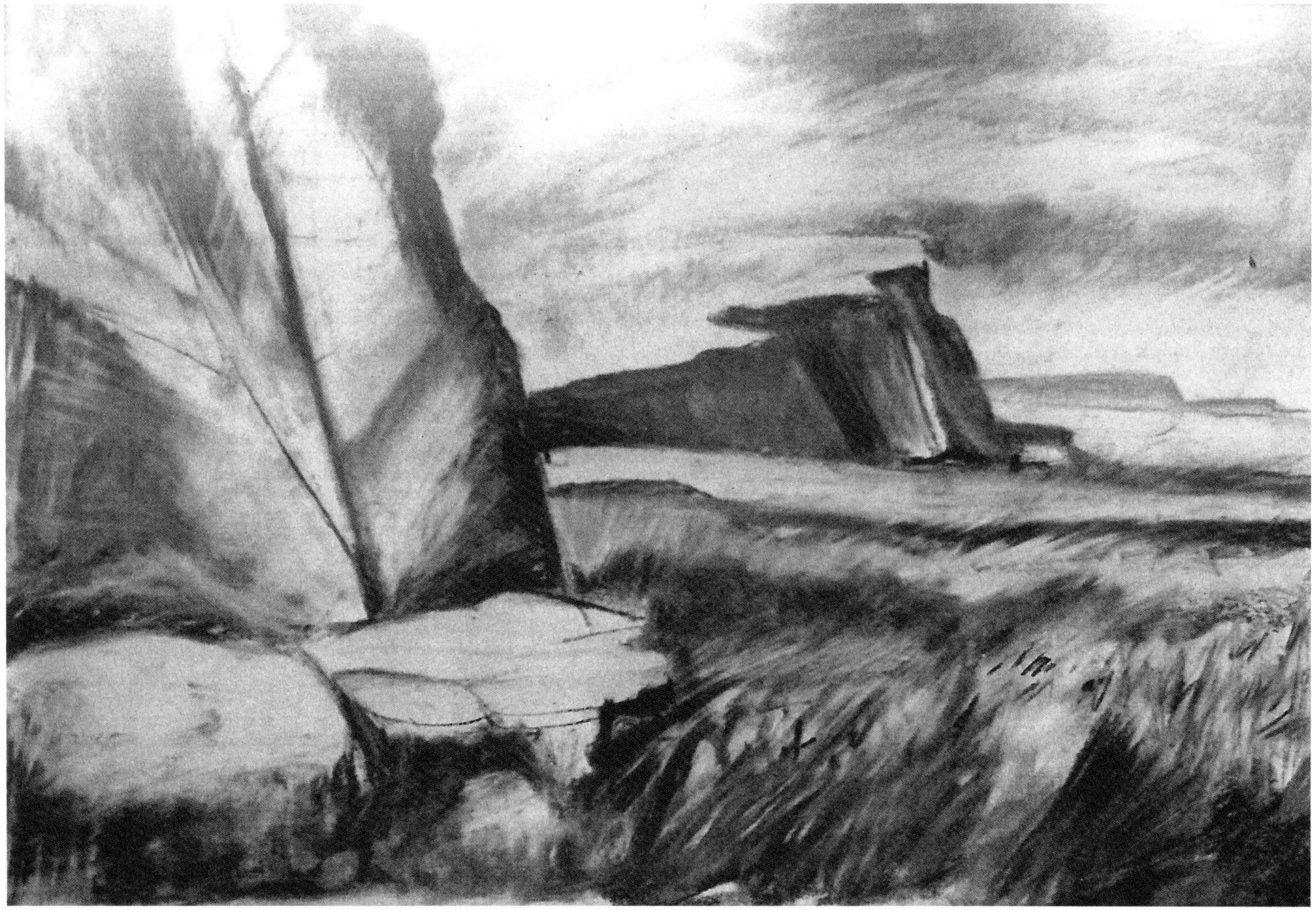

THE WANNEYS (Charcoal)

The sandstone crags of the *"Wild Hills of Wanney"* were the first place I began rock climbing in my youth.

In fact, when I founded a club together with a group of friends, mostly teachers at Ashington Grammar School in the 1960s, we adopted the eponymous name of the Wanneys Climbing Club.

Later the area was to serve as the subject of much of my painting and drawing (*including the "Rain" series*).

Warriors they are, and veterans
of long assaults;
Scabbed by plots where sheep must crouch
to fret the unforgiving grass.
Their heads are emptied out by rain, their feet
abused by pitchfork-tossing pines.
Backs to the wall of sky
and stripped to grit, except
where mist or snow can compromise
their fierce nudity;
they can do nothing but resist.

Stone-shouldered and unkindly twins;
but I have seen their stacks
turn tractable by light,
and as the peaceful clouds unwind
each blown, embattled height
is touched, and taught a mystery.

Then the crags stand in accord
with all whose battles are adjourned for joy;
and those, unlike the rock, who hold it fast
against a time when they may fall
among the kindnesses of light
infrequently, or not at all.

PETER BENNET Light on the Wanney Crags

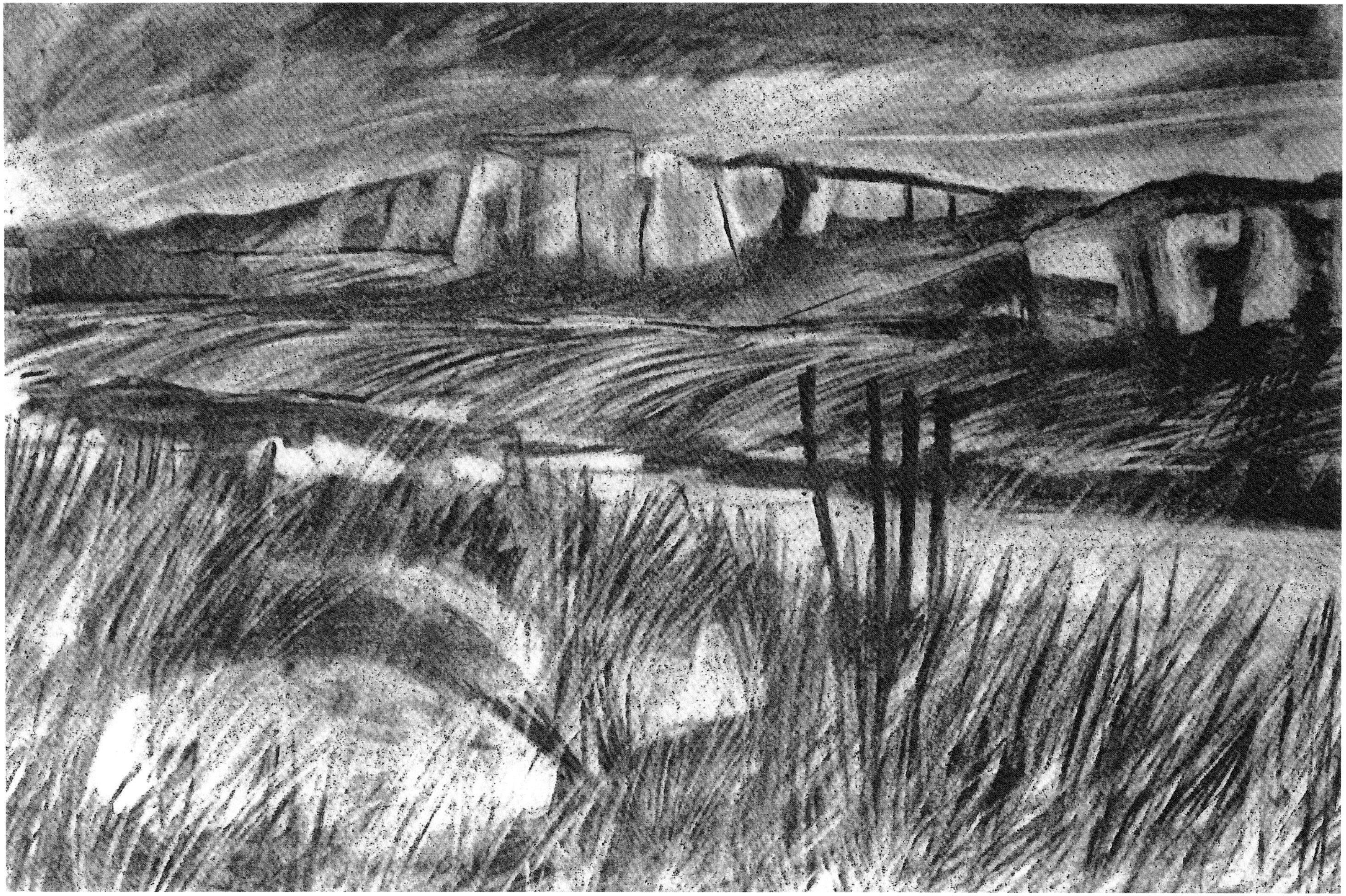

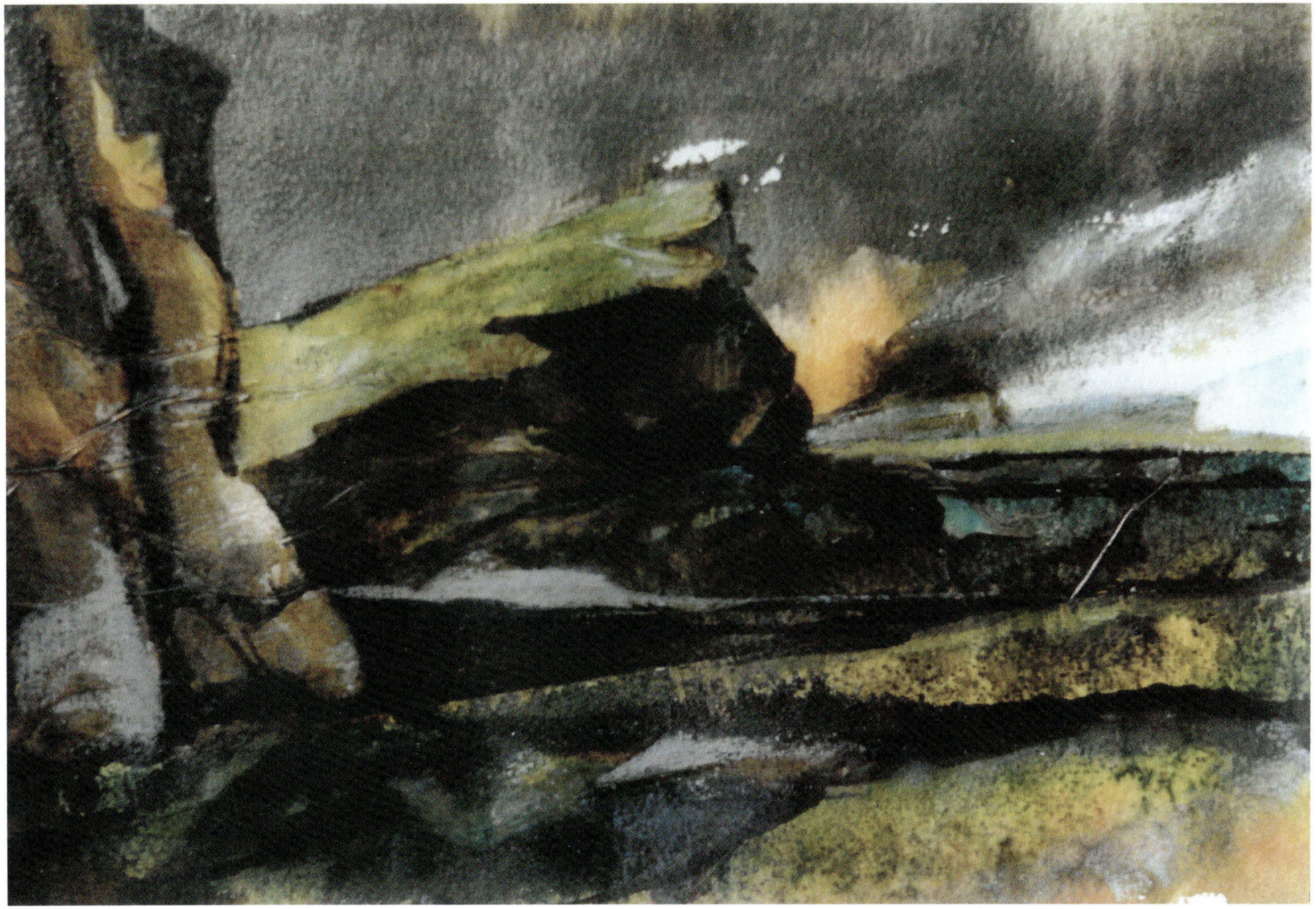

THE WANNEYS (Inks)

The area is subject to many moods and influences which is best expressed in the variety of colours and textures to be found here.

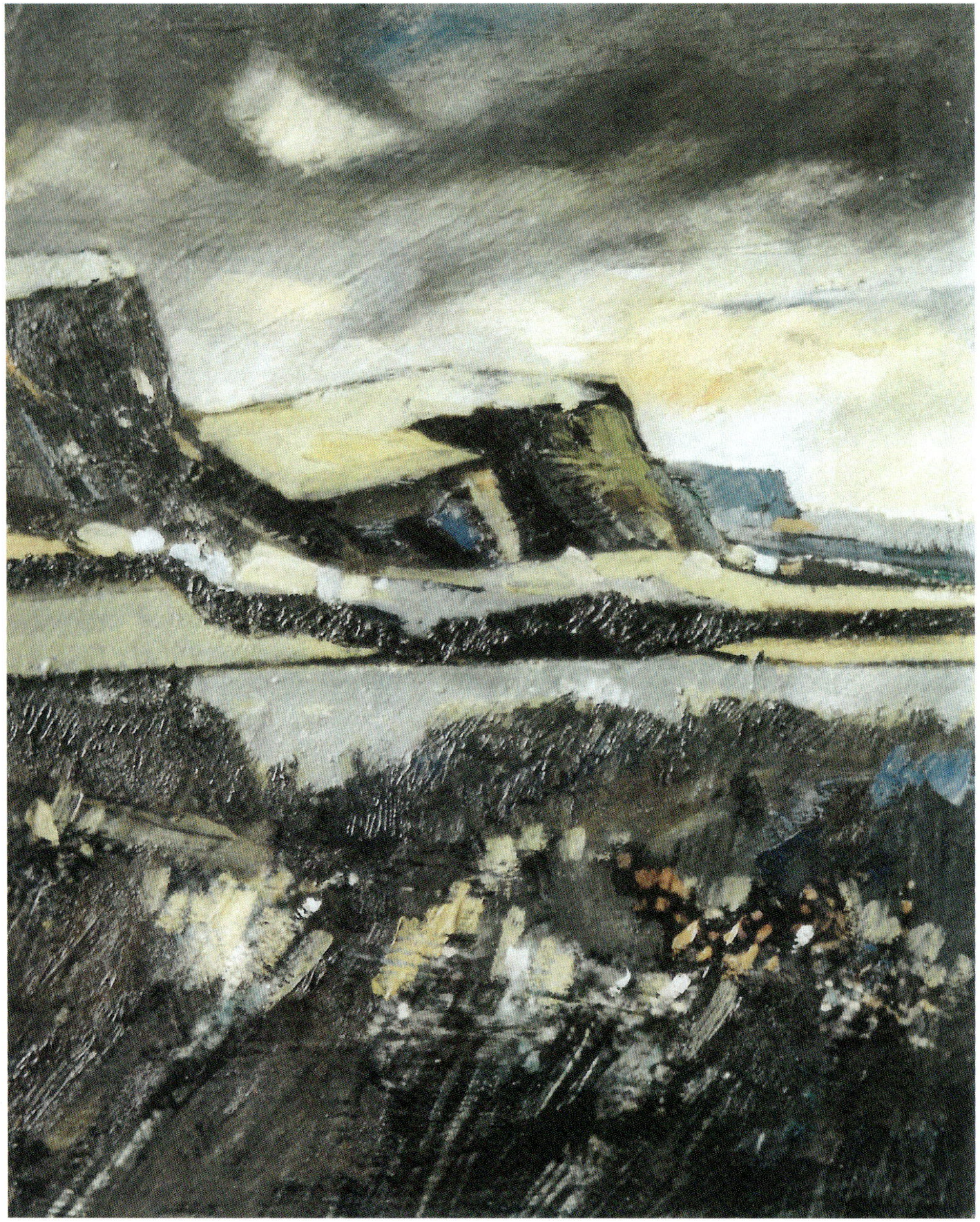

No living creature moves, only the skies'
Slow turbulence; The slanting rain that shakes
In sudden gusts and flurries as it rakes
The stubborn grass; no sound except the sighs
Of wind and ceaseless, hissing rain.
No colour, only varied tones of grey
Against the slate the lowering skies display.
The weather and the landscape speak a pain
That we, not they, must for a while sustain
Until the season break and see, alone,
Close in the foreground the single hunk of stone,
Bleak cenotaph, and one which bears no name.

VERNON SCANNELL Moors Threnody

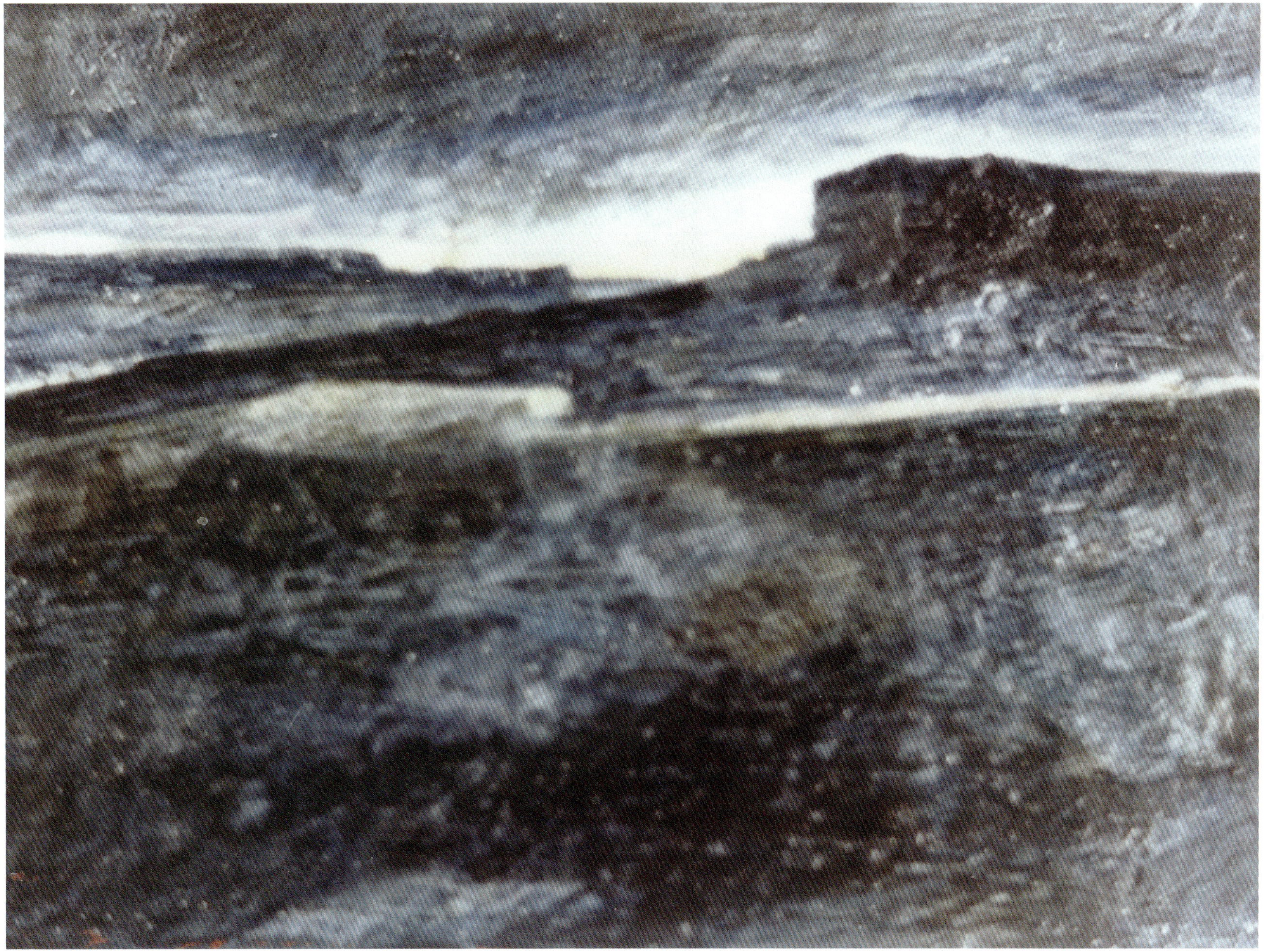

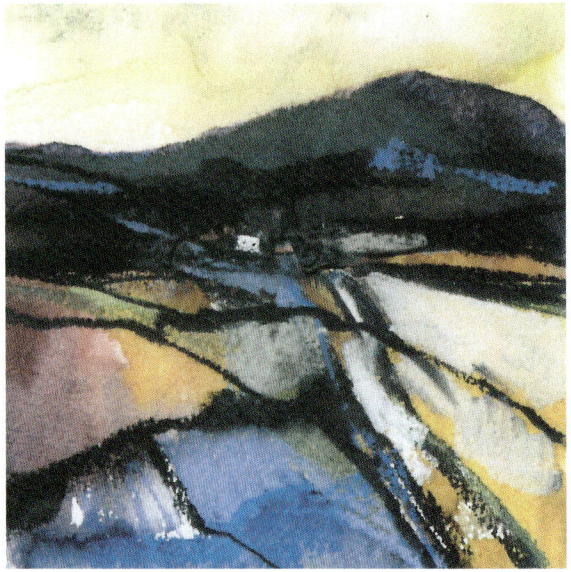
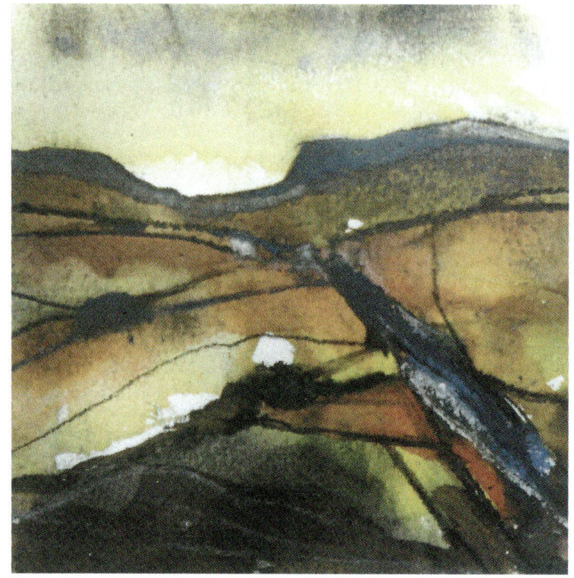
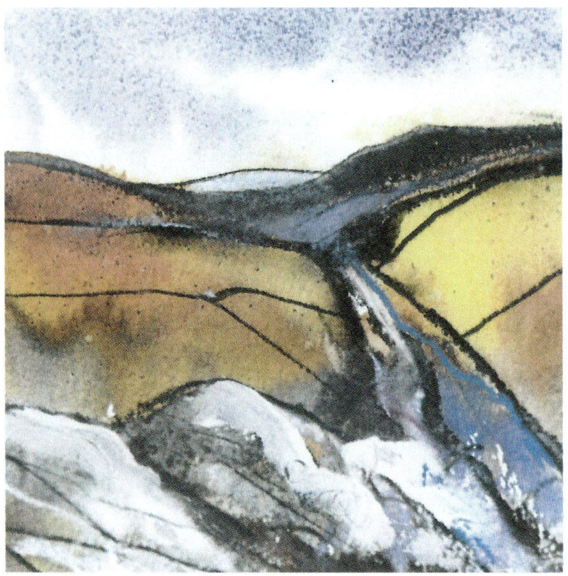
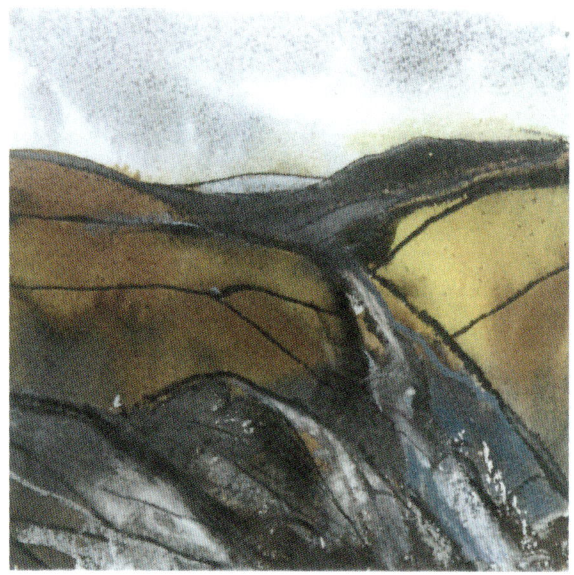

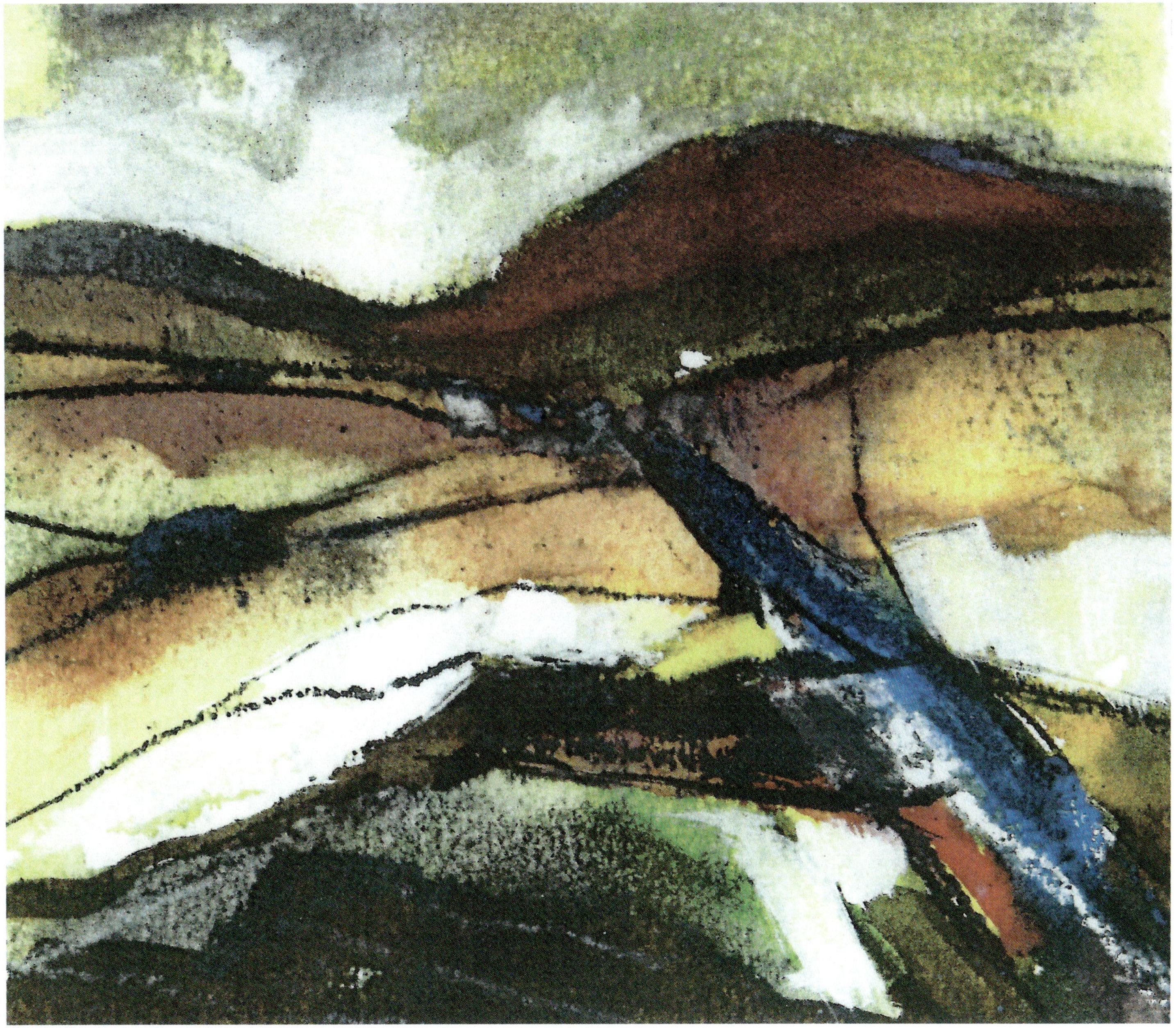

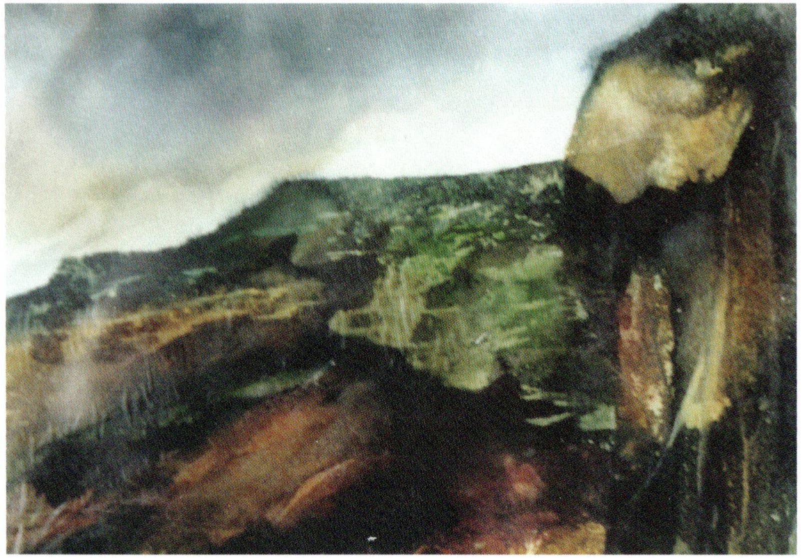

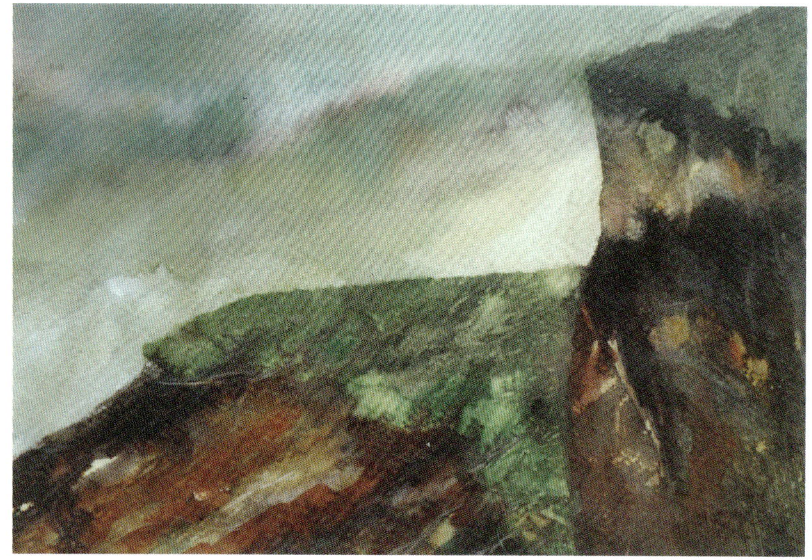

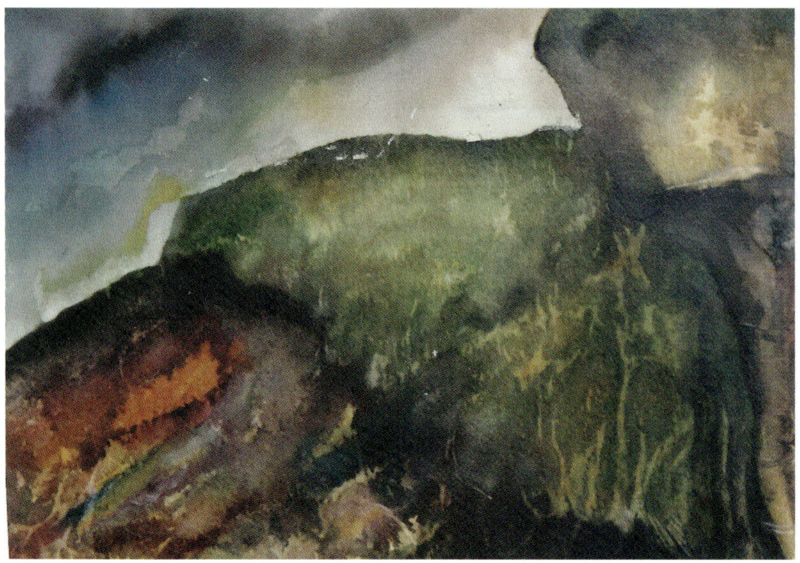

SEA CLIFFS (Watercolour)

Most finished paintings start with notes and sketches in order to clarify one's ideas and often, as these watercolours, are done on the spot.

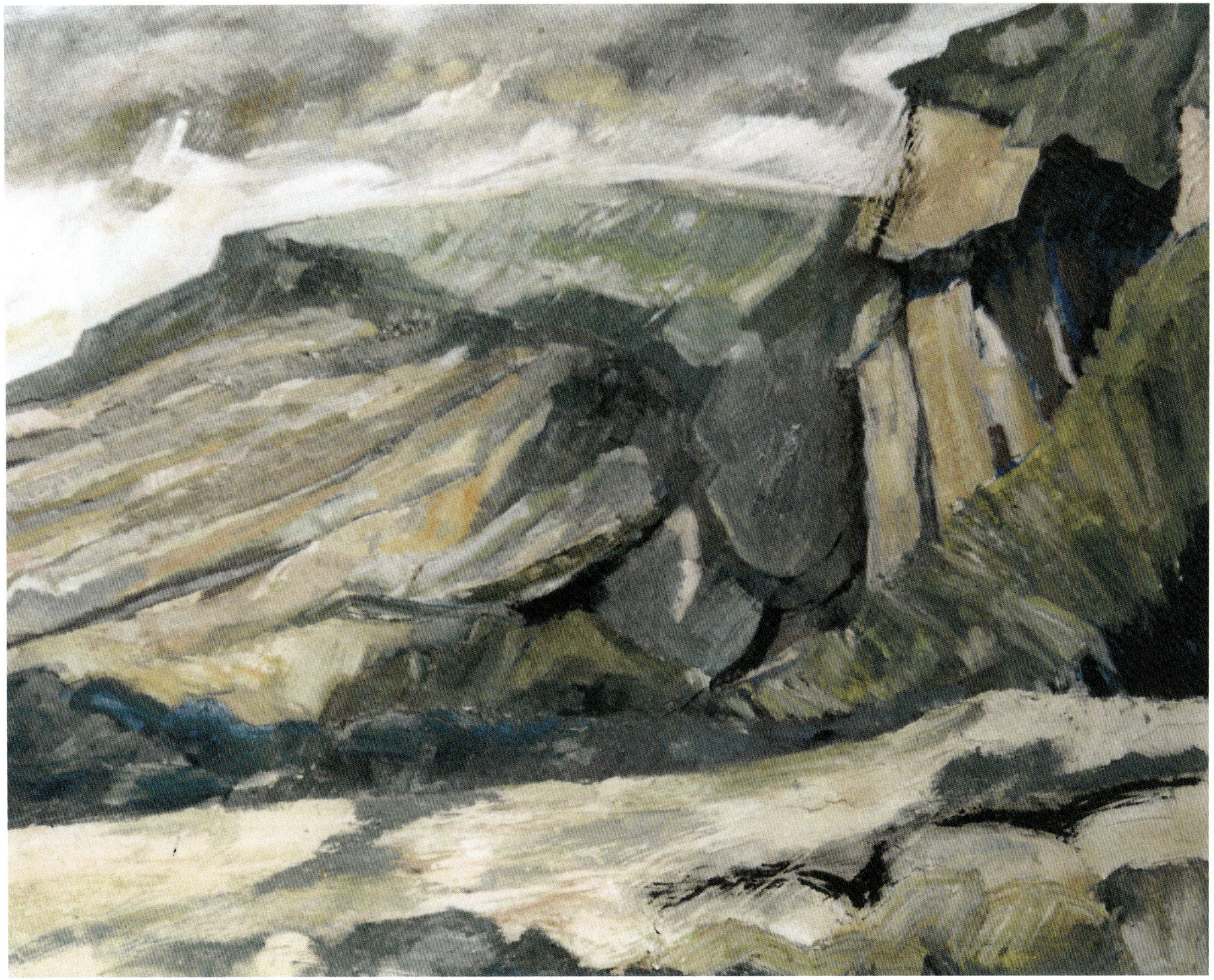

SEA CLIFFS (Oil)

Northumberland abounds in coastal cliffs, mostly of sandstone and dolerite, and which have been climbed on for many years and guide books made.

These rocks at Cullernose Point form a veritable geologists' laboratory being the location for several kinds of rock and shale including limestone.

There's even a dinosaur foot-print hereabouts.

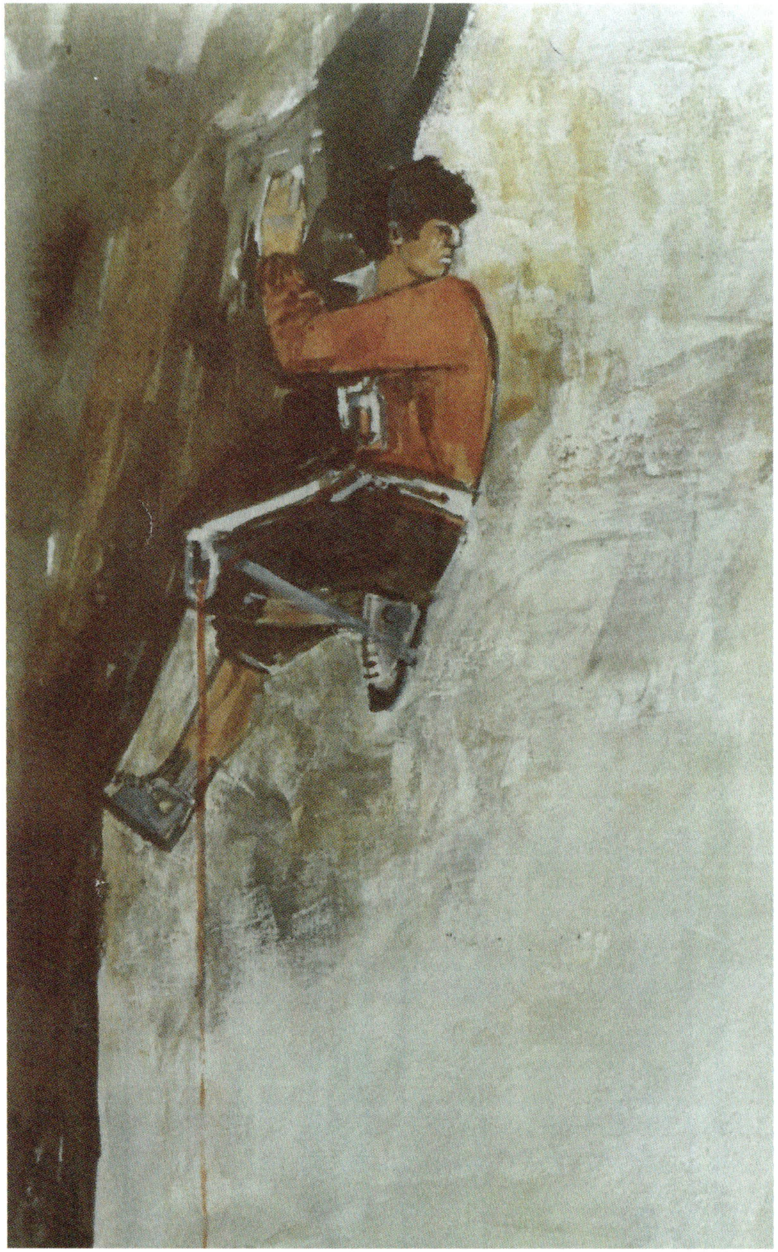

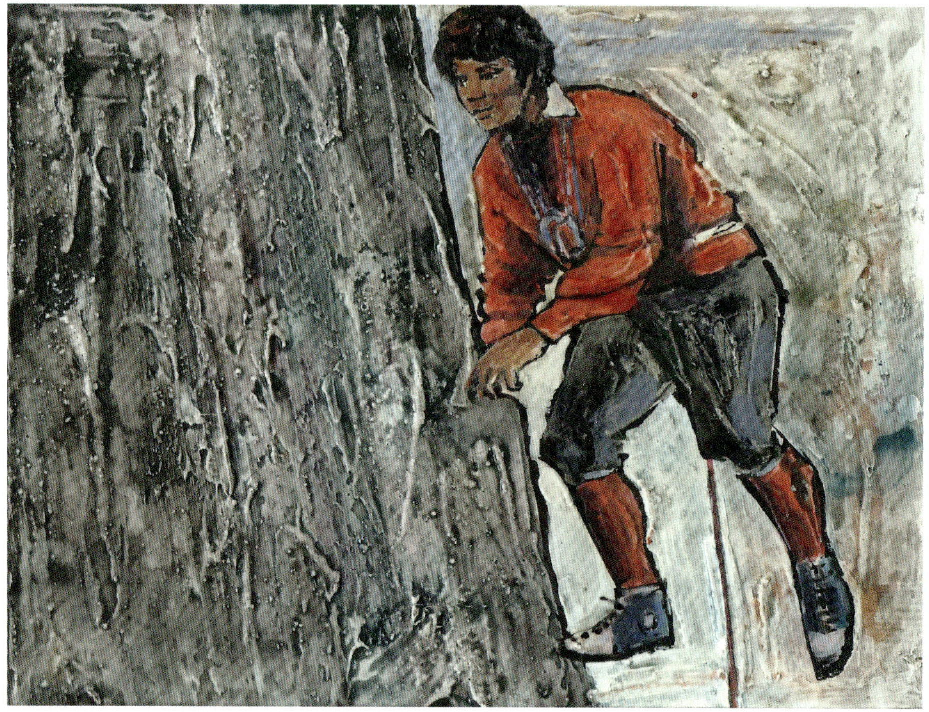

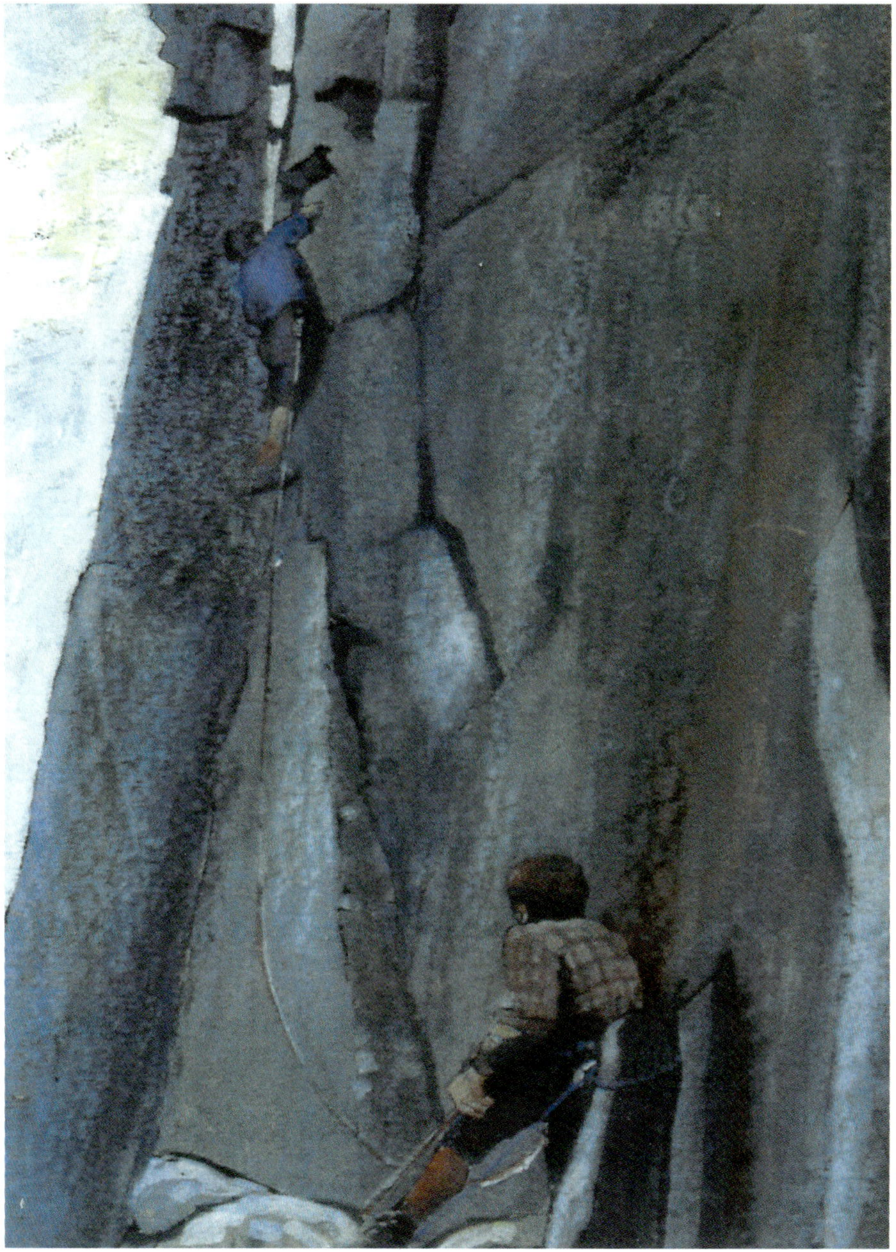

ROCK CLIMBING (Pastel & Wax)

Crag Lough, on the Roman Wall, offers very steep climbing on the grey dolerite of the Whinsill.

Here I am leading the testing WHY NOT (graded Very Severe) while my mate Bill Main carefully pays out the rope. This is the crux (the hardest part of the climb), a strenuous move into the large crack containing jammed rocks where some protection can be arranged.

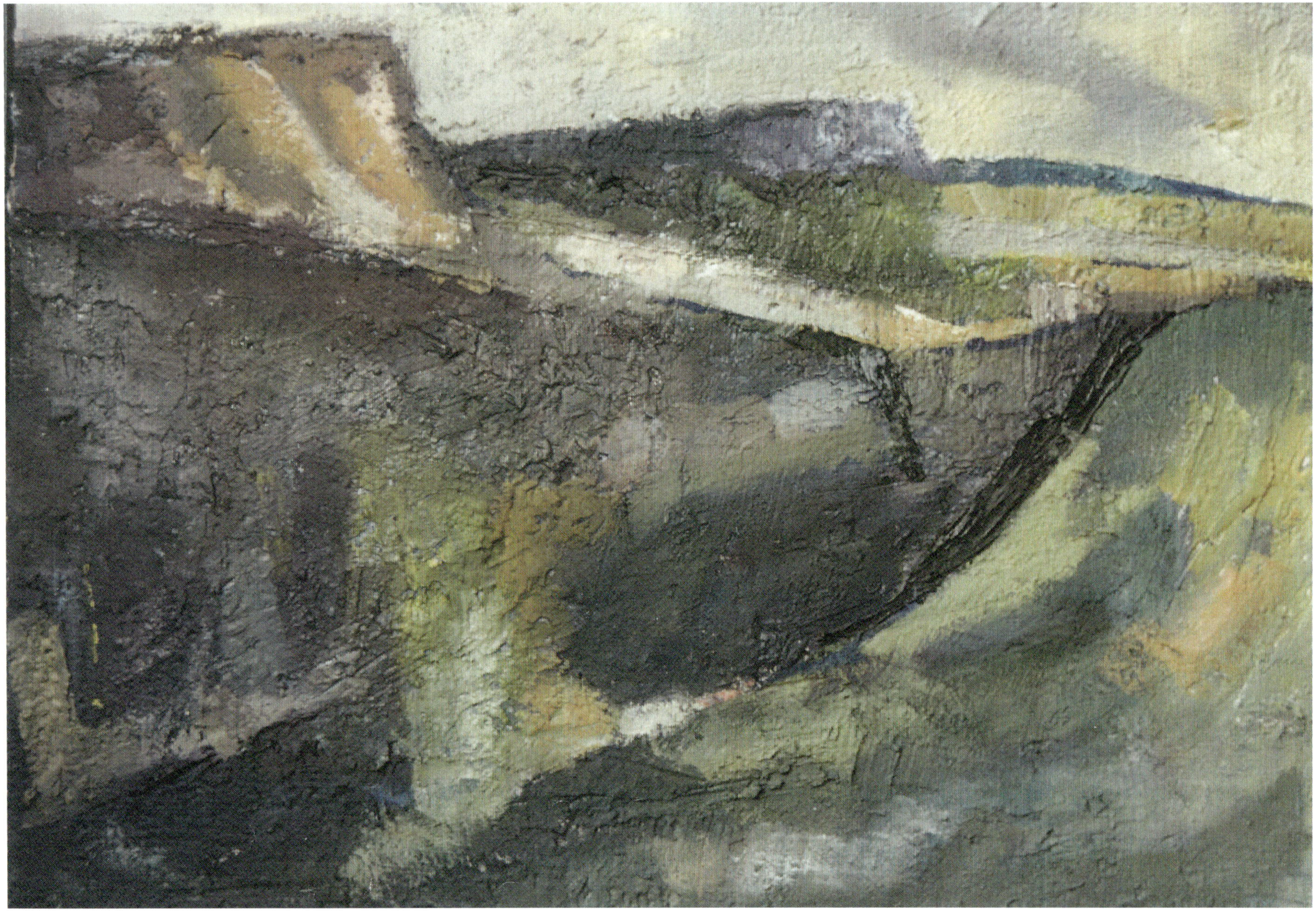

AND SILENT, SHIFT AMONG THE HILLS.......

A series of watercolours, made over a period of weeks in the 1980s, intended to evoke the feeling of shifting rainclouds in a wet Northumbrian sky. These works were also inspired by a poem - *Drifting* by Margaret Gillies (qv) - and the location is the **"Wild Hills of Wanney"** east of the Woodburn/Otterburn road. It is a bleak, largely uninhabited area of moors, rocks, heather and cotton grass where outcrops of fell sandstone break the horizon as they settle in a **cuesta** facing Cheviot itself.

Alas it is also an area identified by those powers who cannot come up with a better solution to our energy problems than to scatter those obscene wind-turbines across the landscape. So far we have managed to stave off the threat as many like-minded Northumbrians, whether born here or enticed here, continue to oppose those who come to destroy our landscape and our heritage.

I watch them,
The rain clouds drifting from the sea,
Imperceptibly moving nearer,
Shrouding the landscape.

Sometimes I stand in their predestined path,
Here in this fertile valley,
Feel their liquid fall
Upon my upturned face;

Sometimes they pass me by,
And silent, shift among the hills
Like drawn veils dimming women's faces.
Softening the bone-clad loveliness
The structured elegance;
Shading the harvest's brazen make-up,
Adding allure,
Heightening the mystery.

MARGARET GILLIES Drifting

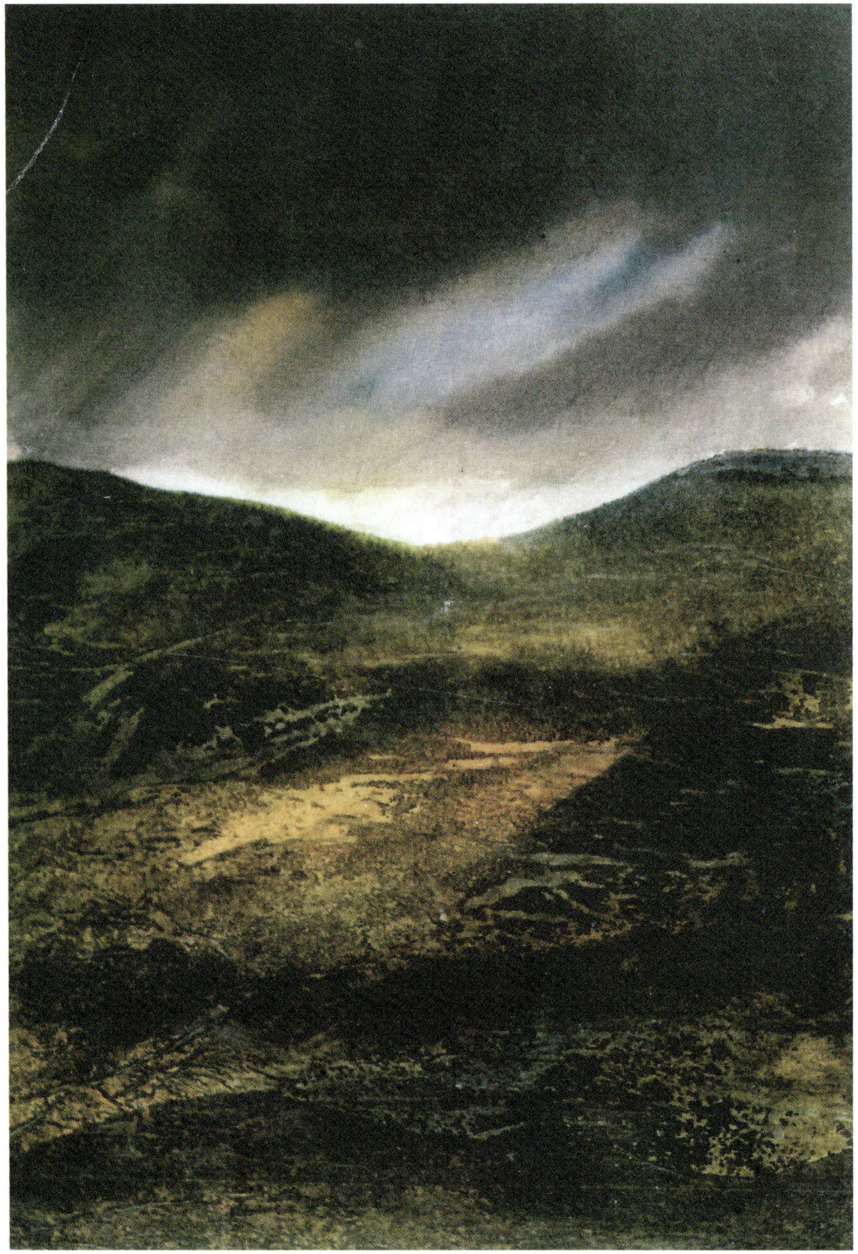

RAIN CLOUDS (Watercolour)

Part inspired by a poem and by music, the watercolours explore the movement of the wet sky over the Wanney Hills.

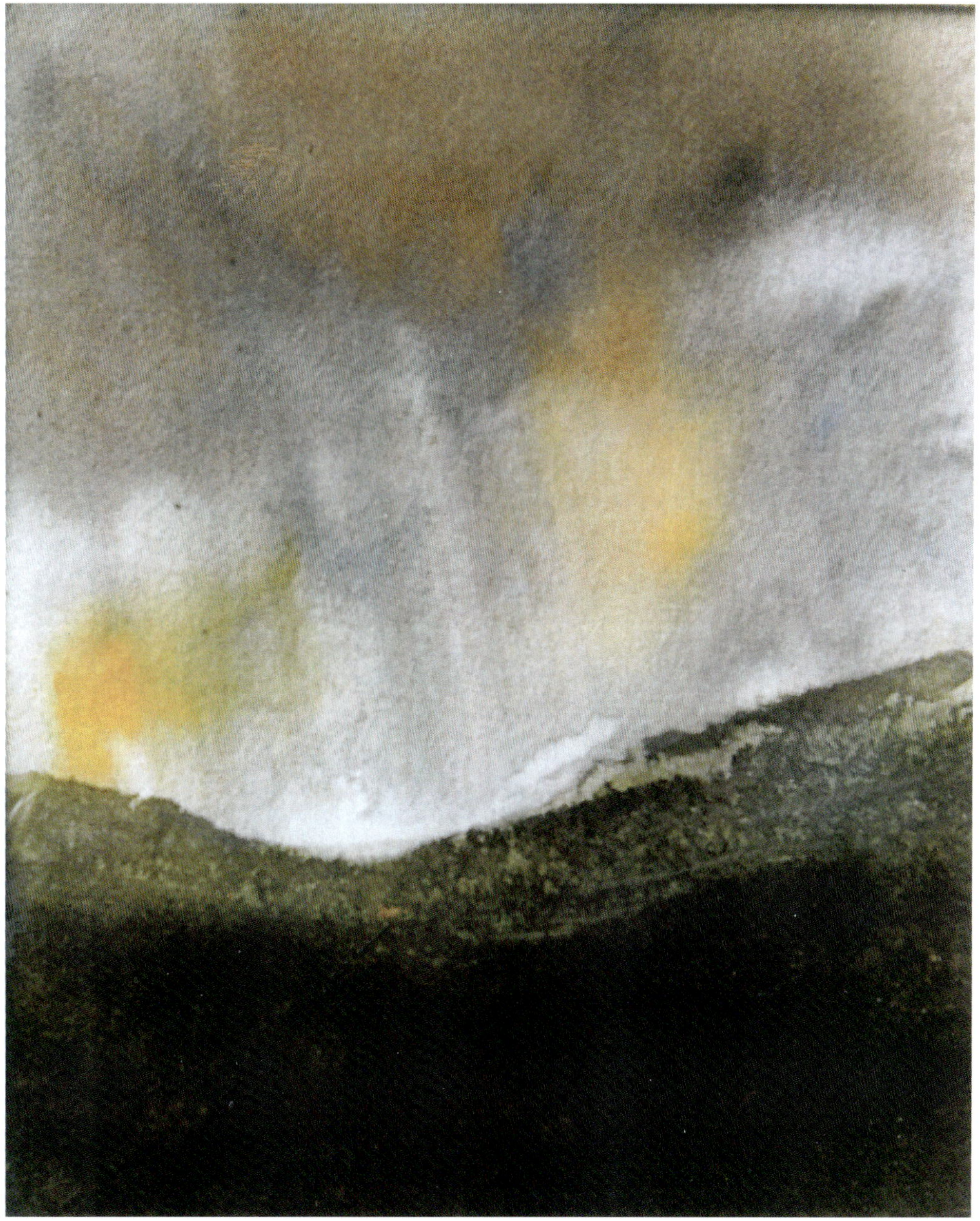

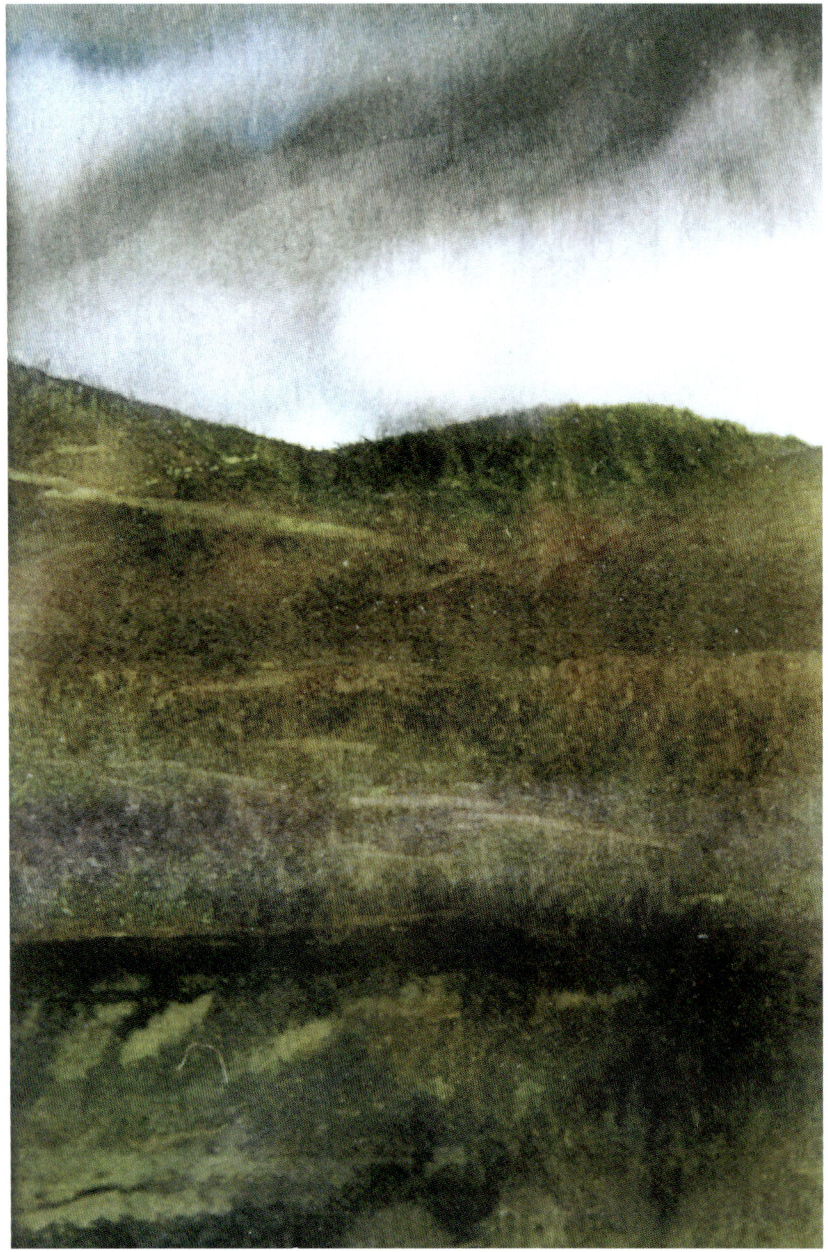

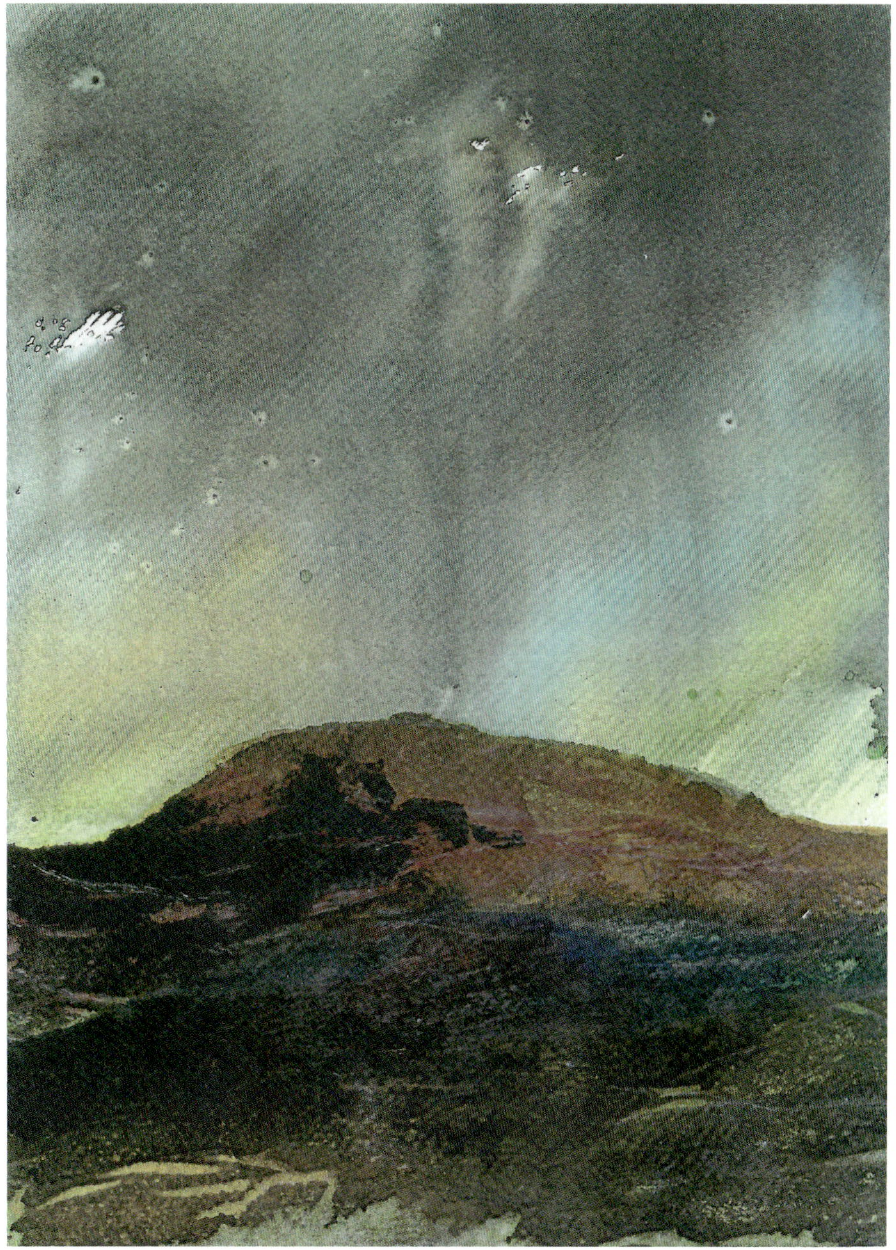

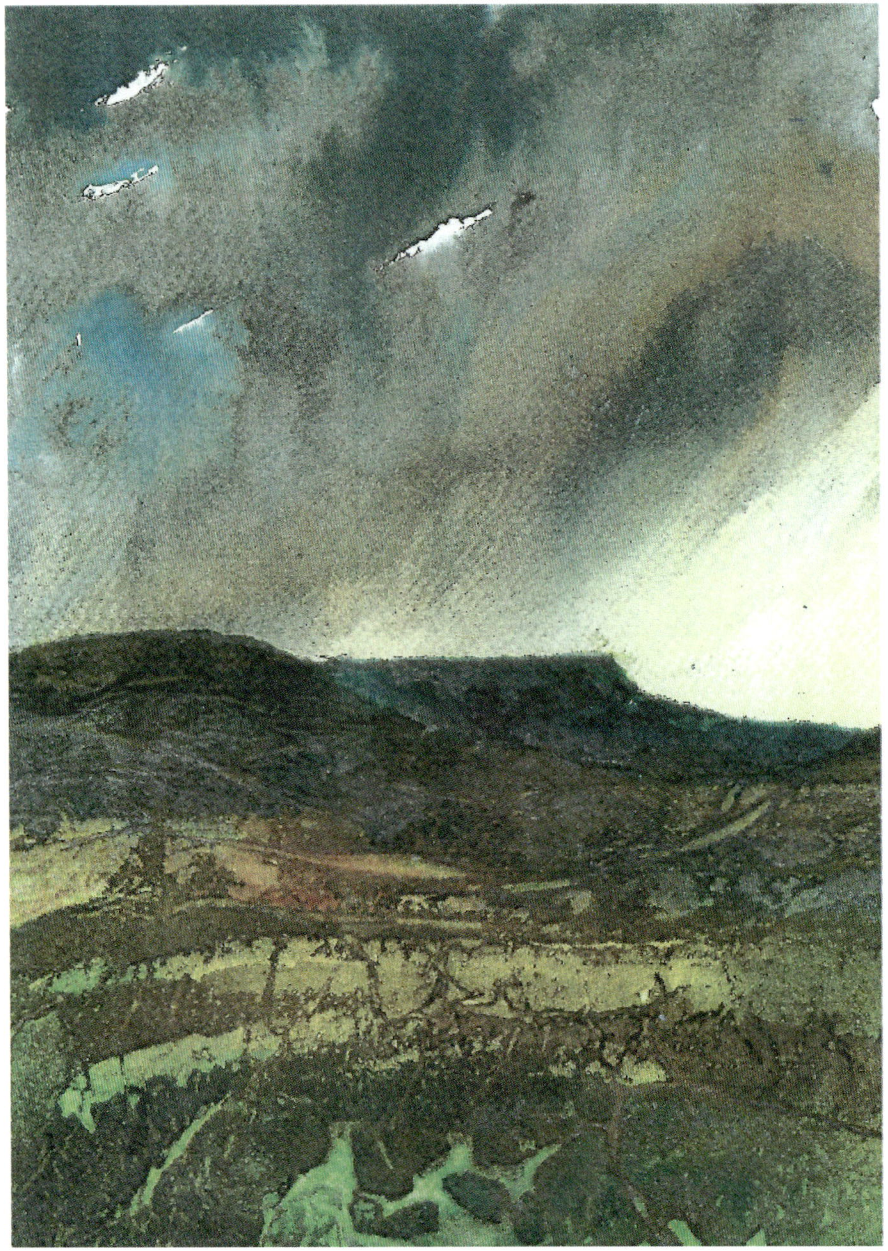

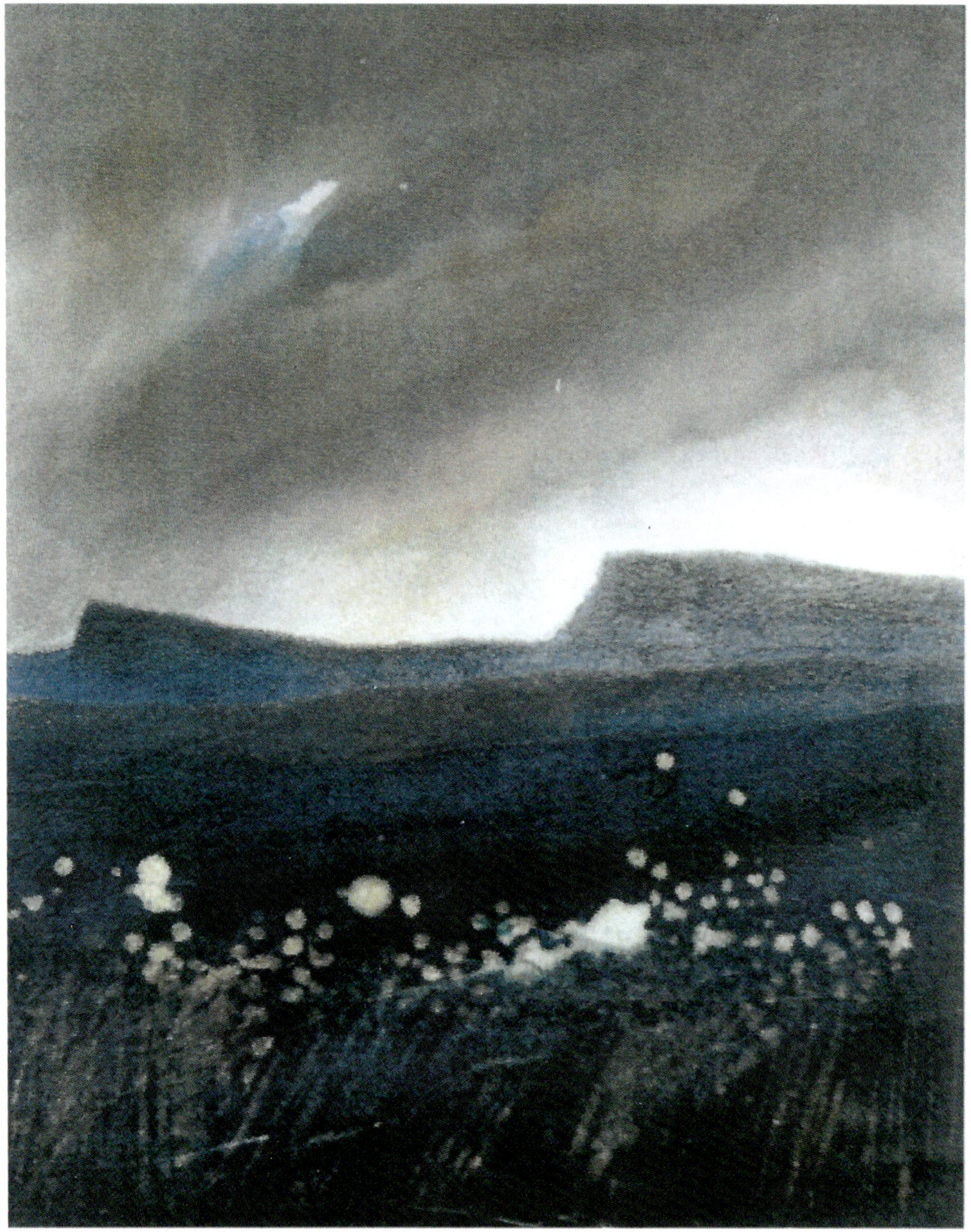

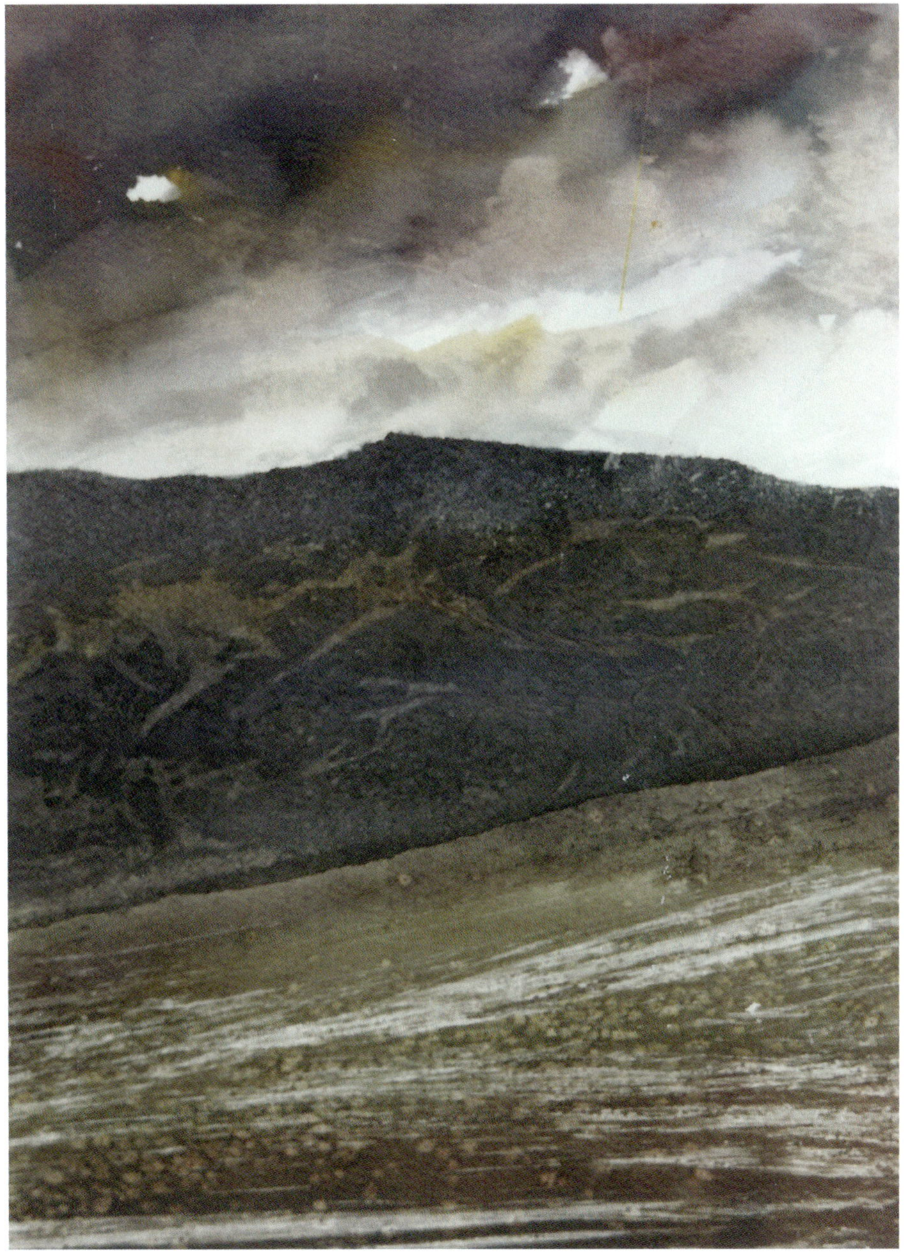

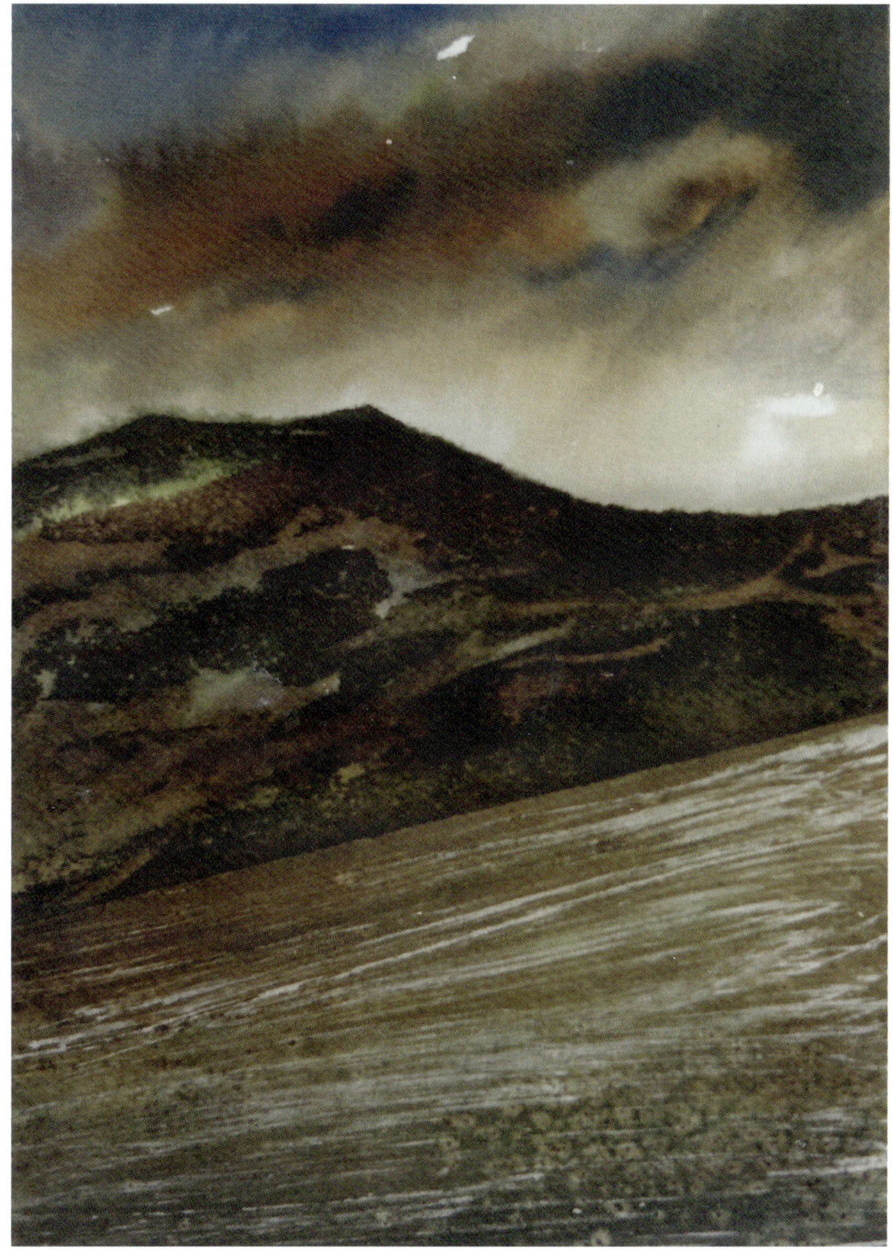

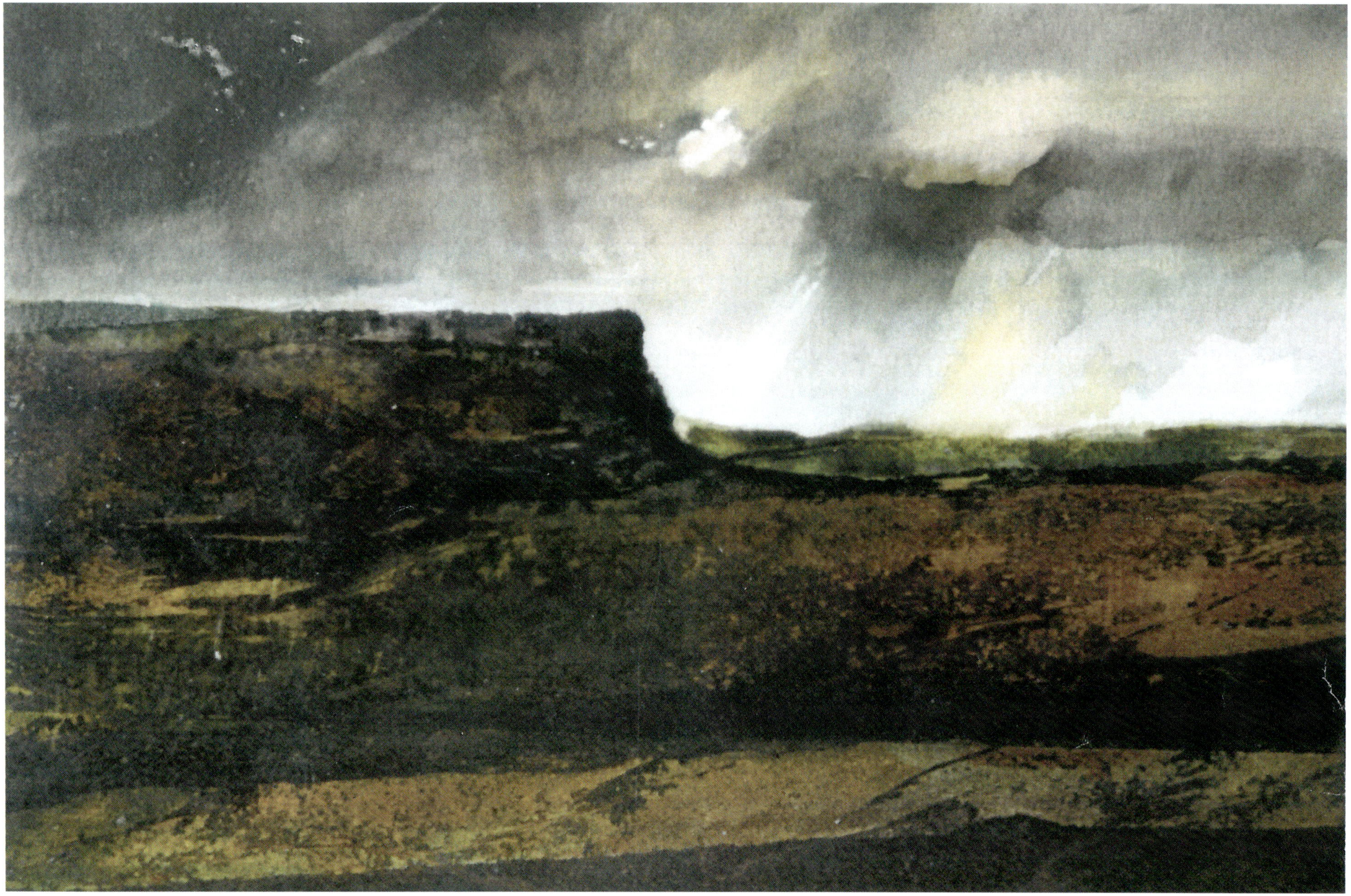

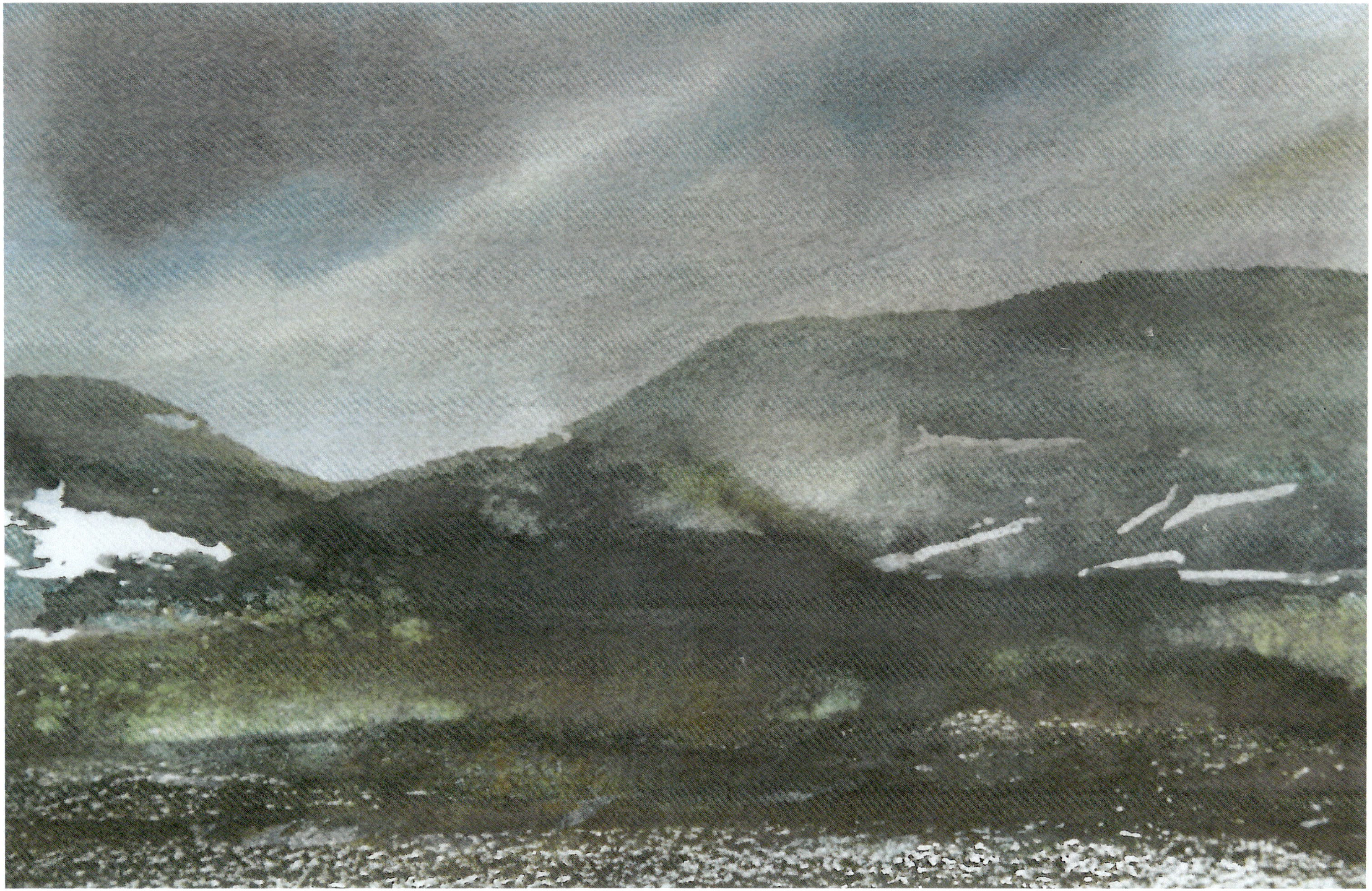

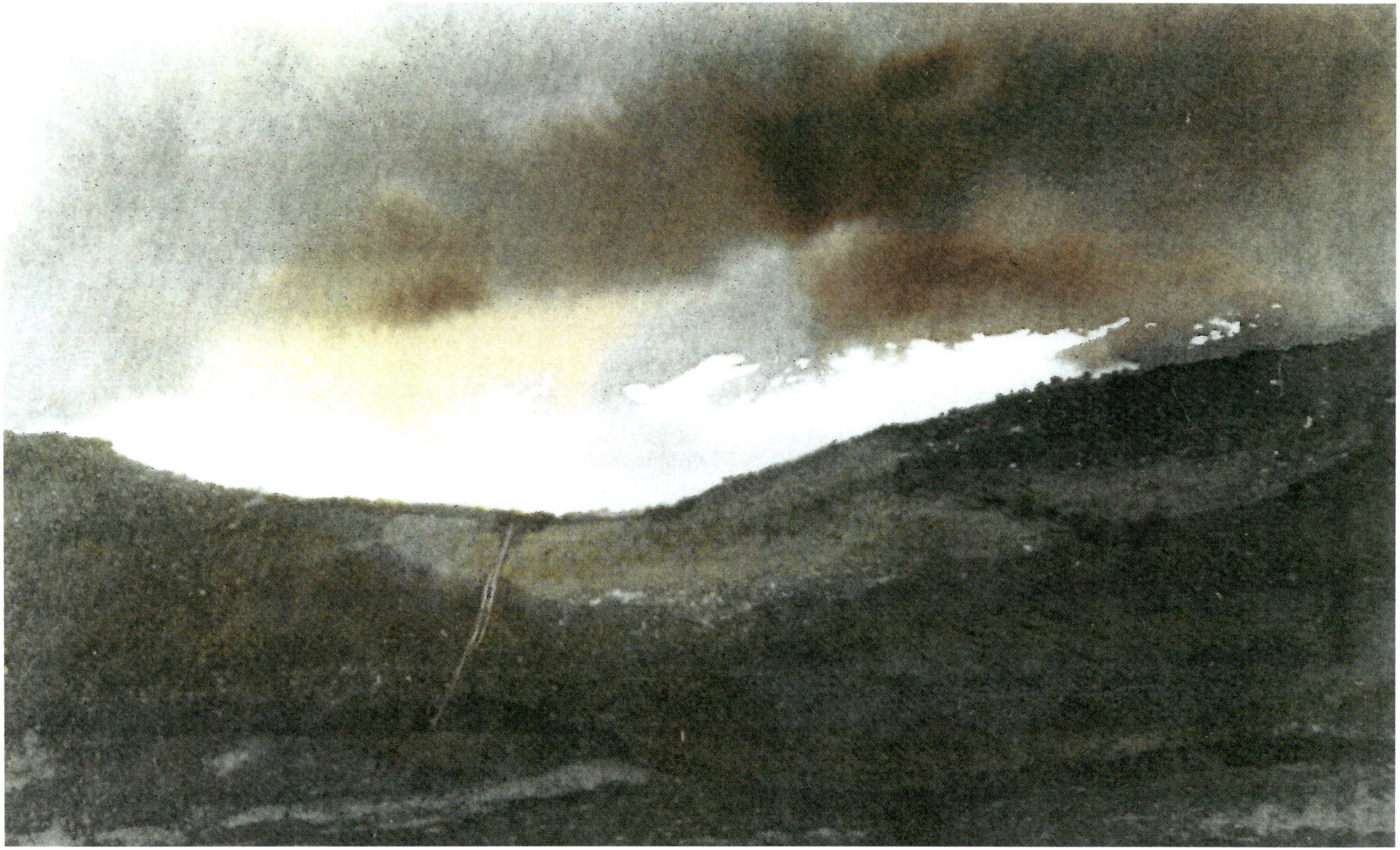

WHO BUILT THIS CAIRN ON THIS WILD HILL.....

The bulk of my most recent work is concerned with the "essence"of my own landscape and what I hope I achieve in these paintings and drawings is a sense of its unique ancient-historical associations. Here I have attempted to create more than mere "views" for the work contains some of the most fundamental themes of nature - the seasonal cycle of death and regeneration and the life-giving power of the sun. Thus specific motifs such as the circle, recur in the work, not only to describe the shape of fort or settlement, or of cup and ring motifs, but as one of the most potent and fundamental pre-Christian symbols.

It is also a textural landscape. Rock weathered by erosion and exposure , dyed by minerals and ores, or bleached by exposure, forms outcrops which, when fallen are used to make walls, to line ancient burial cists, for the foundations of round-houses, or henges and stone circles. These ancient Neolithic places, with their irresistible presence, form the bridge to understanding more about our ancestors, how they lived, fed and clothed themselves, worshipped, buried their dead and made language, art and music.

These paintings and drawings attempt to explore timelessness rather than logic and, although rooted in drawing, definitive figurative statements are subordinated to my primary emotional response. Fox Talbot, in 1839, summed it all up..... *"But after all, what is nature but one great field of wonders past our comprehension."*

Who built this cairn on this wild hill;
Who shaped this pile, rough stone on stone?
Who, toiling here, sought to fulfil
A dream, a promise? Who alone,
perhaps, and lonely, thought in this way
To leave a mark in this wild place?

And for whom - or what? Is a day
a month, a year, some form of grace
commemorated here? A love,
A hope? Or is this pile of stones
a silent supplicatory dove
wooing peace for old, dead bones?

GORDON ALLEN NORTH Ancient Cairn

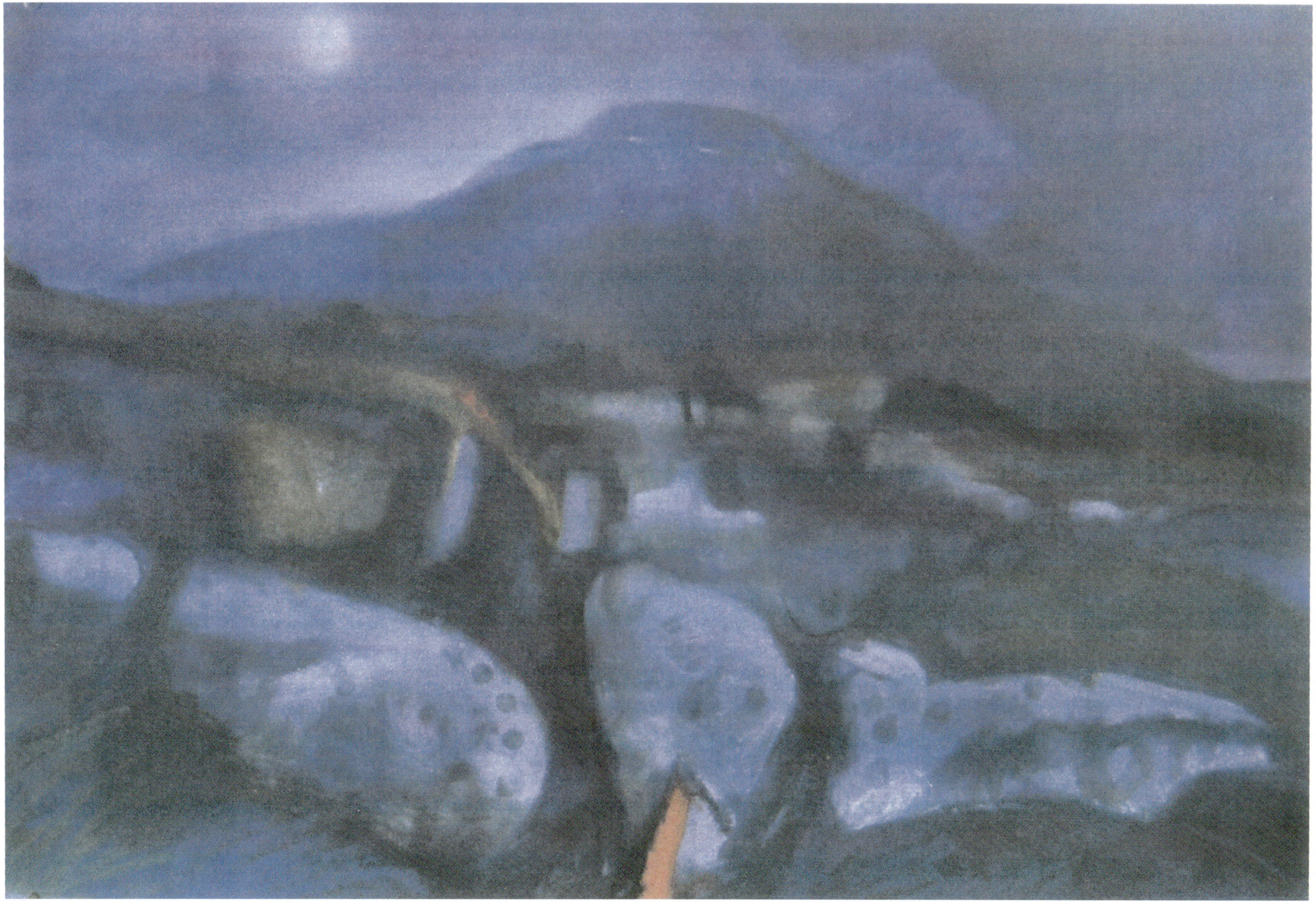

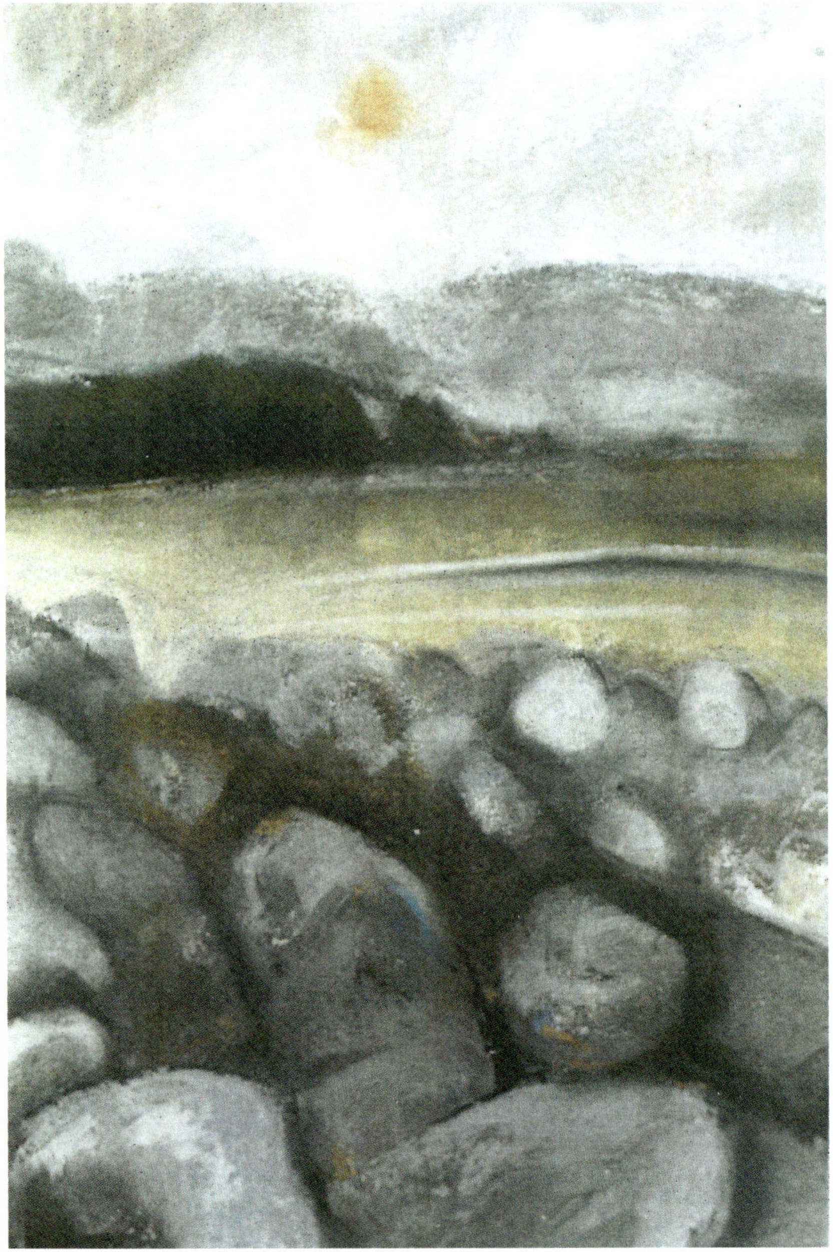

THE POWER OF PLACE (Various media)

Explorations of the Northumbrian landscape which include various themes including echoes of prehistory, burials, standing stones, circles, cairns, and carvings on rock surfaces including the so-called 'cup and ring' petroglyphs. The bulk of the research was carried out on Bewick Moor, the Duddo Stones, Roughting Linn and Corby Crags.

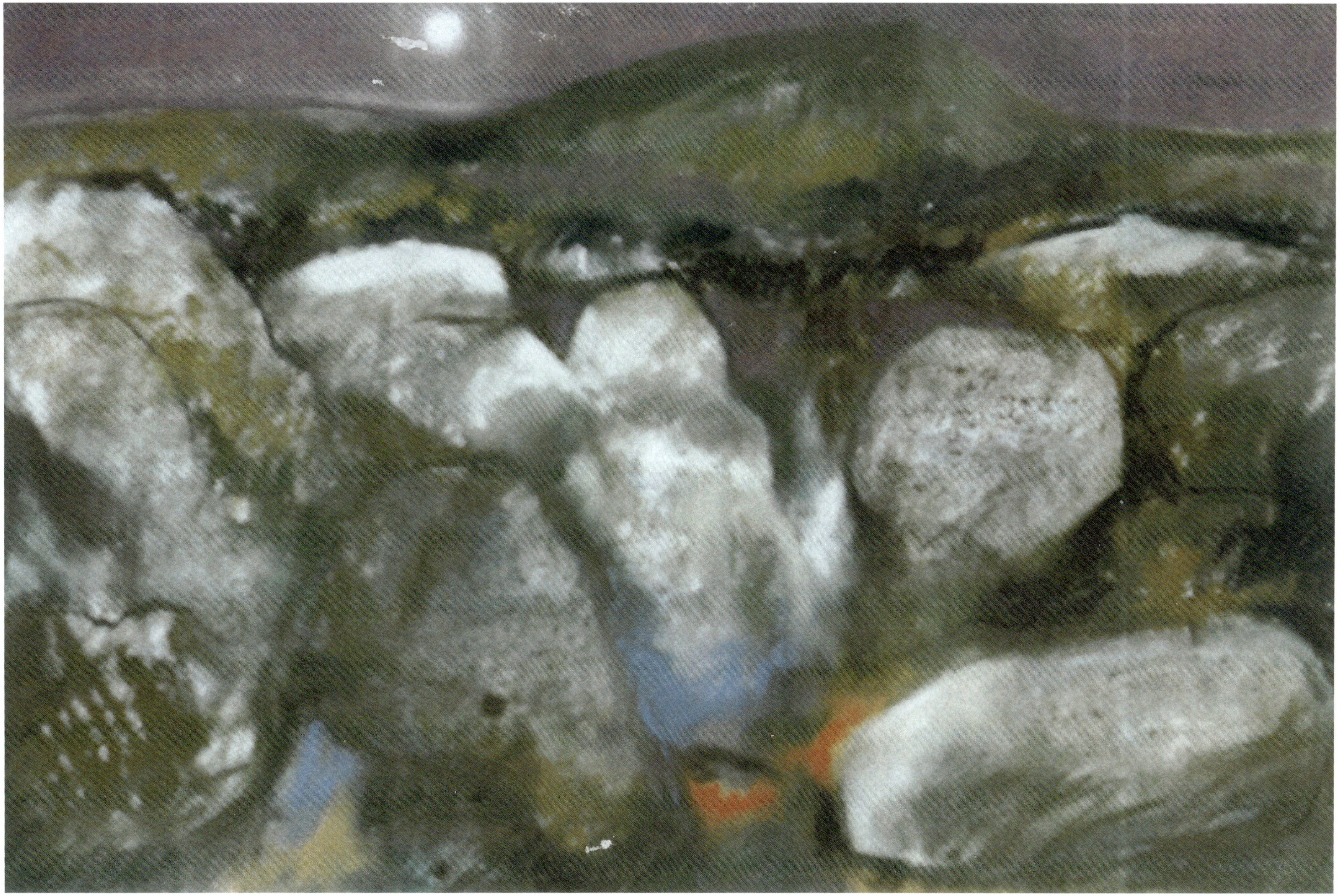

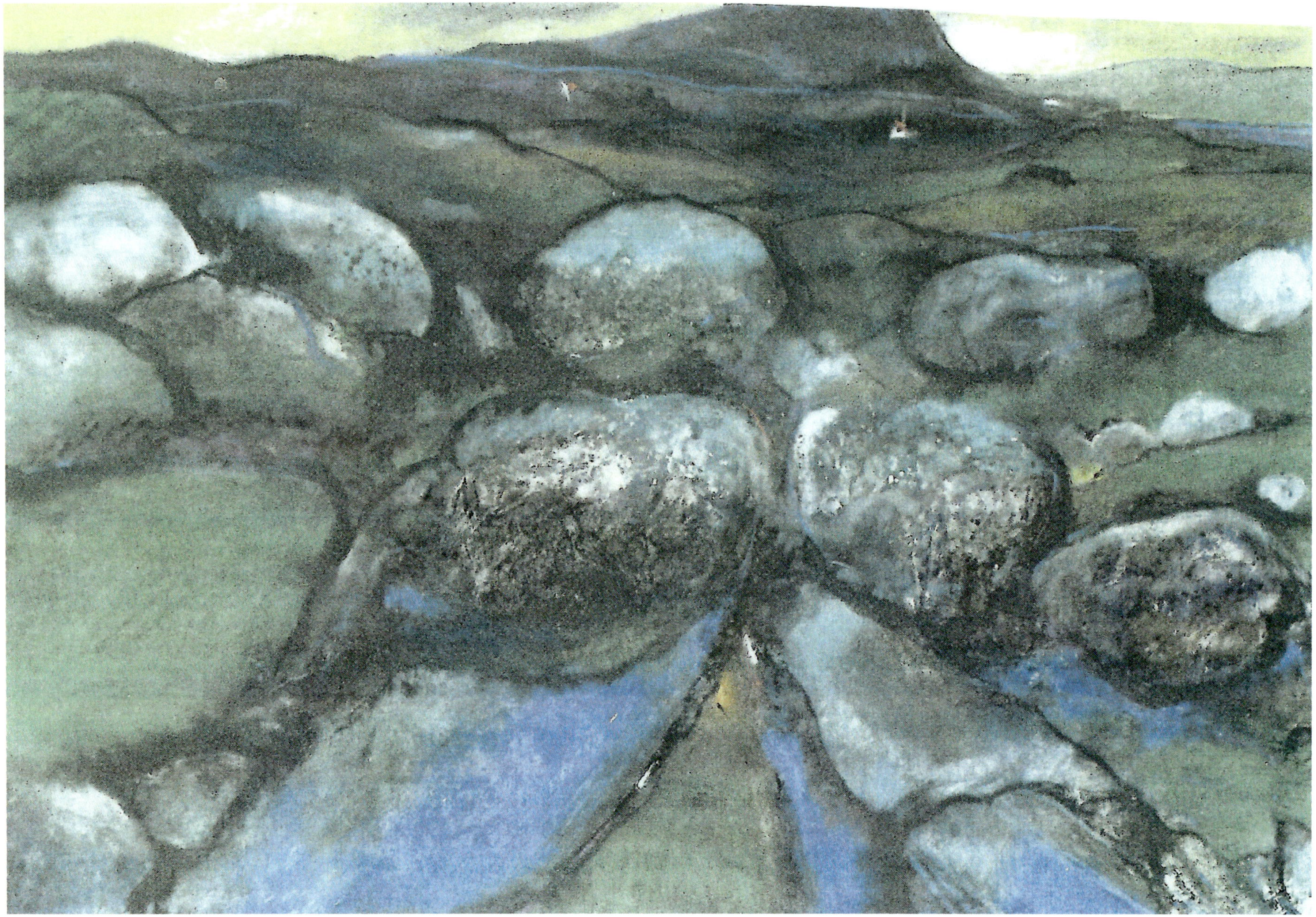

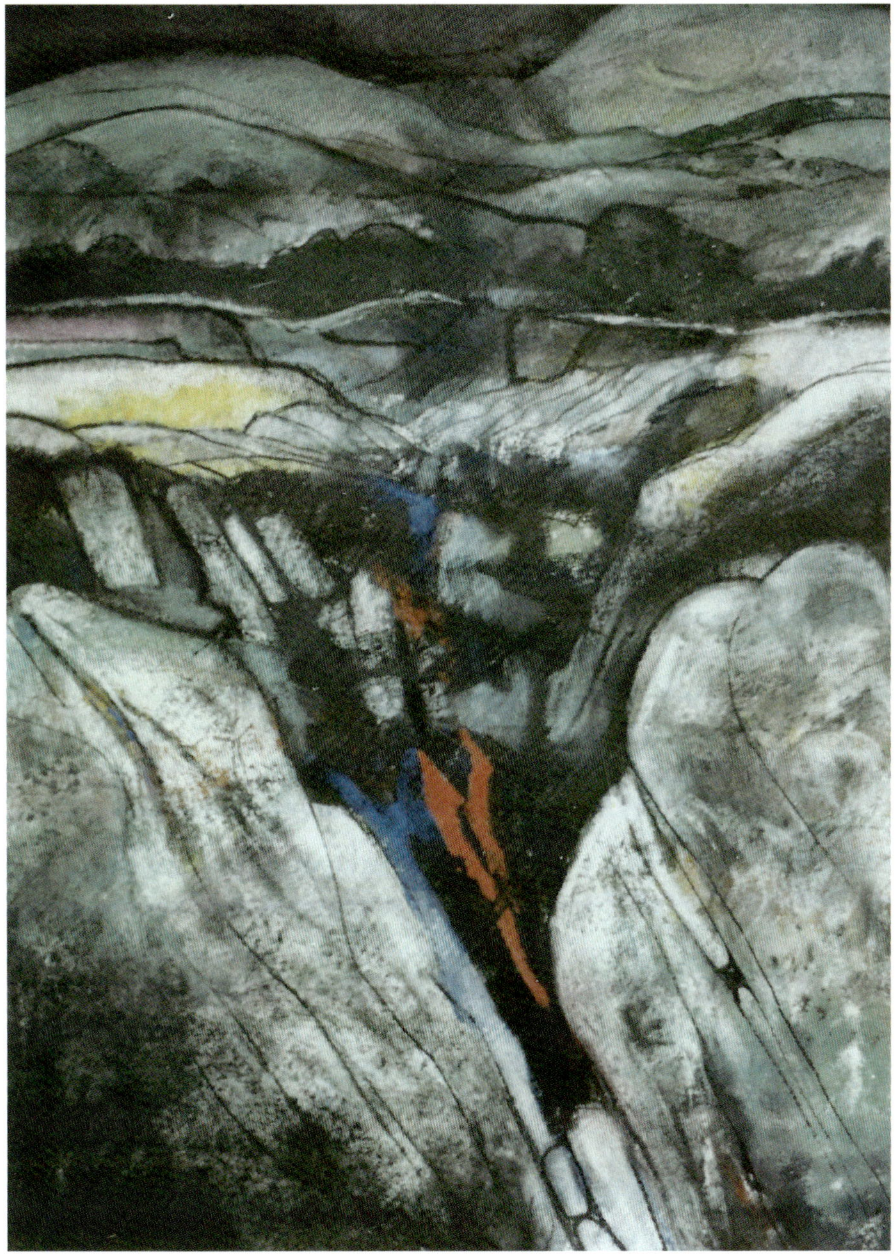

ROCK & RITUAL (Mixed media)

In some works I am fascinated by how much fire would have been important to Neolithic people whether for ritual or purely domestic purposes. It could also have been used for practical tasks: such as clearing land or splitting rock.

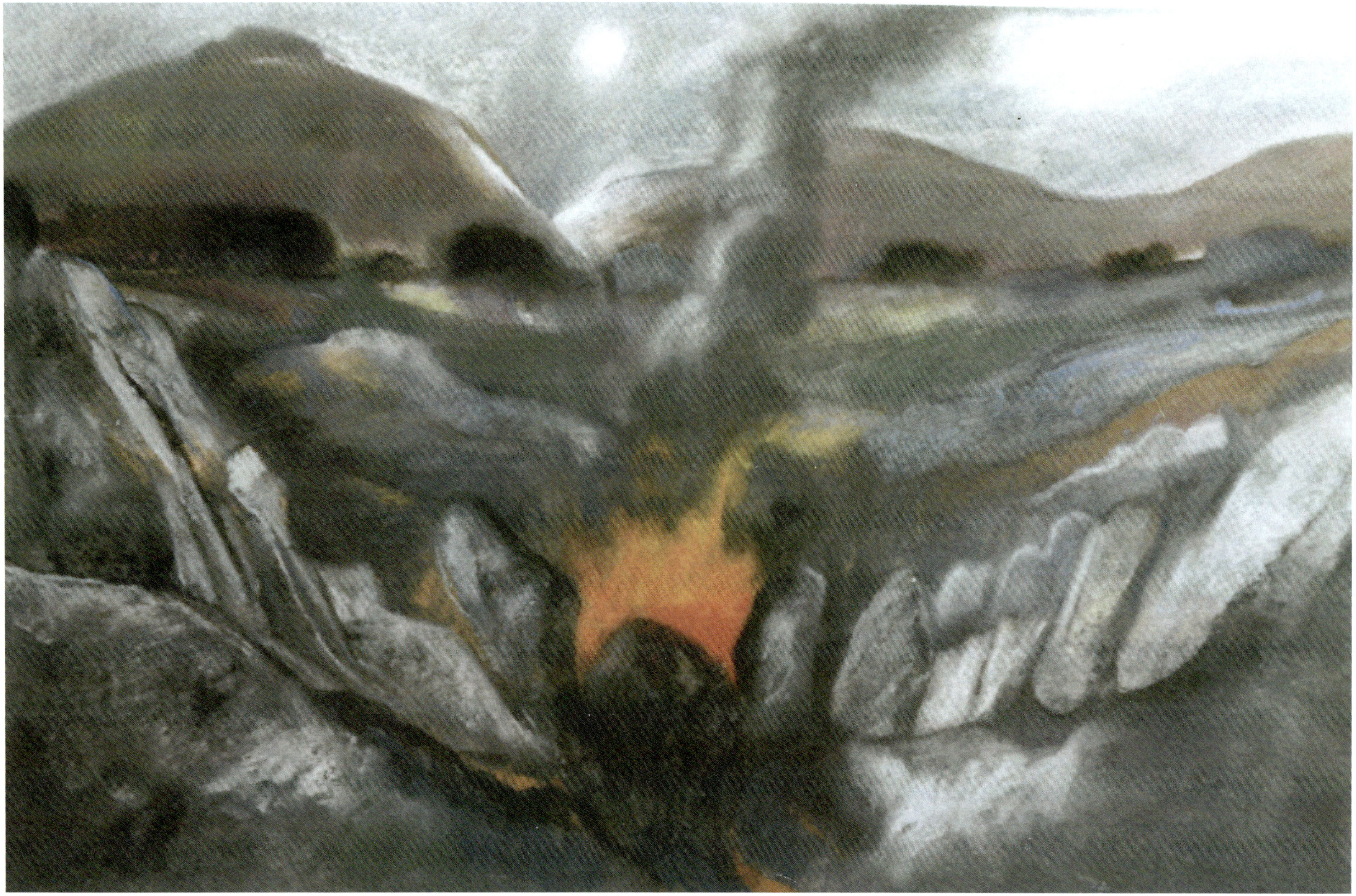

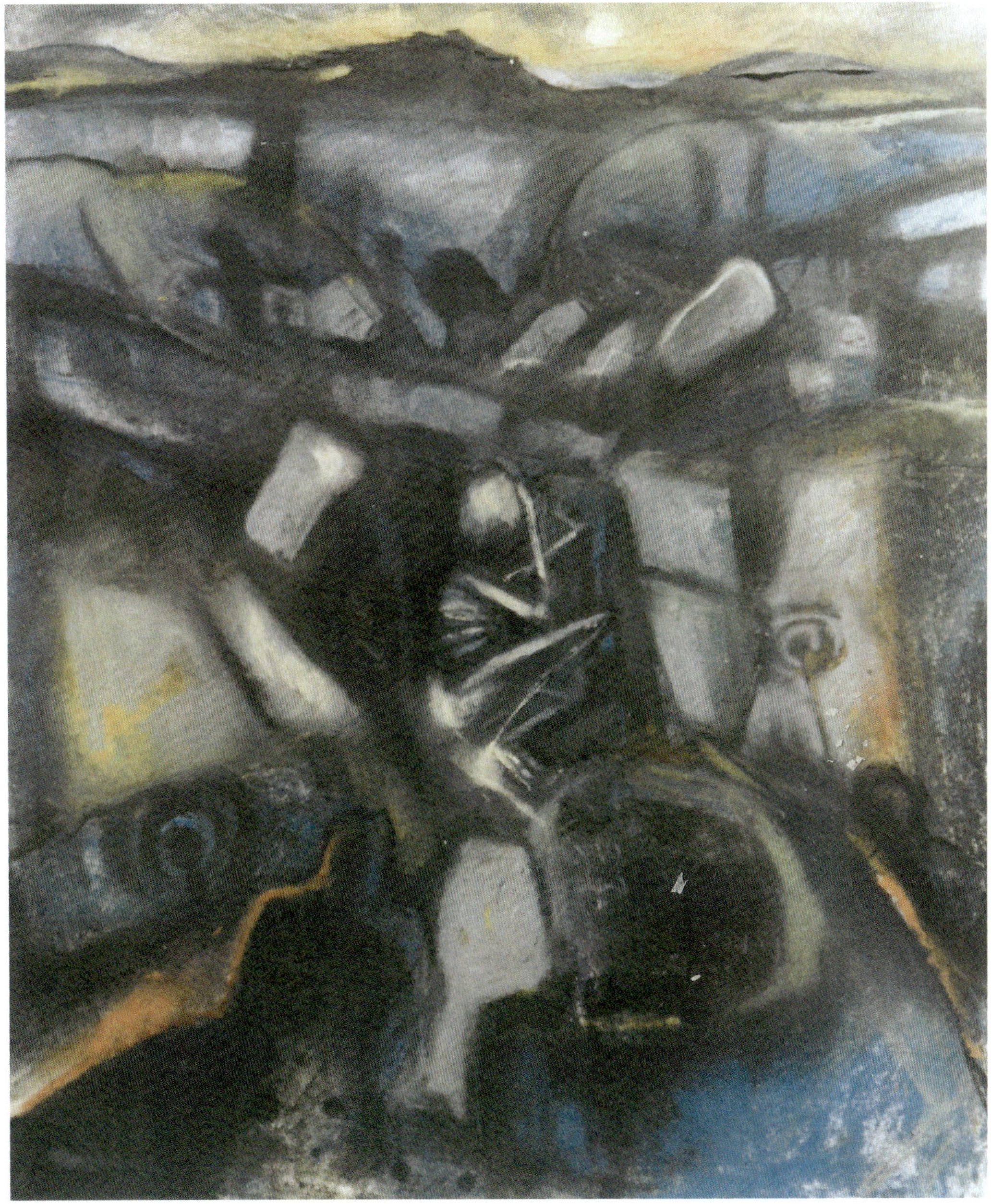

ECHOES OF PREHISTORY (Mixed media)

Structured archaeological digs turn up a plethora of artefacts from domestic pottery for storage or cooking, tools for cuttings and shaping, weapons for hunting or combat, to grave goods and human remains.

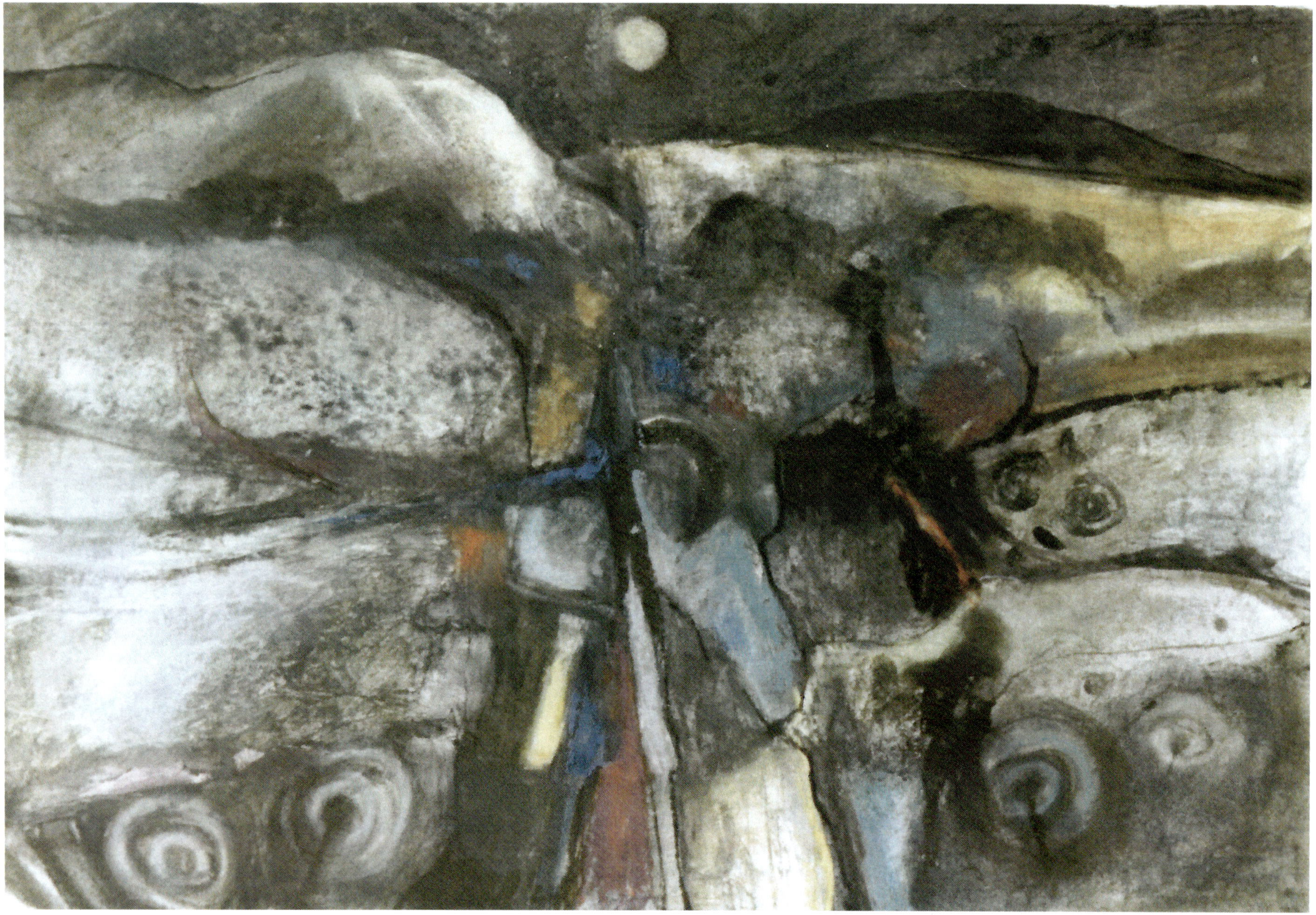

A lingering light upon cold hills and sunward slopes
Coaxes a story thousands of seasons long,
Barrows for the dead, like crusted pimples
Break the sloping ground,
And cord rig combs the hillside, once a bed of grain,
Scarcely a mouthful now for sullen sheep.
Faint hollow ways and intermittent walls
Grow and fade with moving light,
Shallow pits of shadows speak
Of houses in enclosures platform-perched
Or huddled round the hillfort's top.
These soils are wasted now,
Only deep-set lynchets or the massive hillfort wall stands proud,
Only a patient eye can now detect
The traces of the face beneath the veil,
And Humbleton has seen it all.
When moonrise mists the valleys with its eerie light
The dark mass broods and gathers to itself
So many lives, so many times.

STAN BECKENSALL High Humbleton

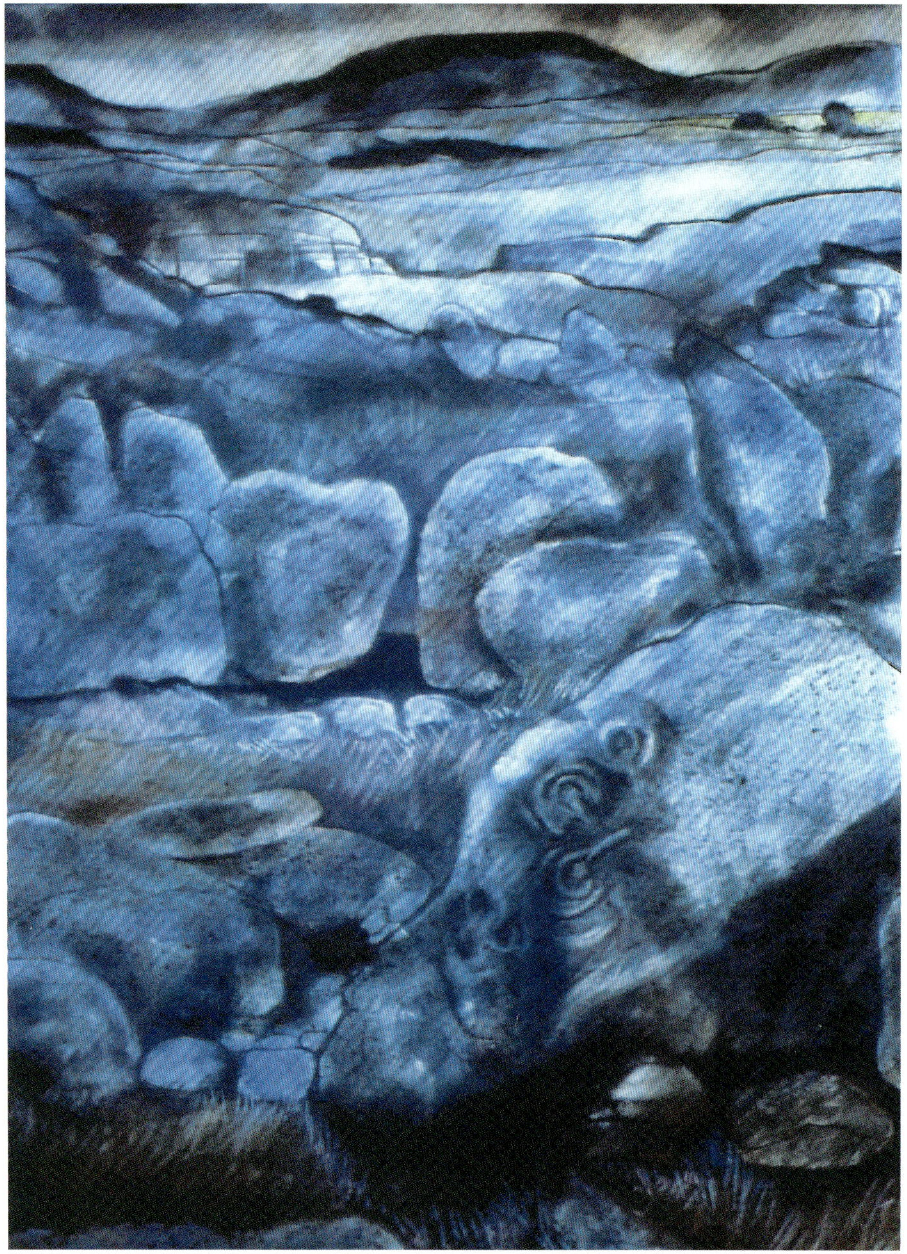

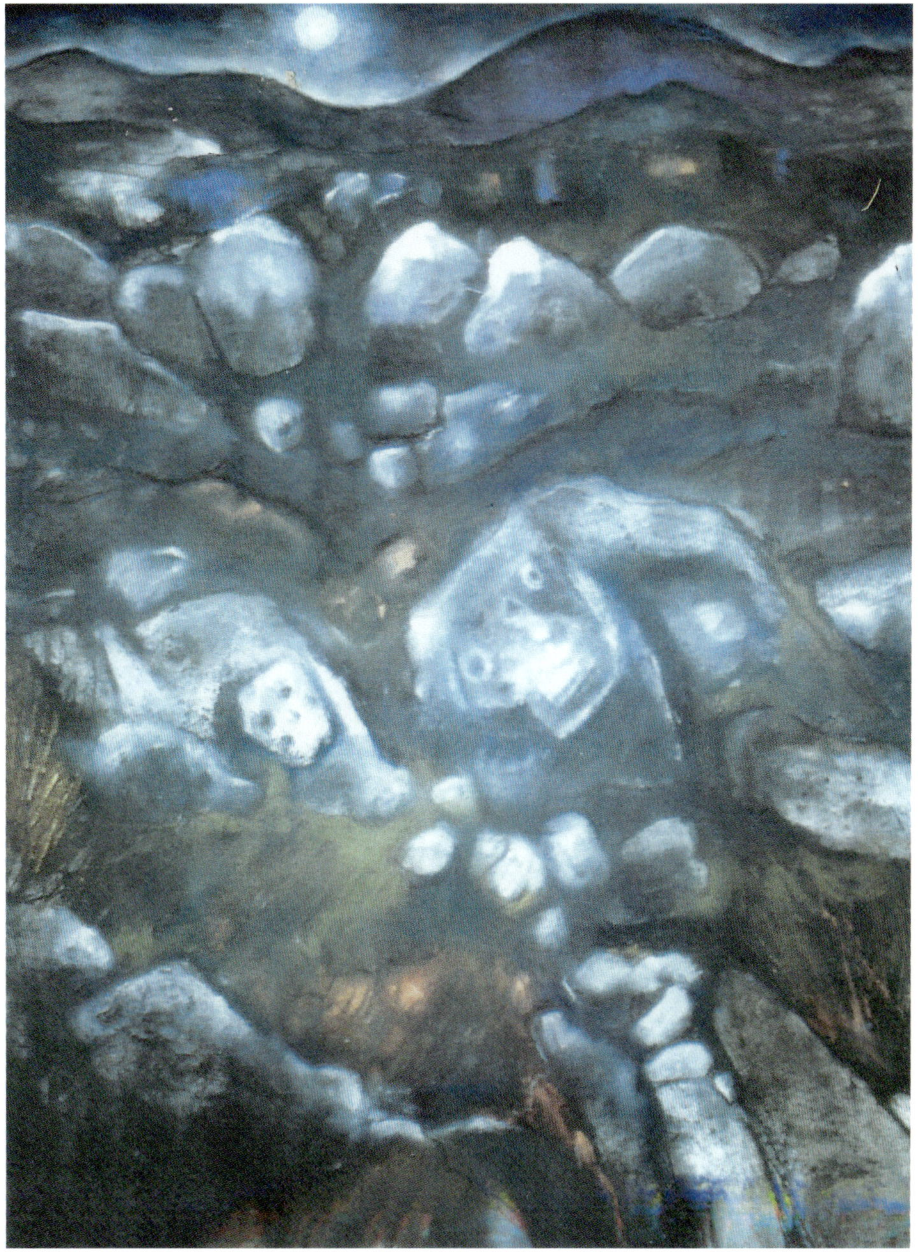

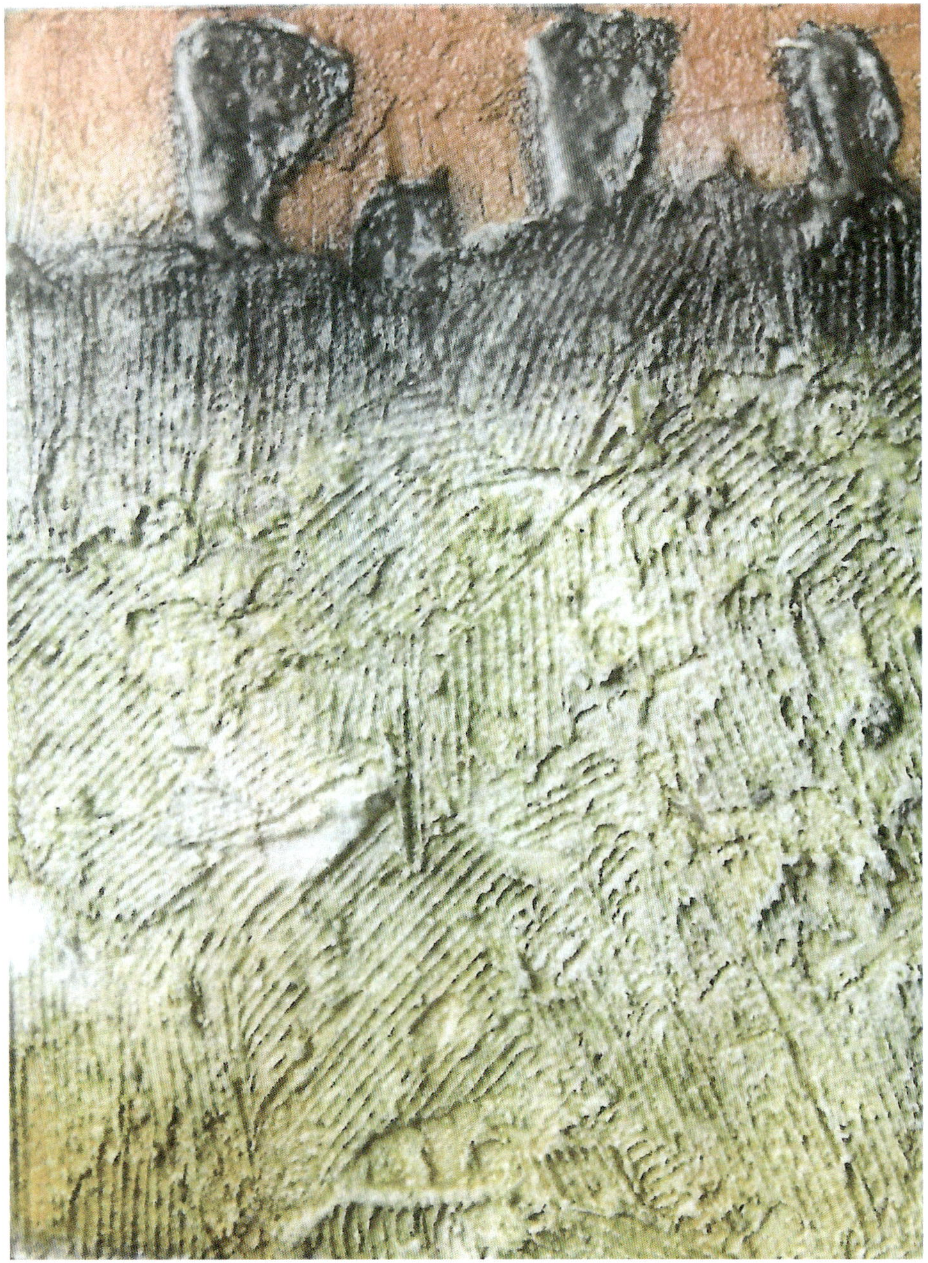

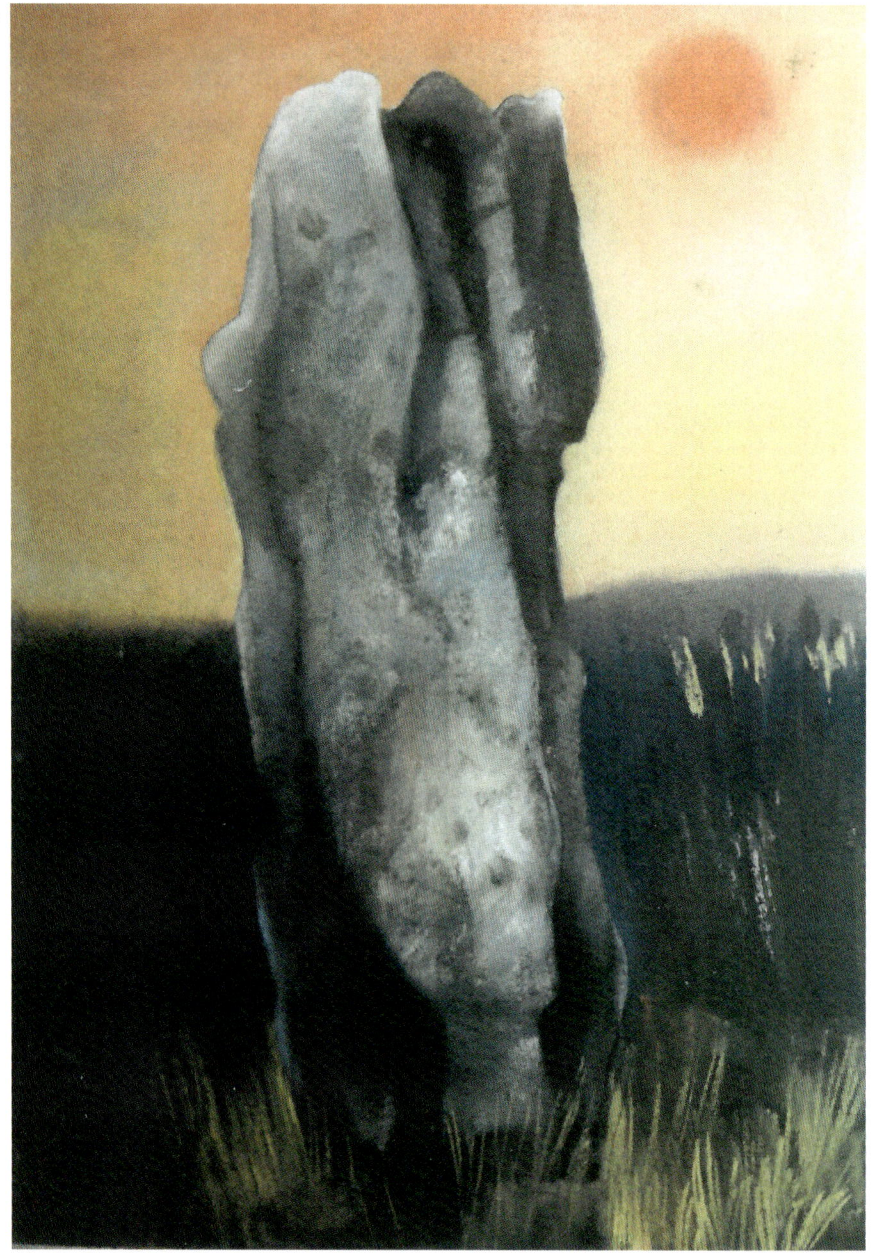

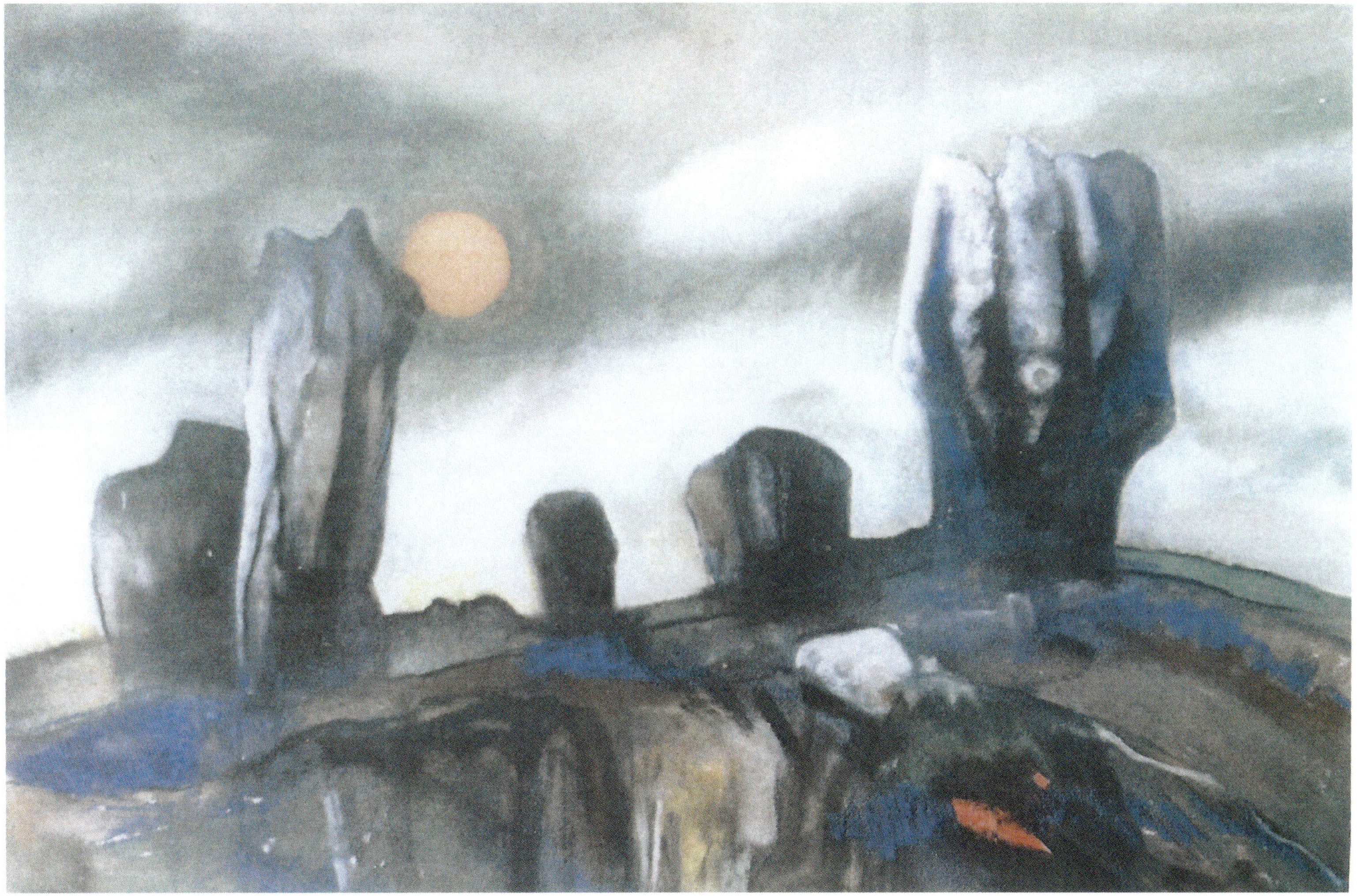

THE DUDDO STONES (Pastel & Mixed Media)

Situated on a knoll near Duddo, in North Northumberland, this site may have been a means of studying astronomy. Several Bronze-Age relics have been found in the vicinity.

A truly wonderful inspiration for a whole series of works.

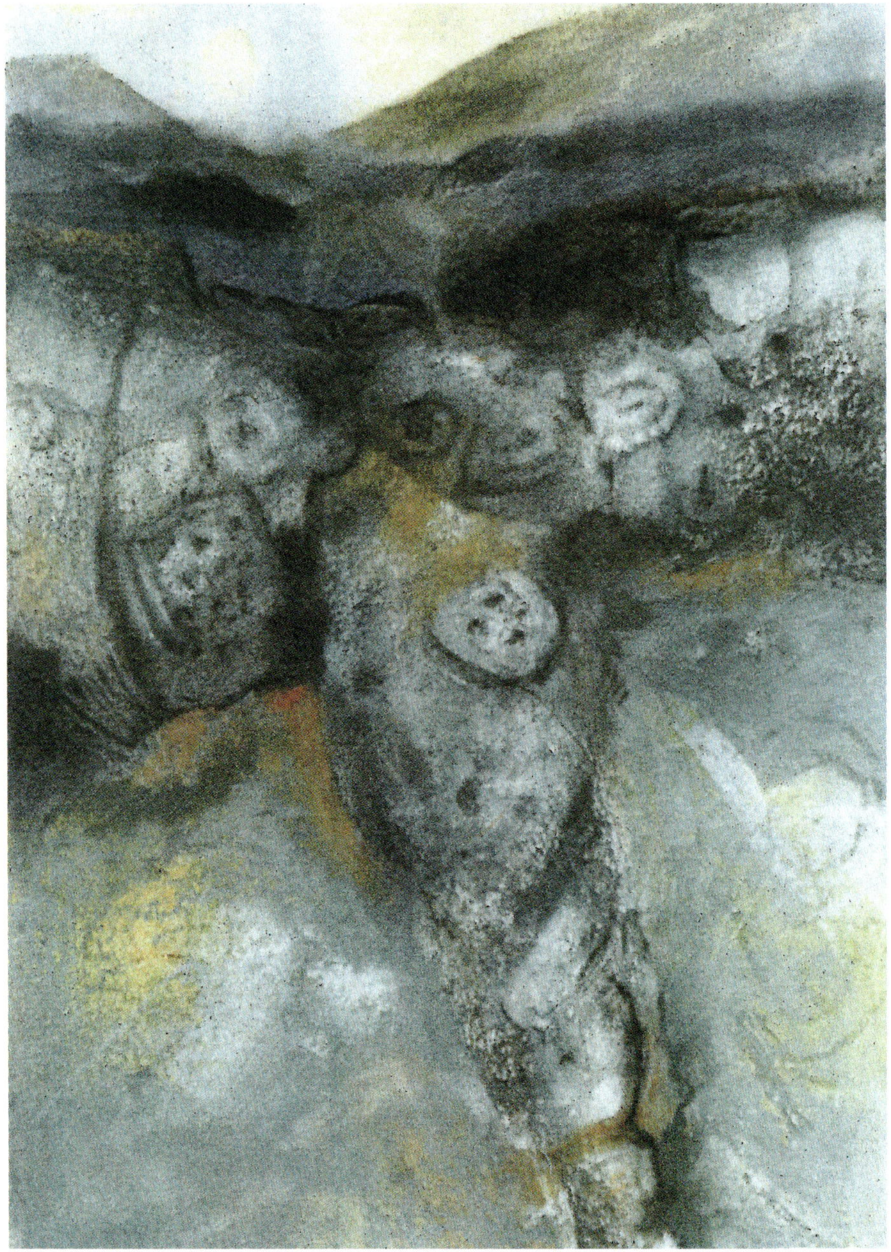

CUP & RING (Pastel)

The carvings on Dod Law are not on raised rocks but lie close to the ground. I was, at first, struck by the 'cruciform' nature of the rocks before noticing the many differing varieties of motif, claimed to be some of the finest In Britain.

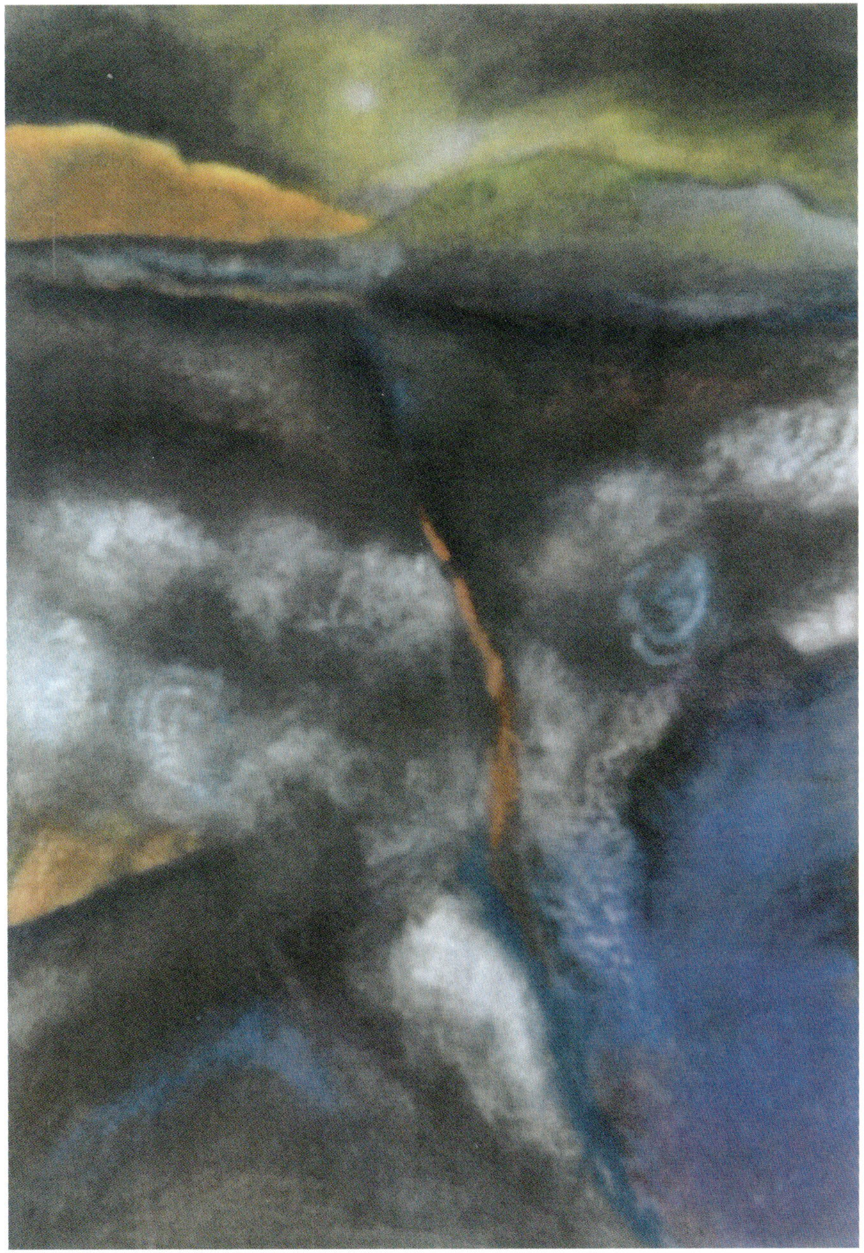

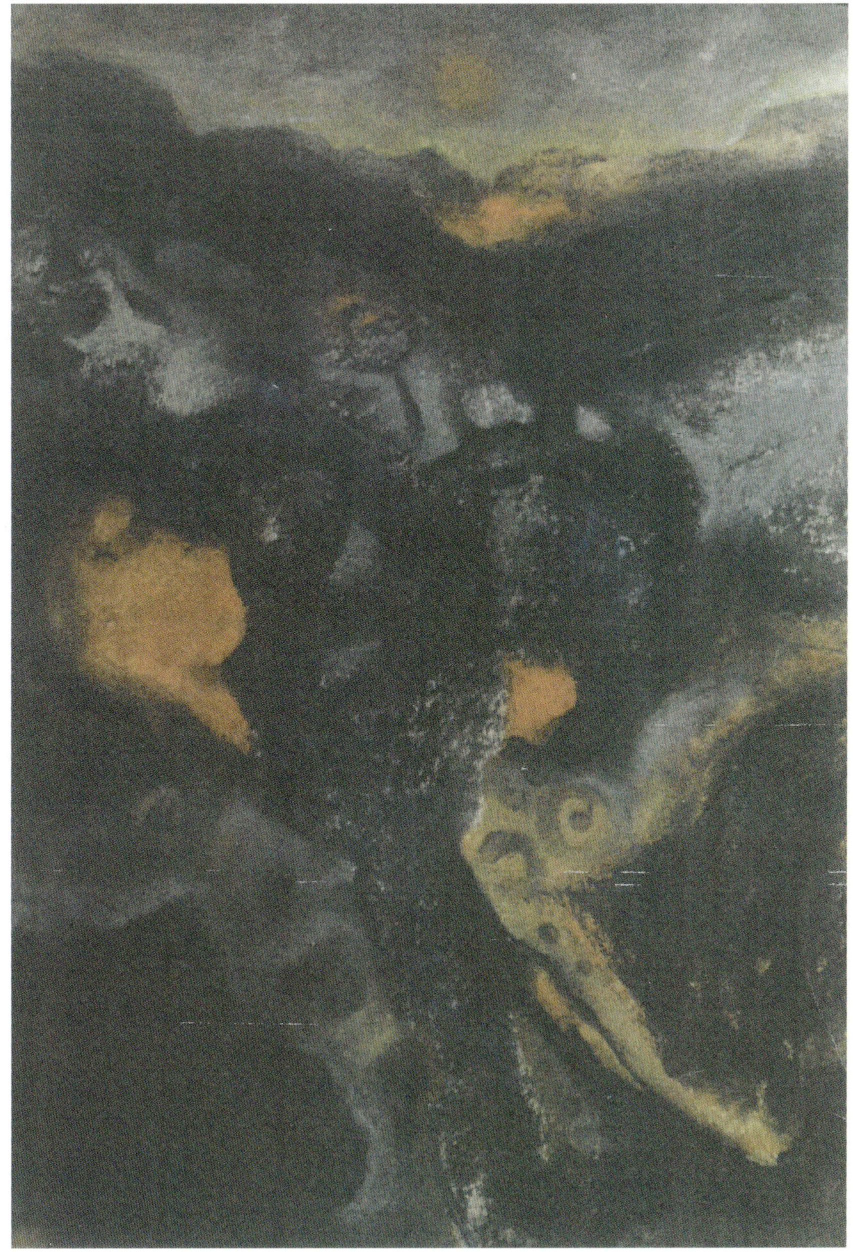

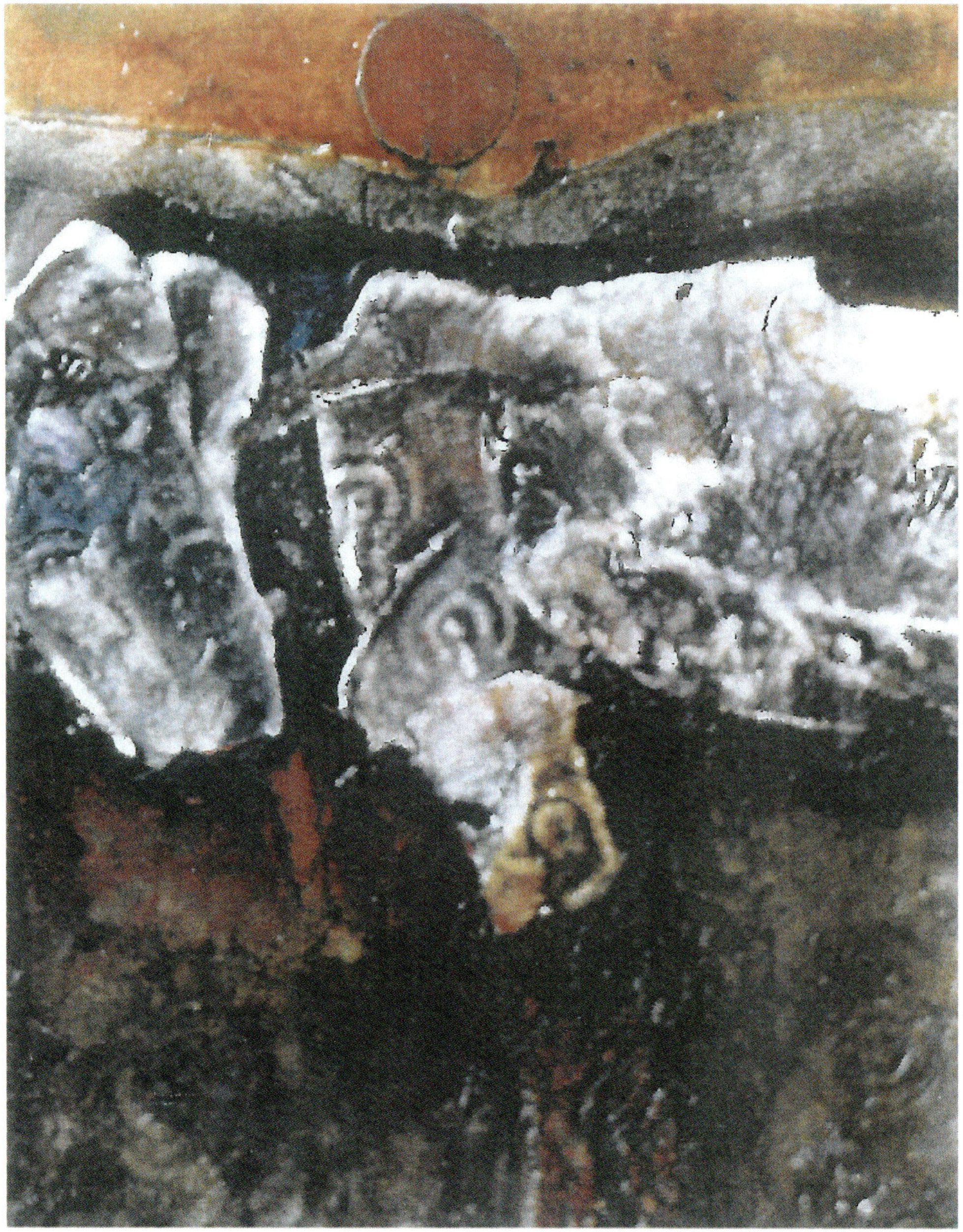

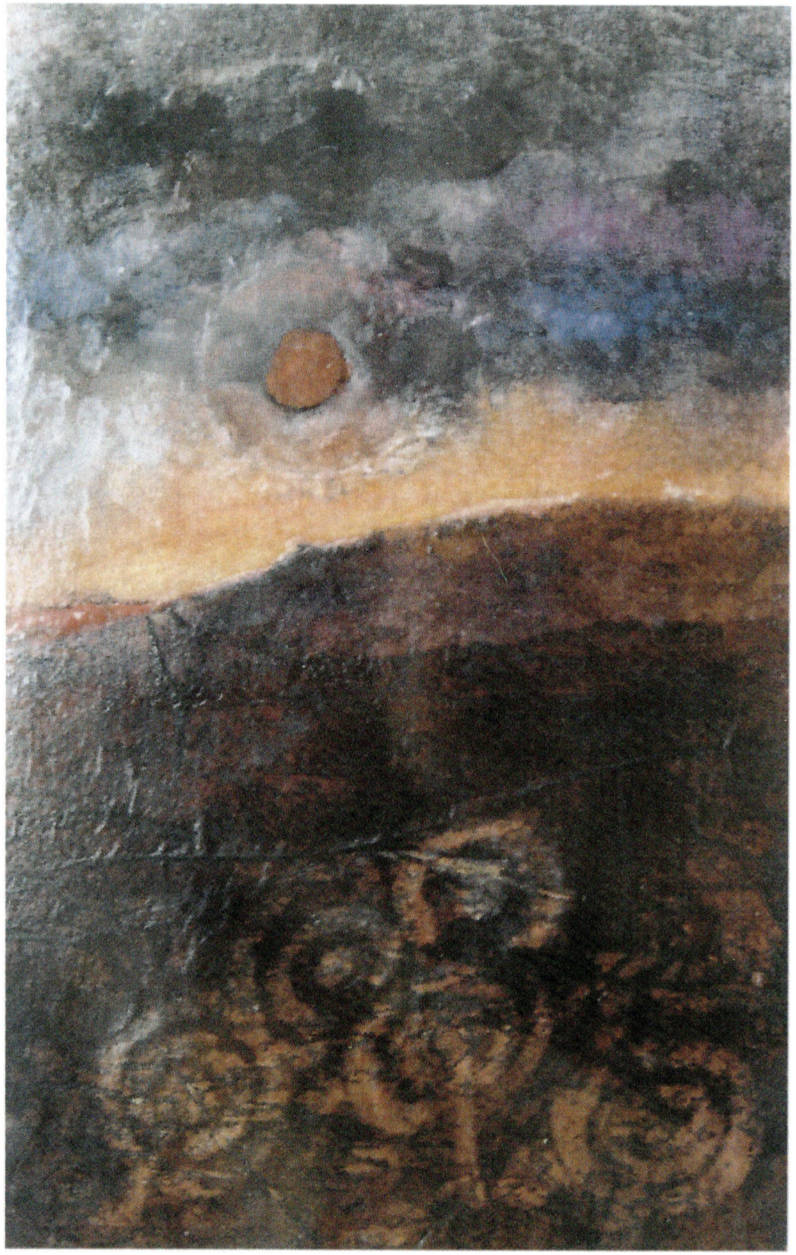

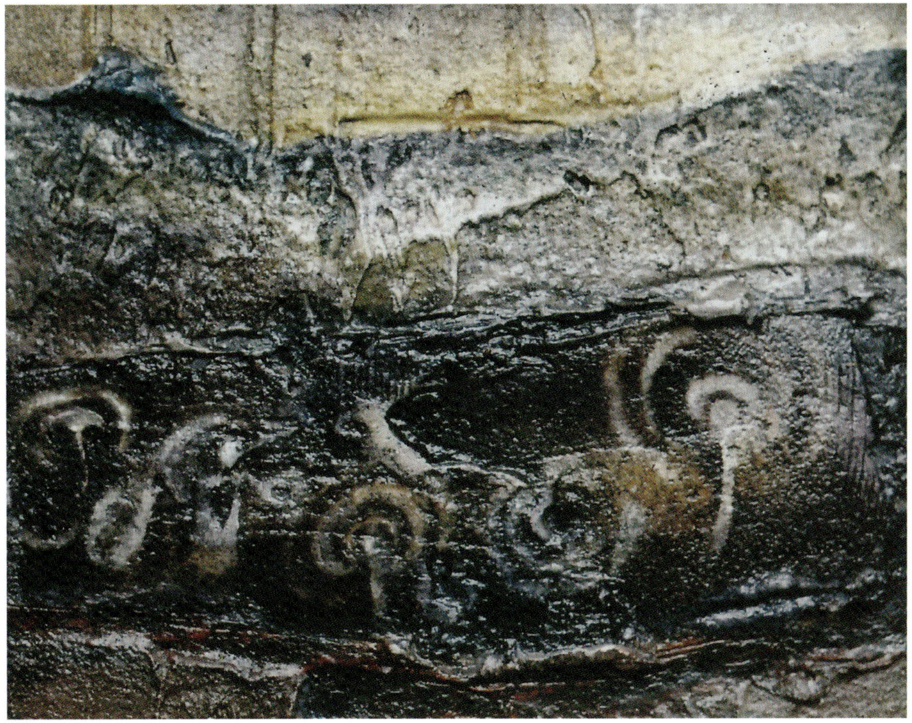
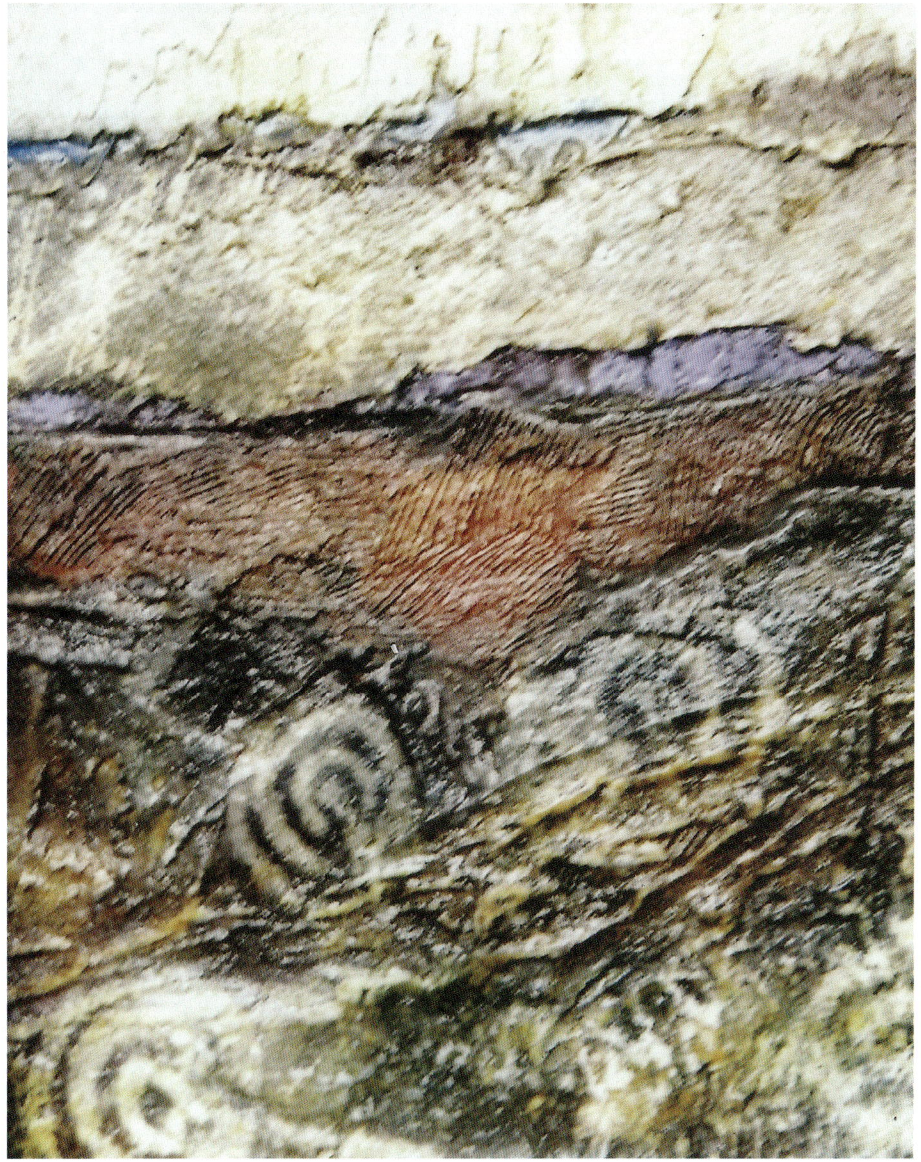

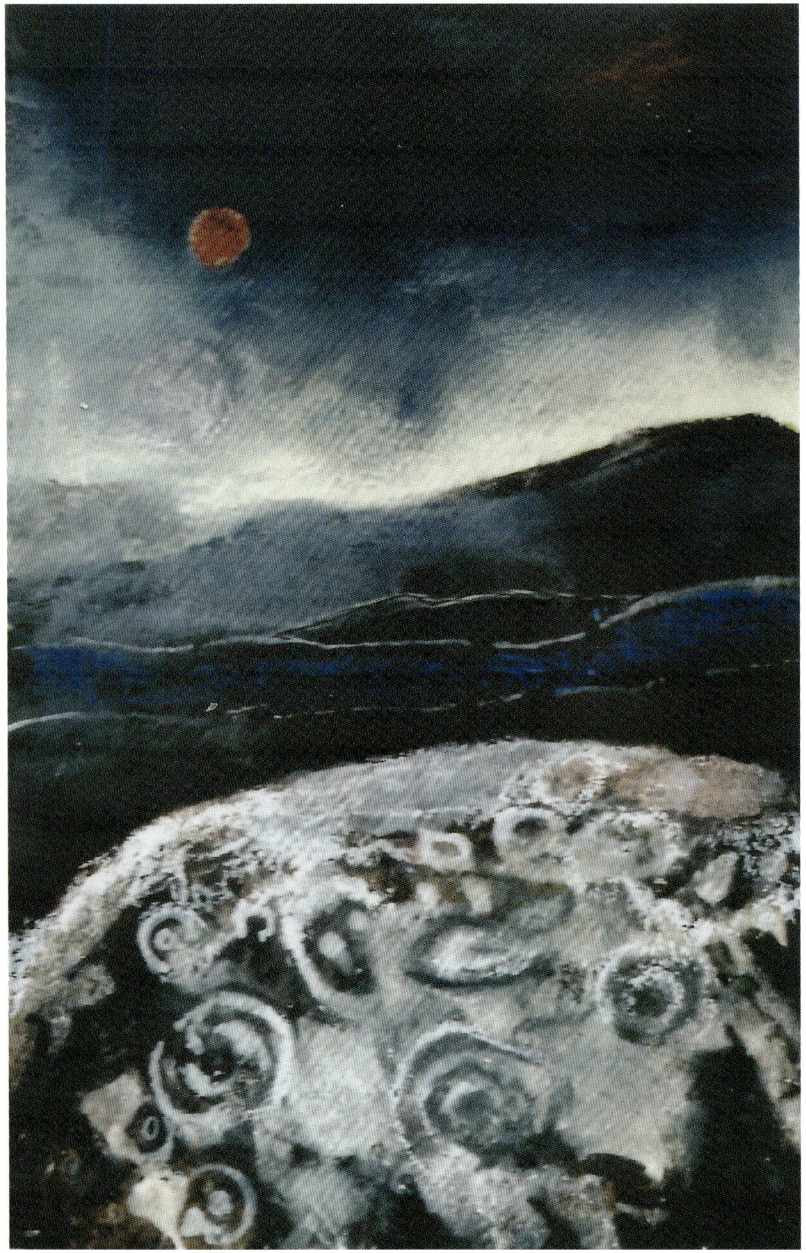

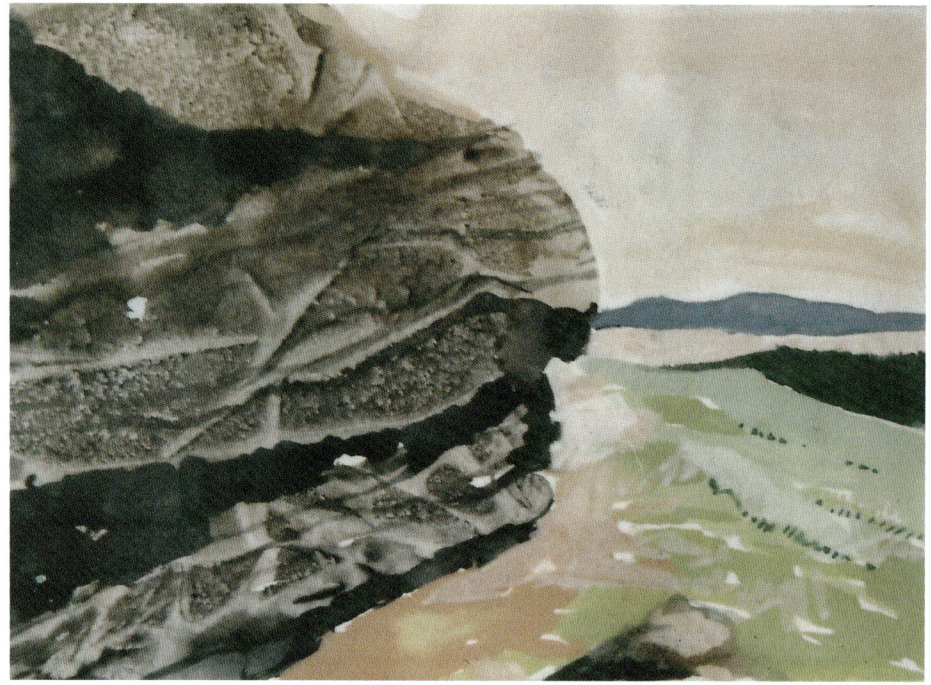

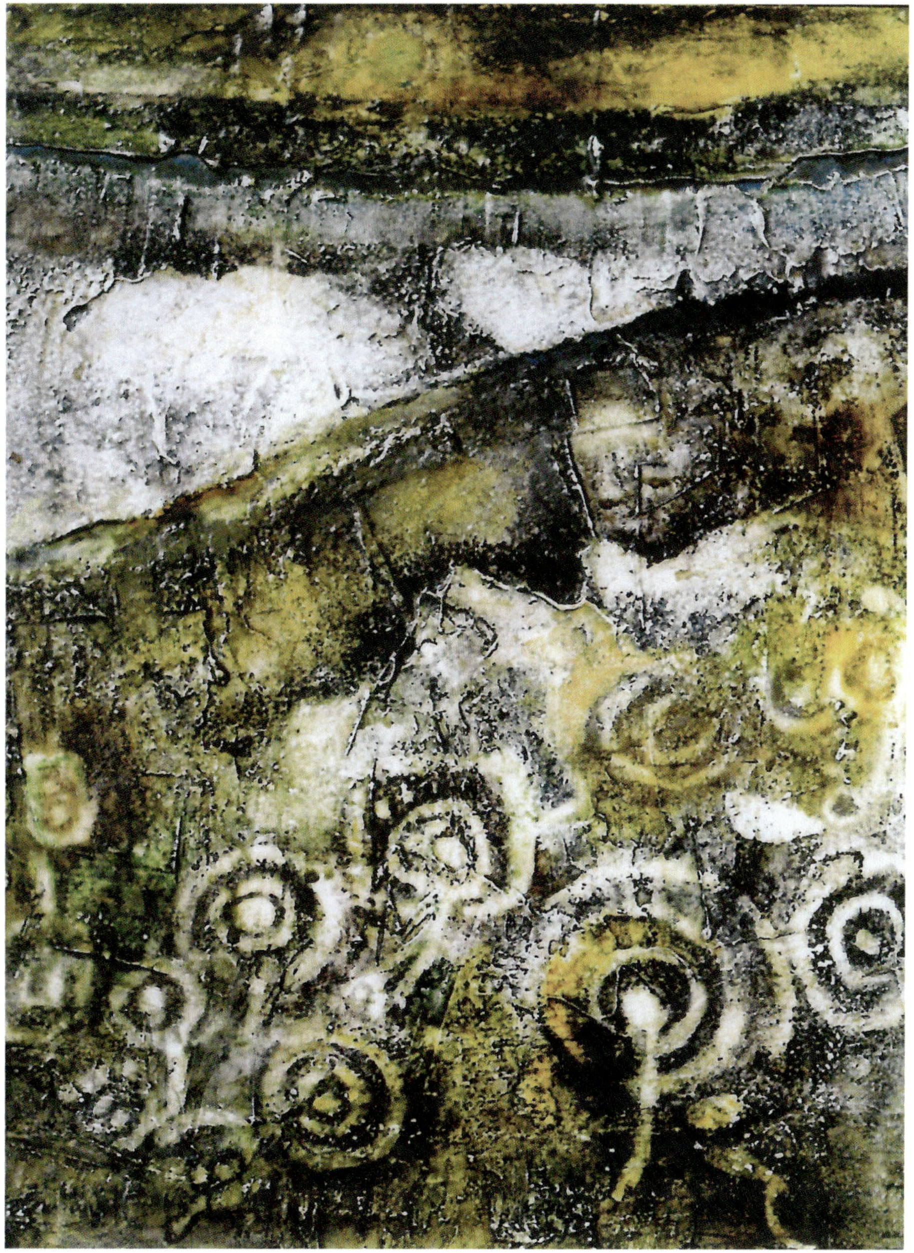

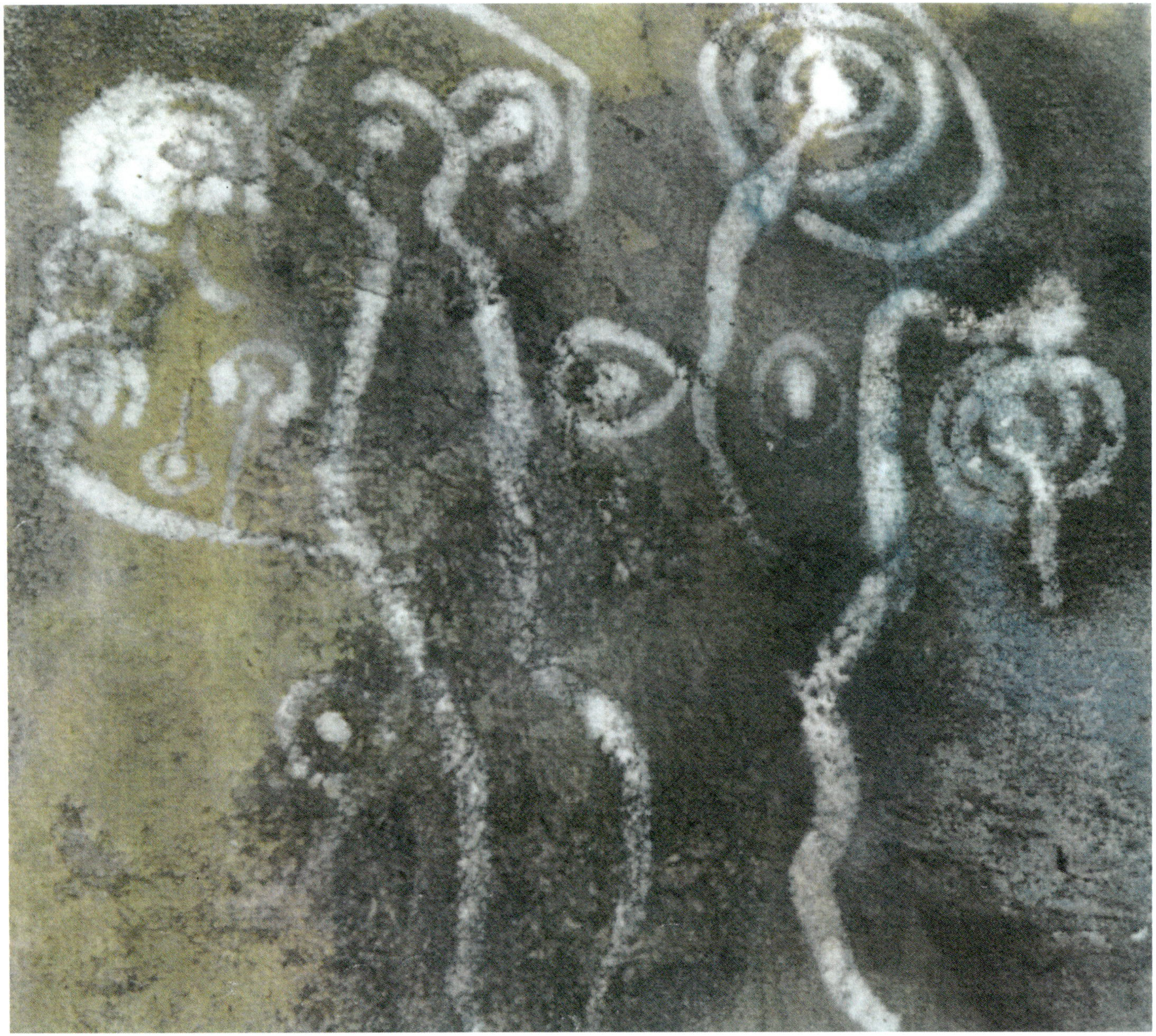

PREHISTORIC ROCK CARVINGS
(Mixed media)

Although I stubbornly refuse to follow the habit of calling these carvings "rock art", there is a fascination to be found in both the complexity of the marks themselves and their aesthetic nature. From time to time, however, I have allowed myself to be seduced by certain configurations and their relationship with the weathered sandstone rock on which they are to be found, to want to paint them, such as these at Horton.

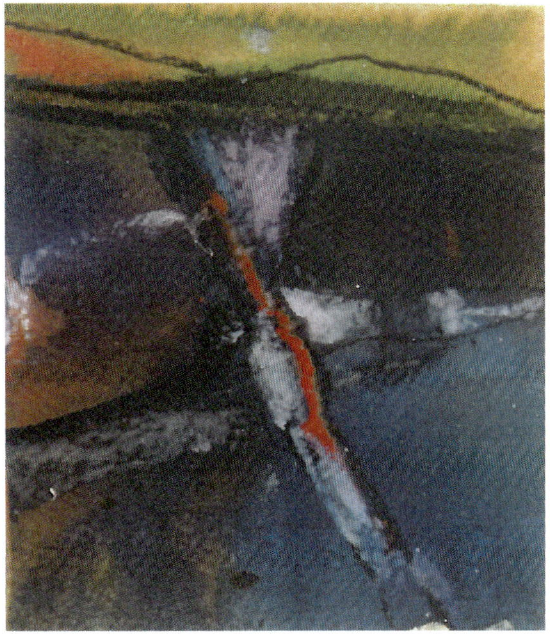

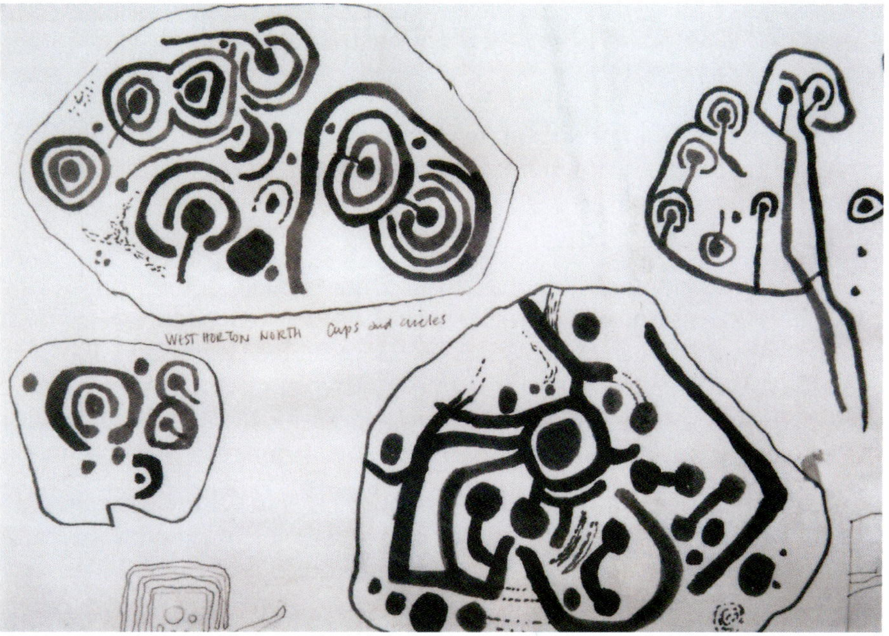
WEST HORTON NORTH
Cups and circles

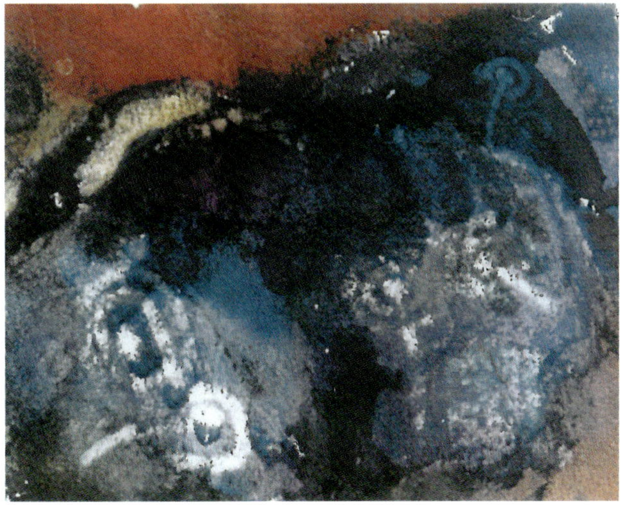

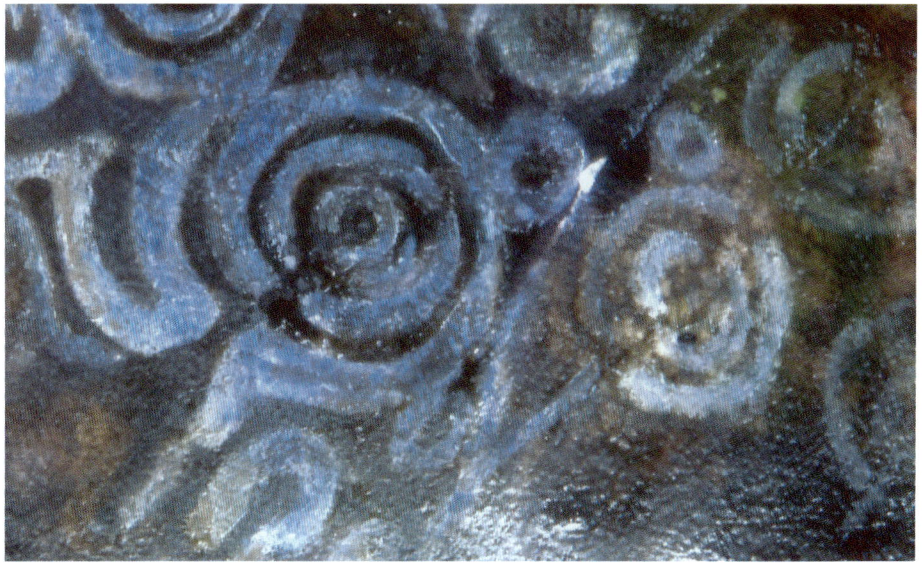

ECHOES OF SURVIVAL...

After experiencing criticism by some who challenged my right as an artist to make what are both speculatory and conjectural statements concerning our landscape, I wanted to make my point in a series of works.

Putting aside the fact that there have been some major works produced in response to various archaeological sites by a host of brilliant artists, men such as Stuckley, Constable, Turner and John Piper (see text), we need to examine some fundamental anomalies which are raised by the activities of collectors, souvenir-hunters, antiquarians, historians, museum-owners and, dare I say, archaeologists themselves.

A brief excursion around ancient-historical sites and museums alike, will reveal a range of sins, from a basic lack of humanitarian care to despoliation and downright vandalism. Rock sites containing unique carvings, for example, have been quarried away to provide building materials, rockery-gardens, or simply mantelpiece decoration, symptomatic of a magpie culture which finds these symbol-stones, flint arrow heads or bronze axe-heads in Alnwick and other castles too. Worse still, what are actually precious relics, languish unseen sometimes, or in glass cases, hundreds of miles from their original source (shades of the Elgin marbles). In other sites, whole tracts of precious moorland have been destroyed in military manoeuvres or ploughed over by farm machinery in land clearance. Other monuments suffer from neglect, lacking protection or information boards. And it is well documented that a local Victorian cleric, Canon Greenwell, would pay young boys to dig up bumps and small hillocks and deliver to him any grave goods found therein.

So far, I have only highlighted five sites in this series, but watch this space.

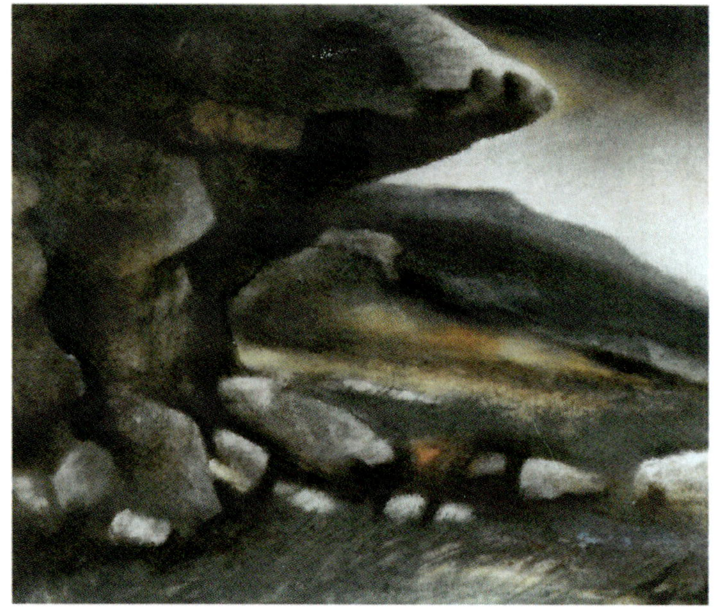

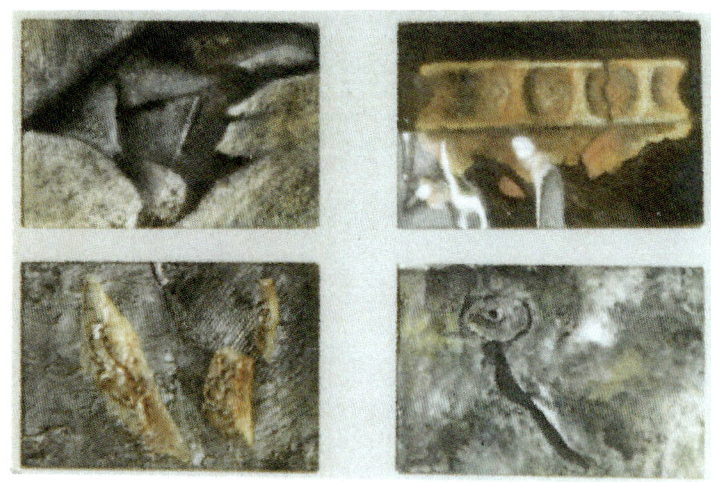

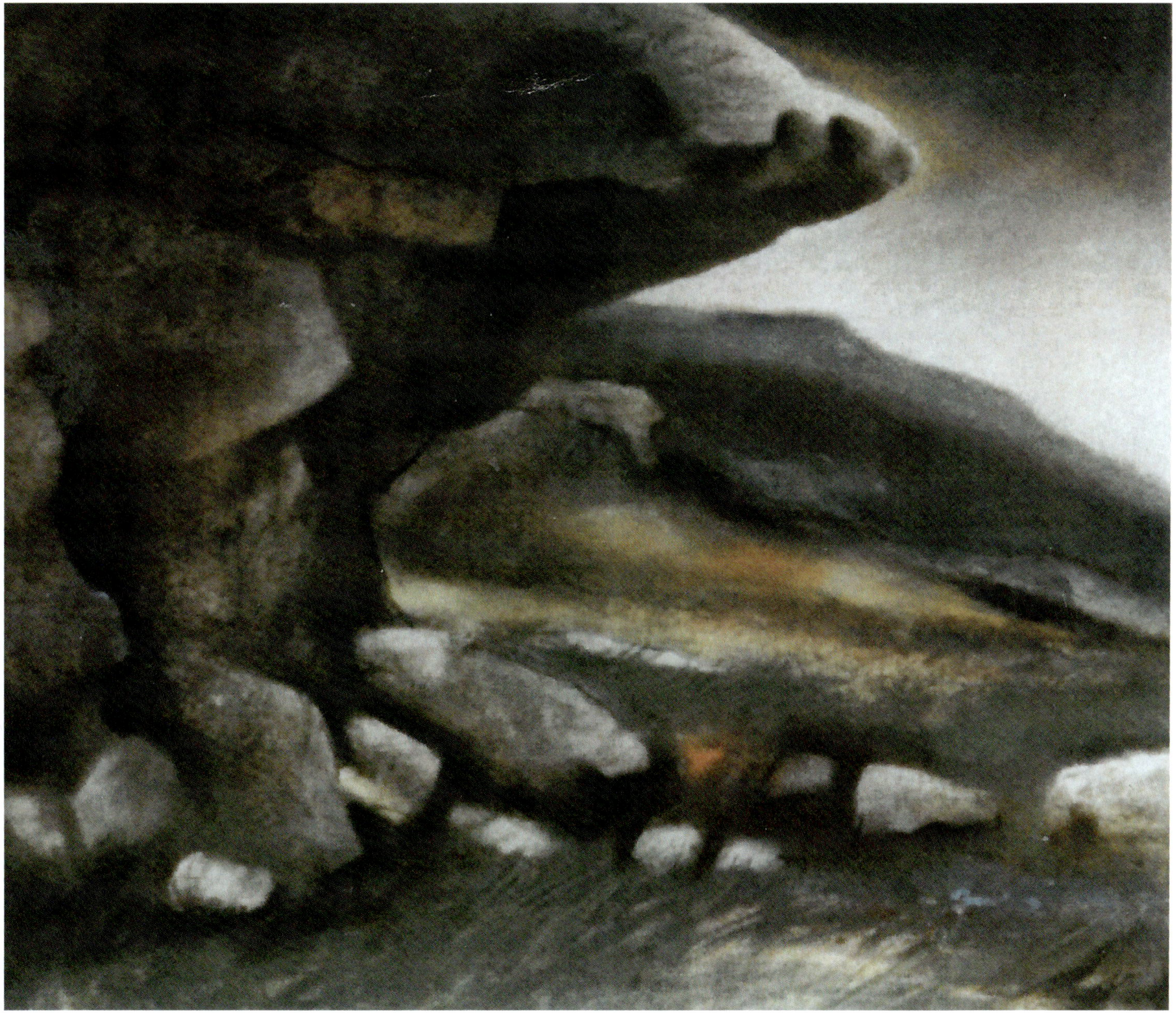

BURIAL - CORBY CRAGS
(Pastel & Mixed Media)

Projects about sites which have been robbed, neglected or even vandalised, and suffer from lack of recognition. Often the grave goods are taken away to various museums not even in this area, the "boxes" referring to how, what are sacred remains, are shown to the public.

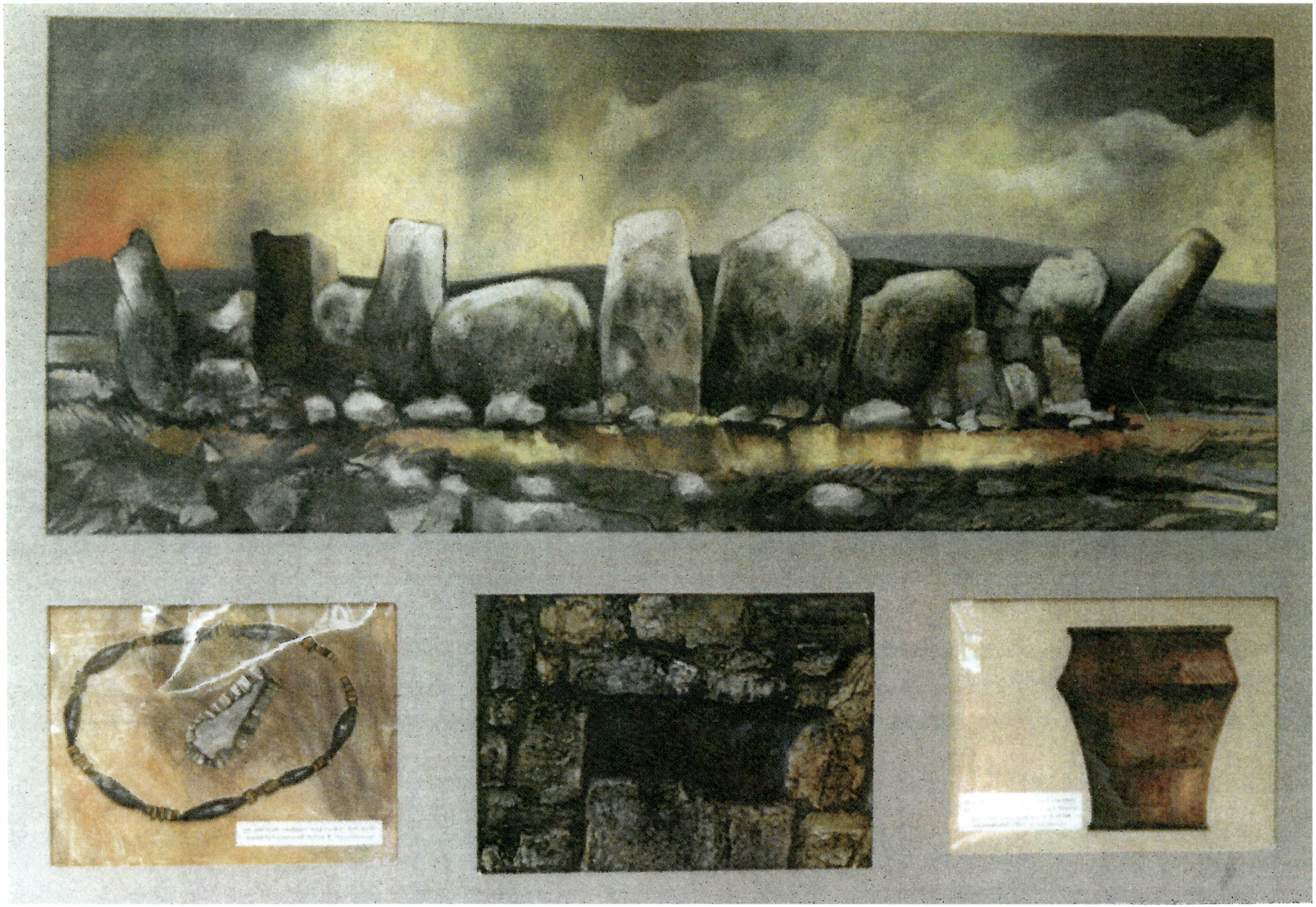

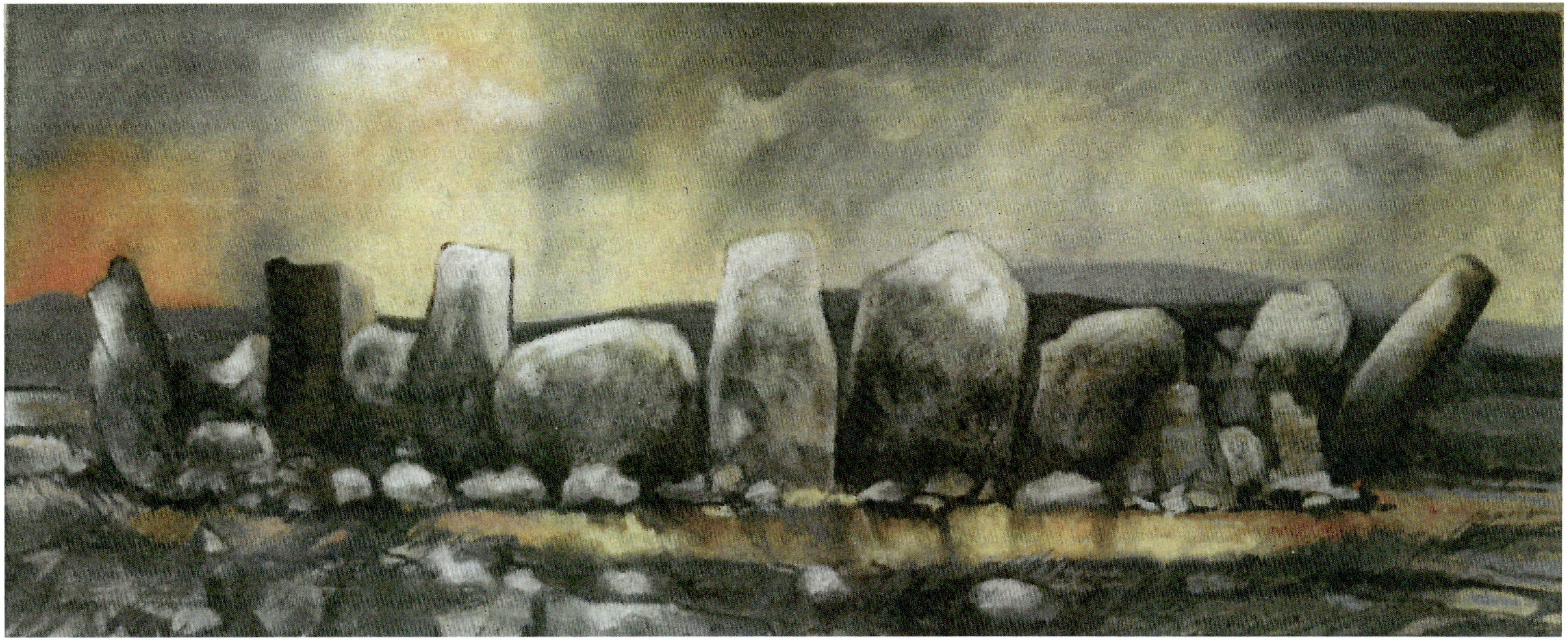

BLAWEARIE CAIRN (Pastel & Mixed medium)

Originally a Canon Greenwell victim, this monument was re-excavated by Stan Beckensall in the 1980s and more grave goods discovered. Unfortunately they were then removed from Northumberland where they should rightly belong.

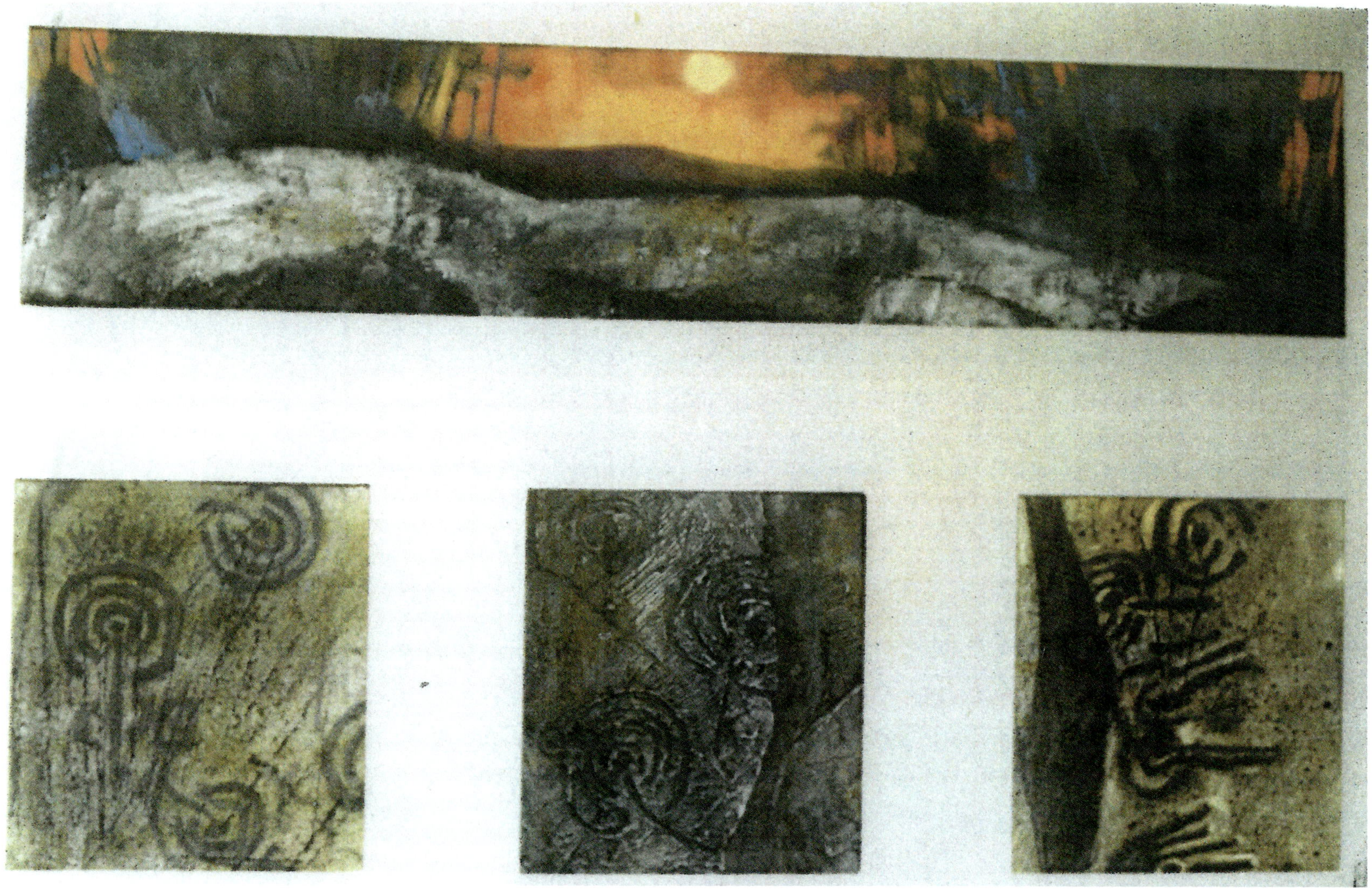

R0UGHTING LINN (Mixed medium)

The name is given to a small linn or pool into which a waterfall 'bellows'. The rock on which are the carvings is a huge 'whaleback' set next to a multivallate defensive enclosure while to the east is Goatscrag Hill, an outcrop of sandstone which contains more carvings and burials under the rock overhangs. It is included here because large wedges have been removed for some reason.

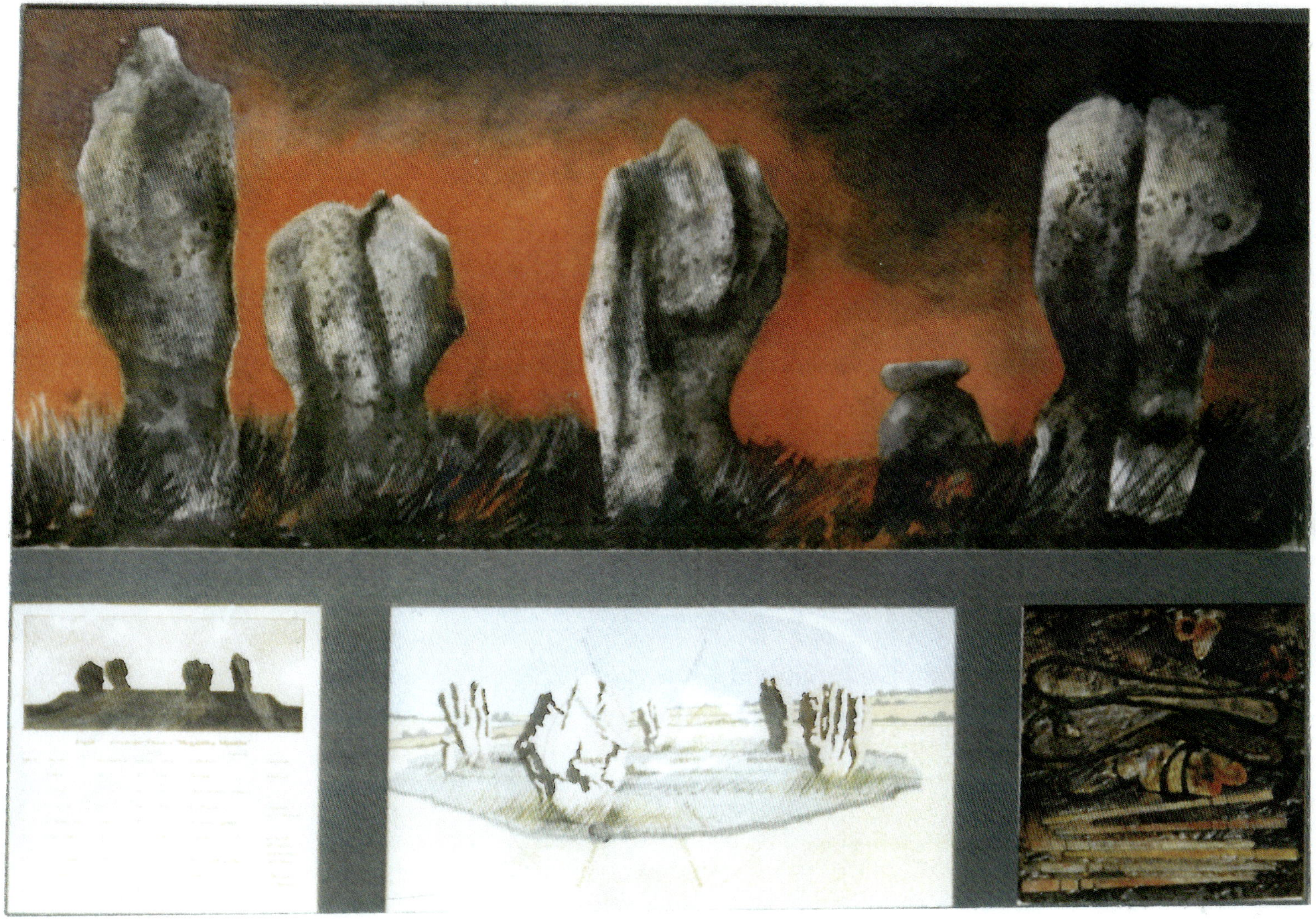

THE DUDDO STONES (Mixed media)

Although the circle has clearly lost one of its standing stones, it hasn't been so vandalised as other sites despite any grave goods being removed. This piece is about what it was erected for and what mathematical systems were employed in its construction.

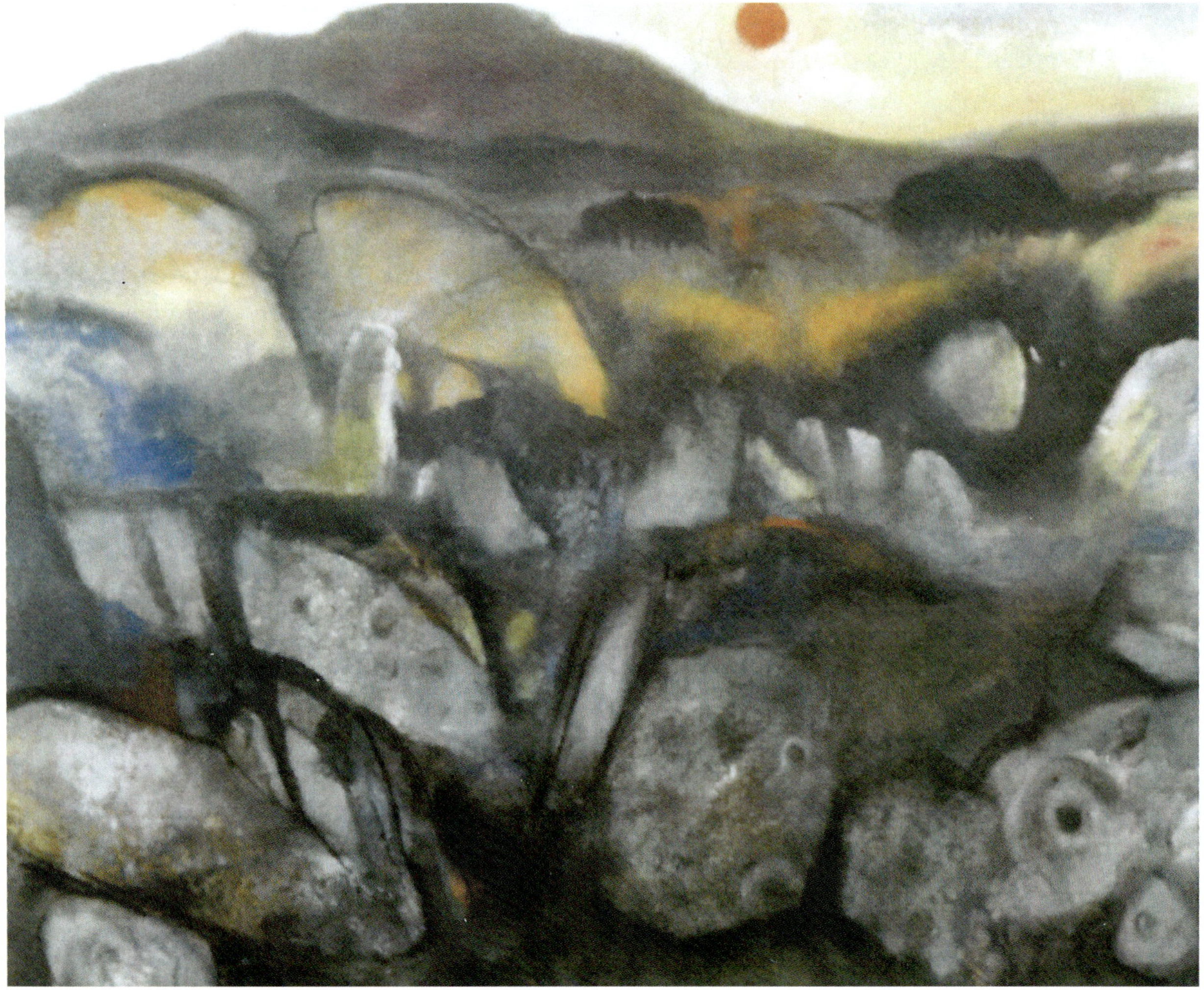

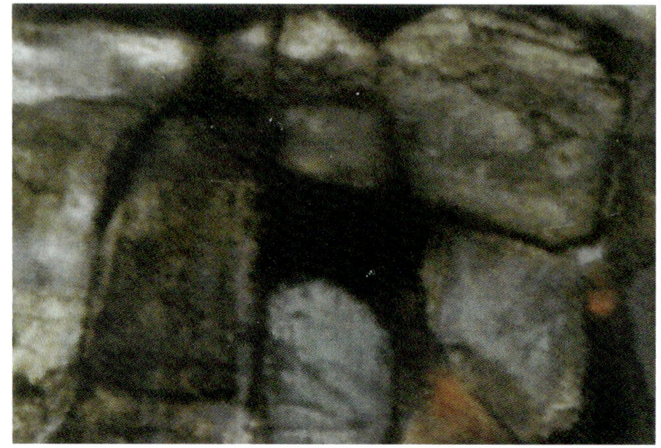

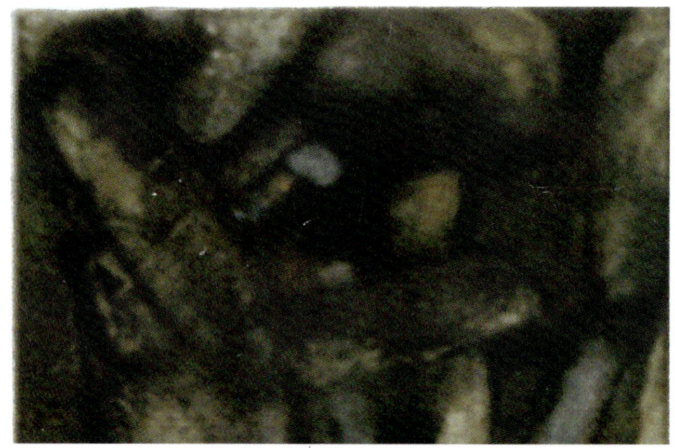

BEWICK MOOR (Mixed media)

Dominated to the north by Ros Castle, the moor is a splendid location containing numerous burial cists, enclosures and other sites including Blawearie. The army however, saw fit to use it as a location for tank trials, ranges and other war-games with the result that much of the archaeology has been spoiled or destroyed.

SING OF THE ROCKS ONCE MOLTEN....

It may be argued that the spirit of certain ancient-historical landscapes can best be evoked through full-orchestral music such as that of Vaughan Williams or Delius say, and only acceptable as full-colour oil paint renderings.

What then of drawings? What I have tried to show here is how important DRAWING in fact is, both to me personally and as a potent force in its own right. These essentially monochromatic pieces therefore are not intended to be merely preliminary studies for paintings, but as works which have their own voice. They are made mostly in charcoal which is a much more versatile medium than many people imagine. Most of them are large.

Although I made etchings as an art student, in the 1990s I was introduced to a new medium, that of COLLOGRAPH, which uses similar inking and printing processes. But the preparation is quite different from the metal plate, etched in acid of the classical method. Instead, the surface to be printed is raised by the use of various surfaces, such as paper and card, plaster and even car body-filler. In spite of the limited print run, it gives a wonderful textural print, which I found ideal for the type of work I wished to produce.

Here nature is barely sketched out
All is a threadbare mat of grass,
Brutal rock, the dark-wet gash
Of peat, the call of the peewit and the lark's far shout
A place where under thin stretched sky
A man may walk and wonder how he'll die.

Here where the savaged or mis-born
Lamb rots by the shedding burn
Or the wild crow dies in the sun
Is the graveyard of aestheticism
Moors are not for the squeamish or lonely
They are the playground of the solitary.

Theirs is a proud drabness of flint and stone
Where grass is tough as wire
And the winded rocks ache like old bones.
Deserted they do not invite much growth;
Man and history would pass them by the while;
Yet in legend and question they're strangely fertile.

WILLIAM OXLEY The Moors

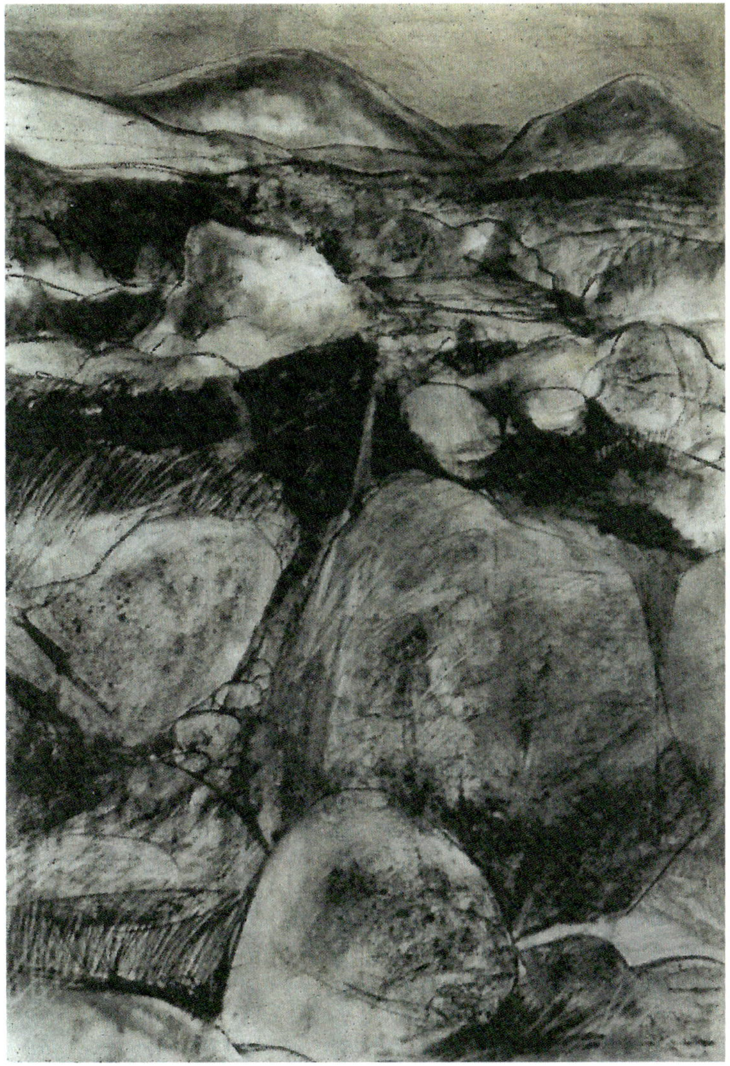

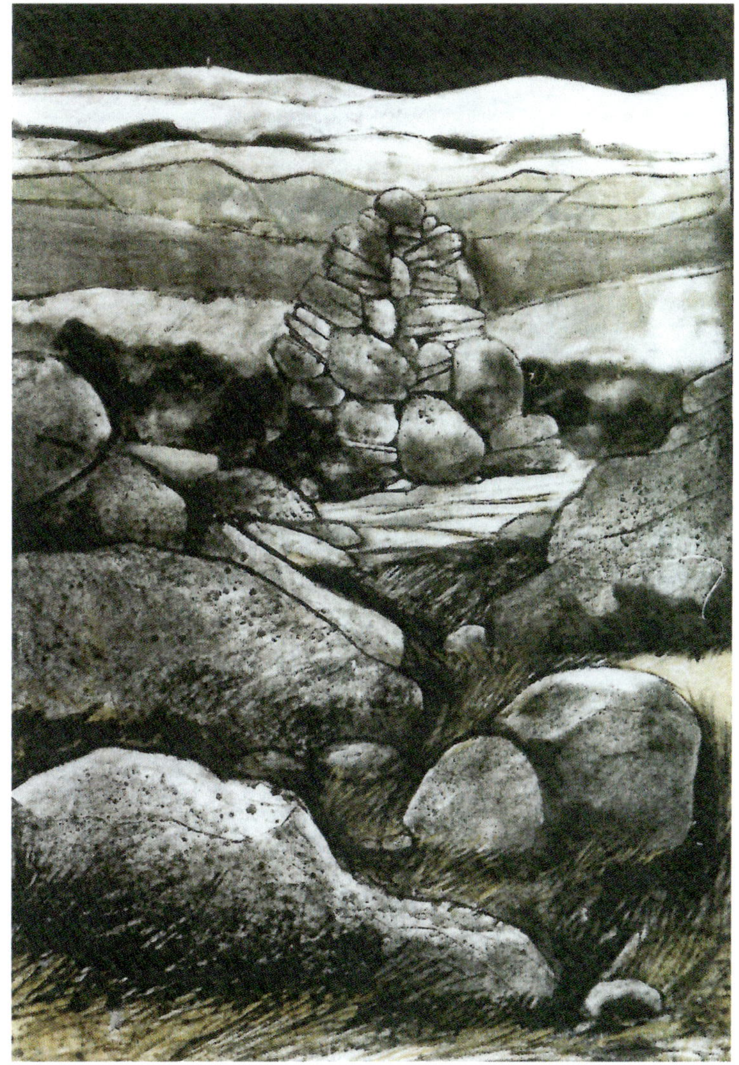

DRAWINGS (Charcoal)

Mostly large drawings some incorporating natural colours from the earth or plants. They represent various locations in Northumberland

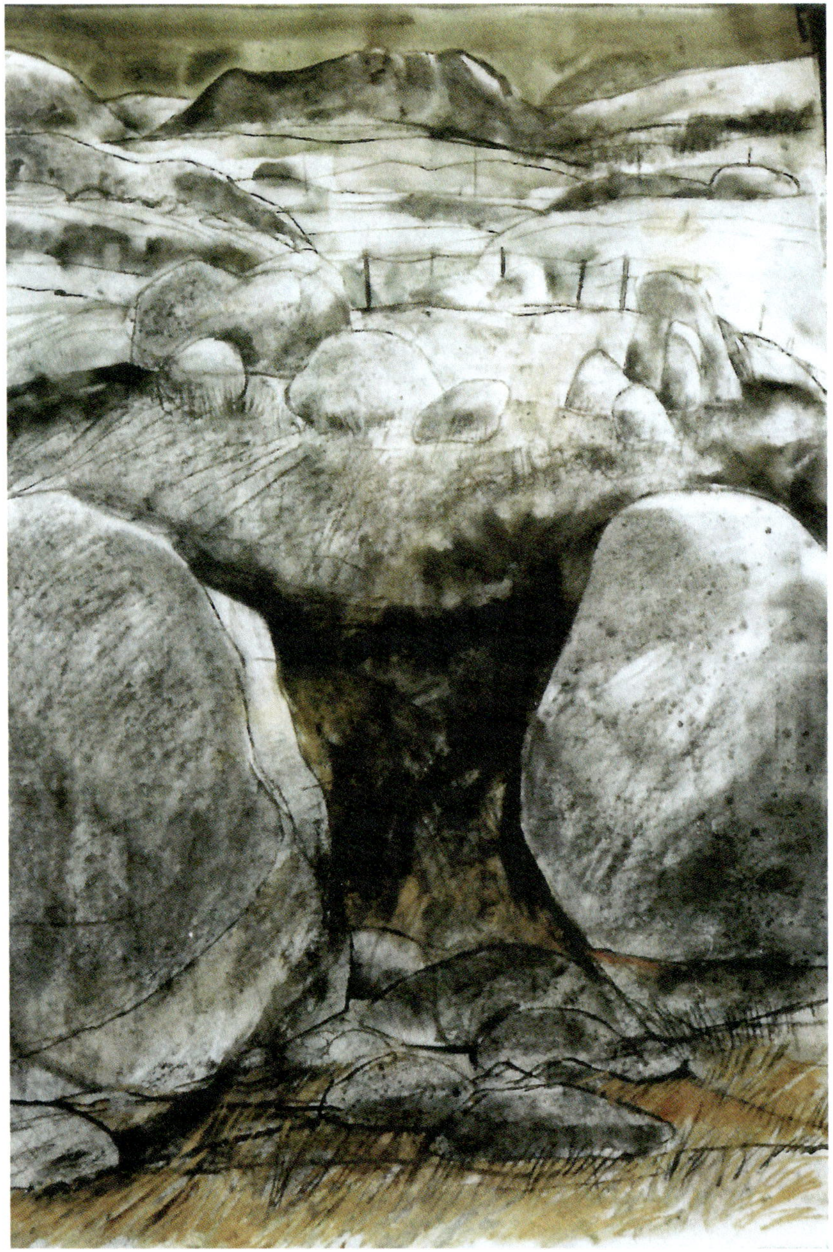

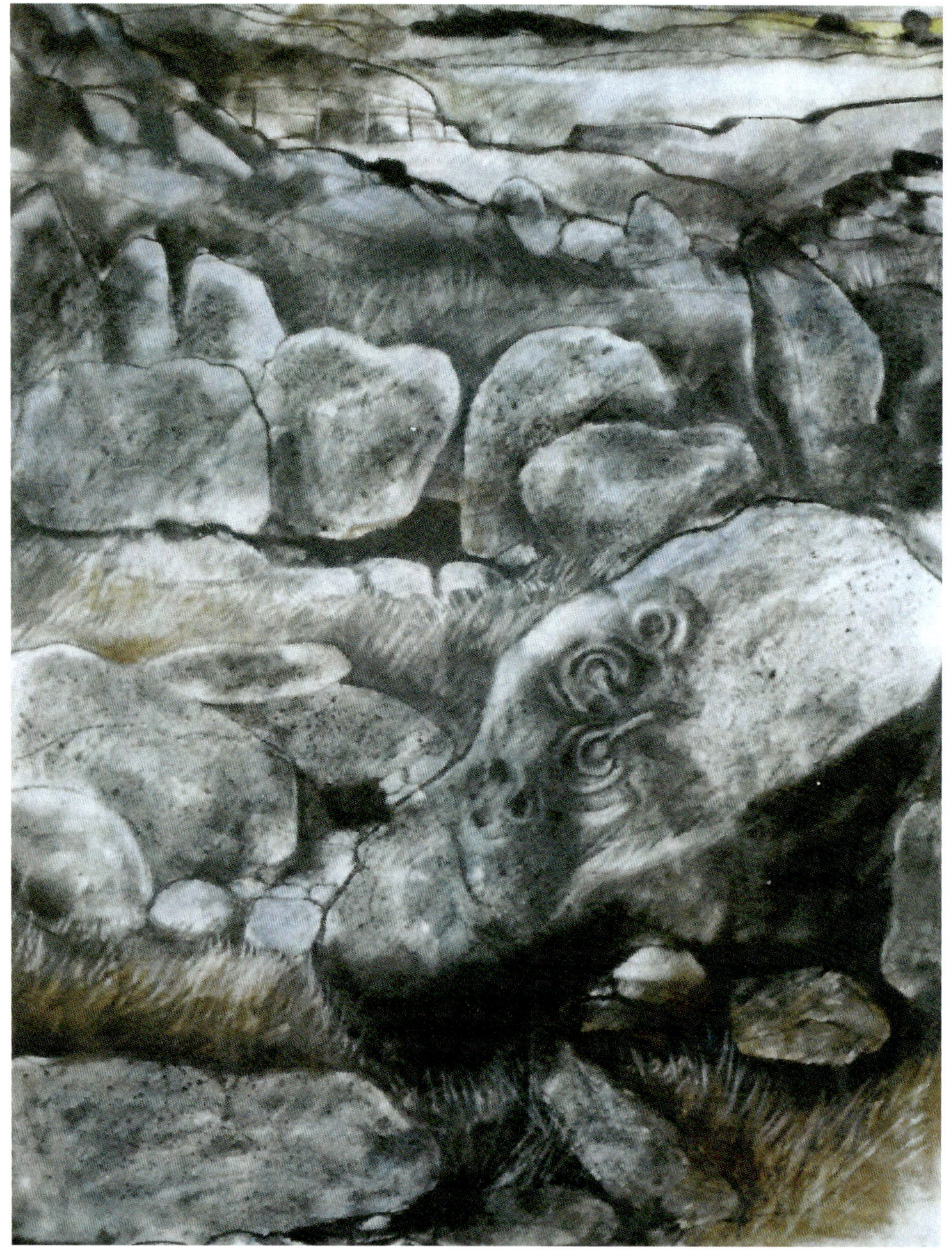

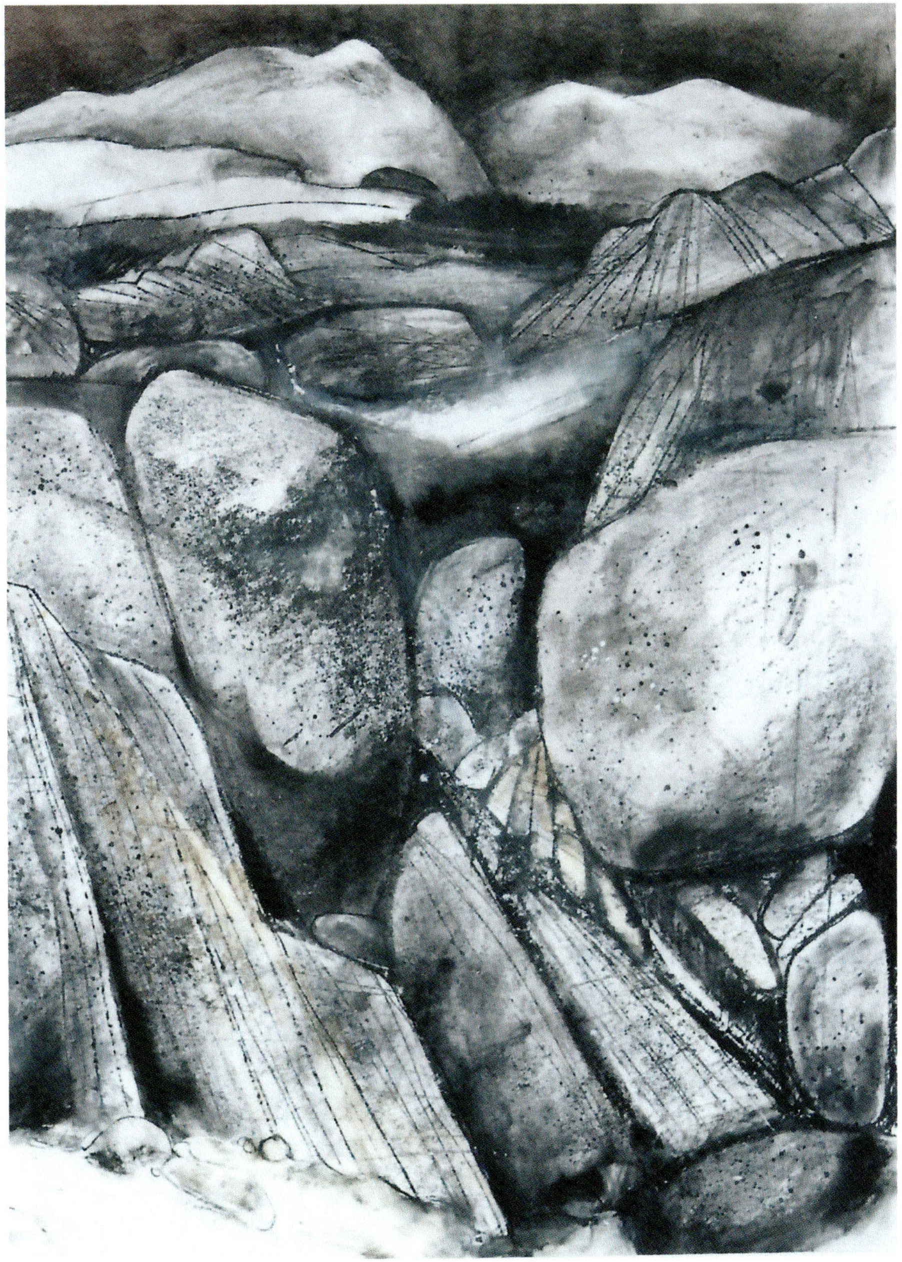

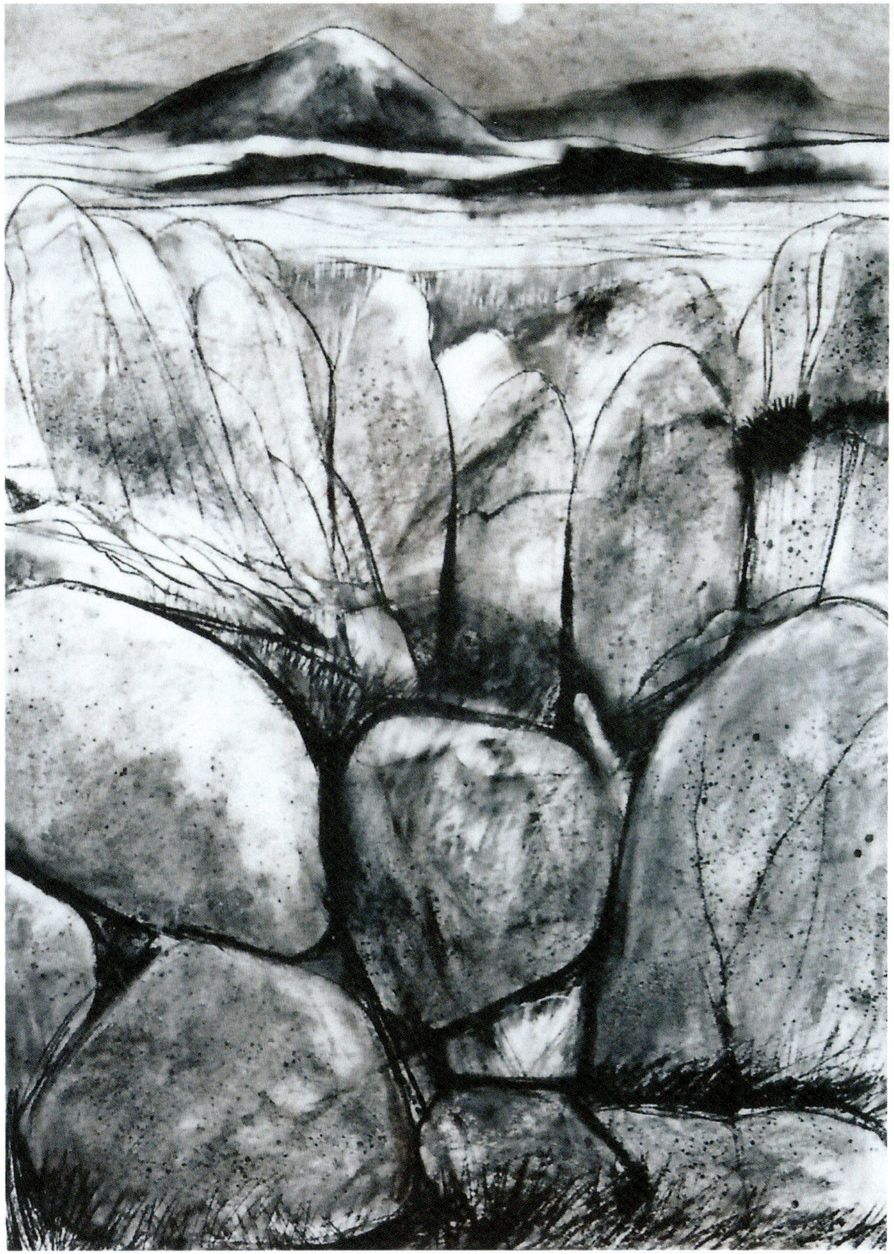

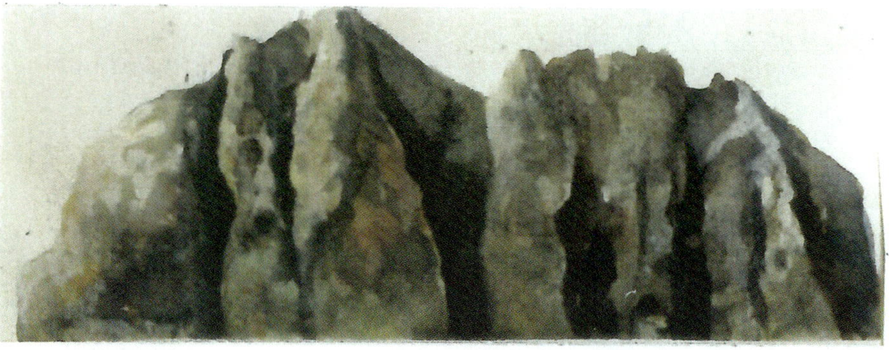

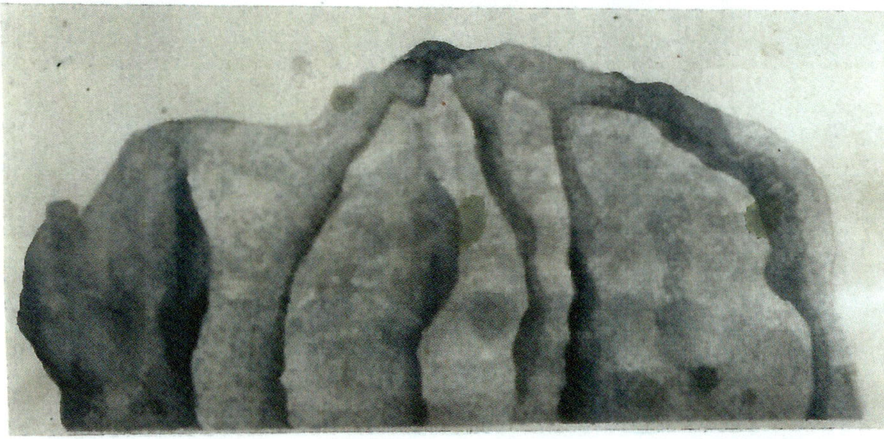

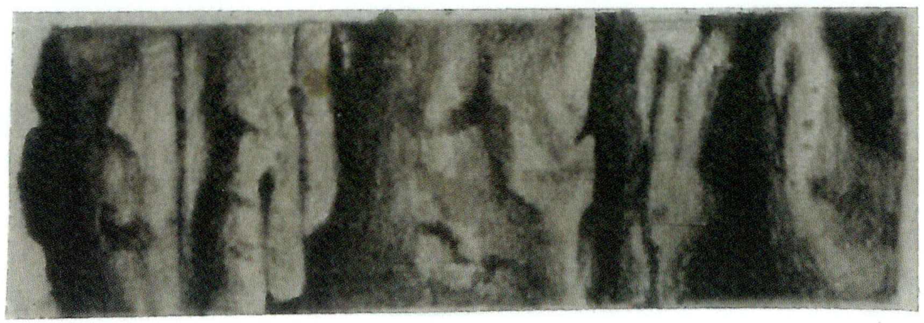

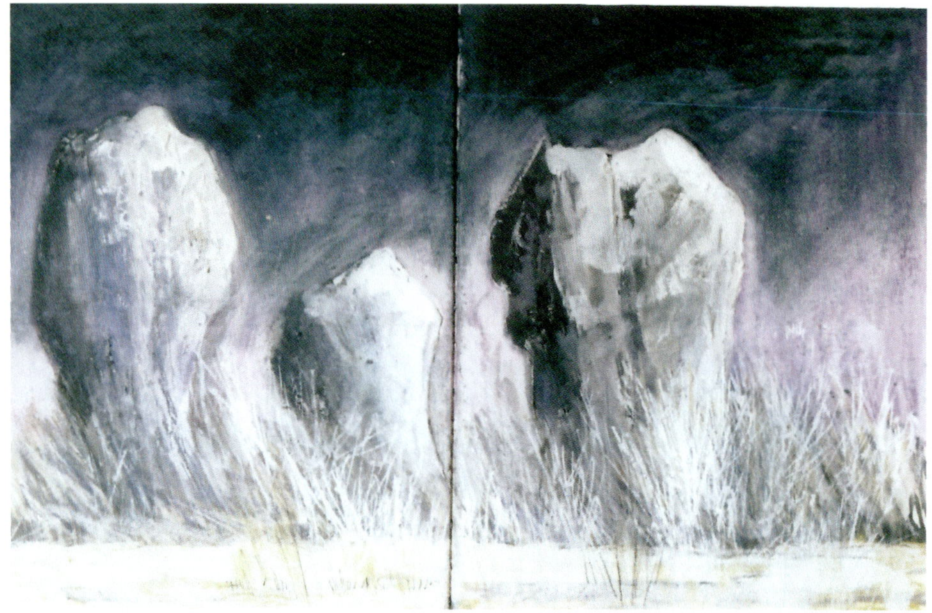

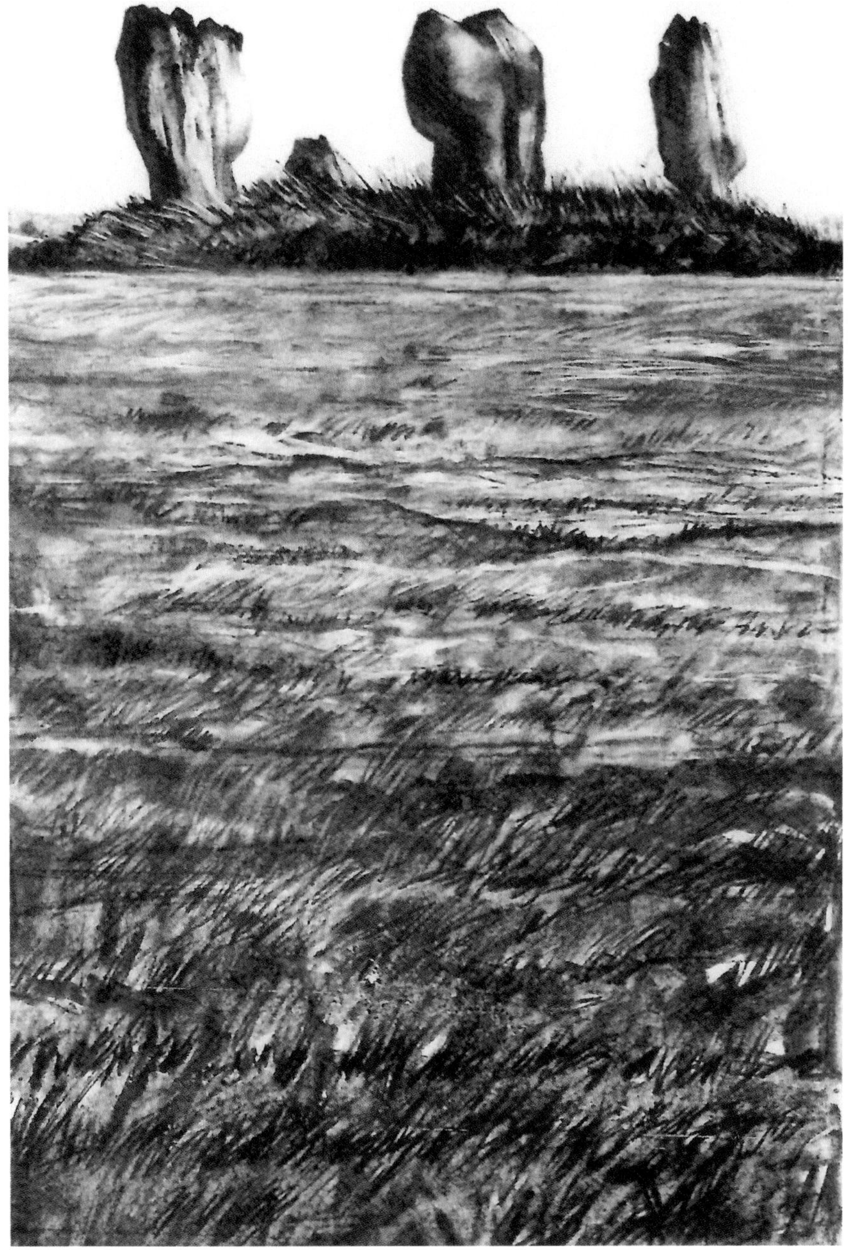

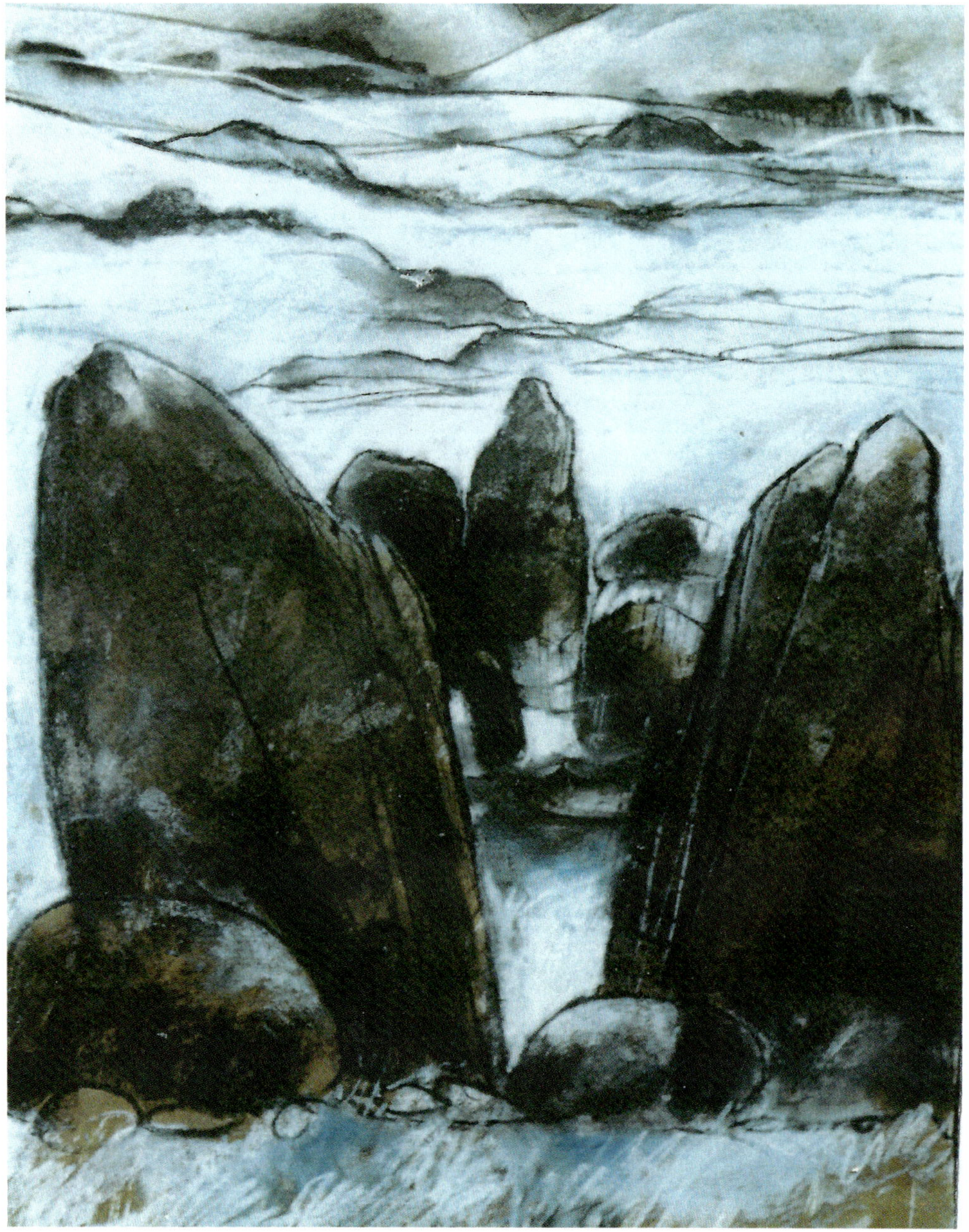

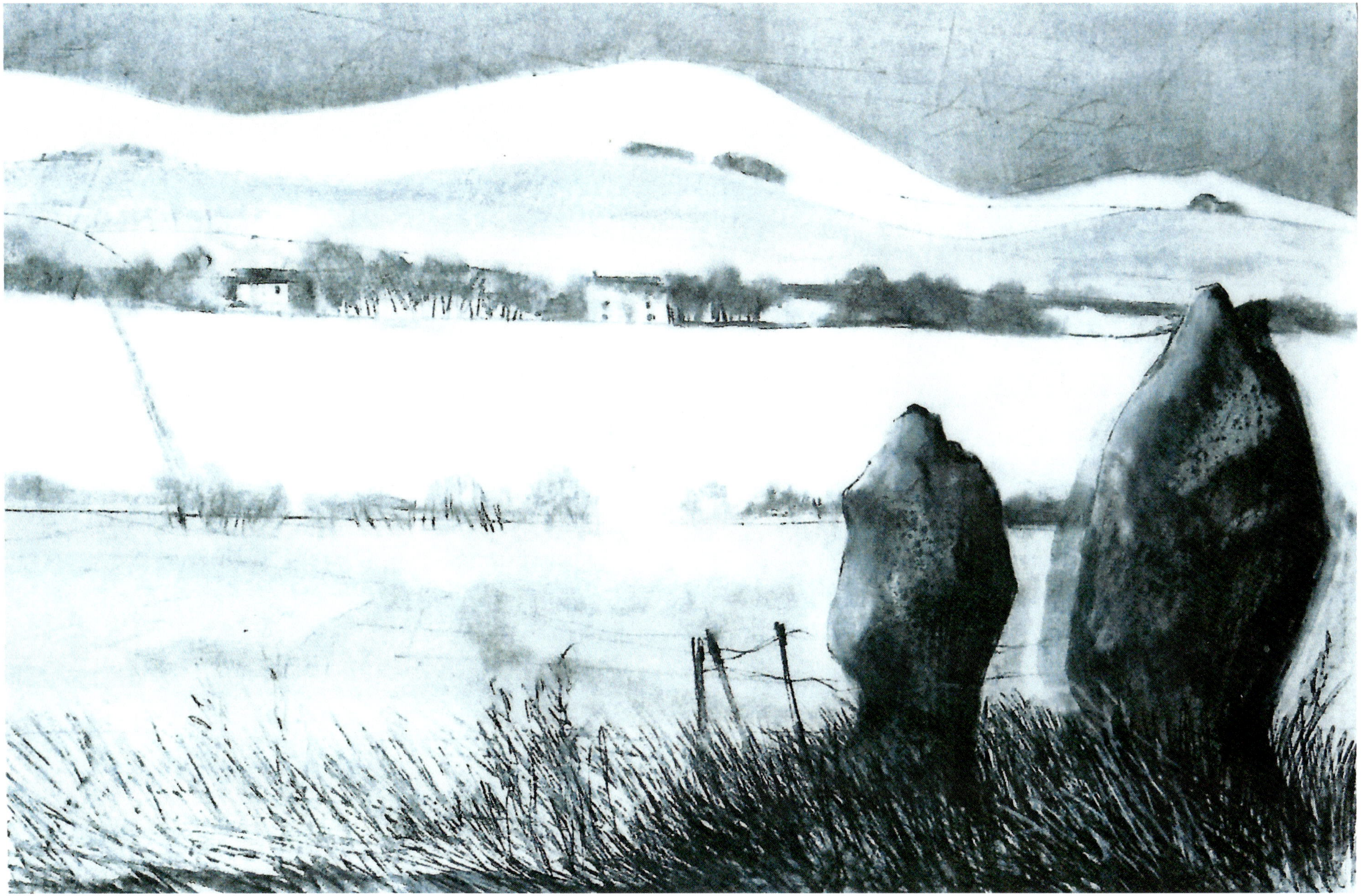

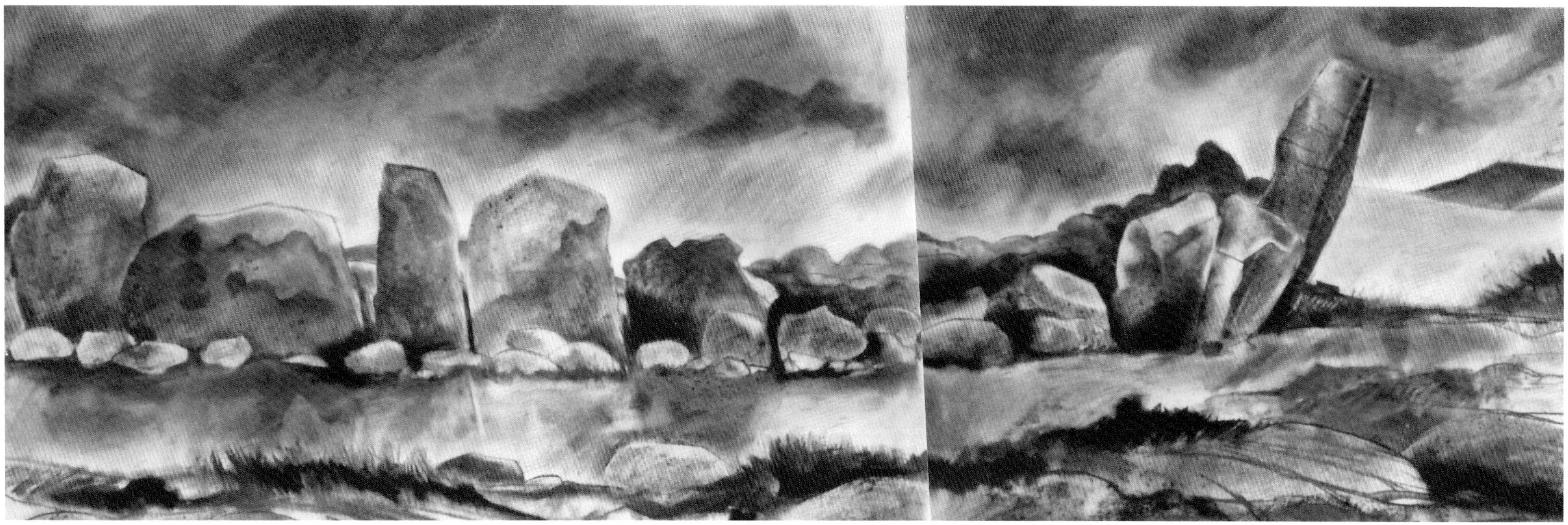

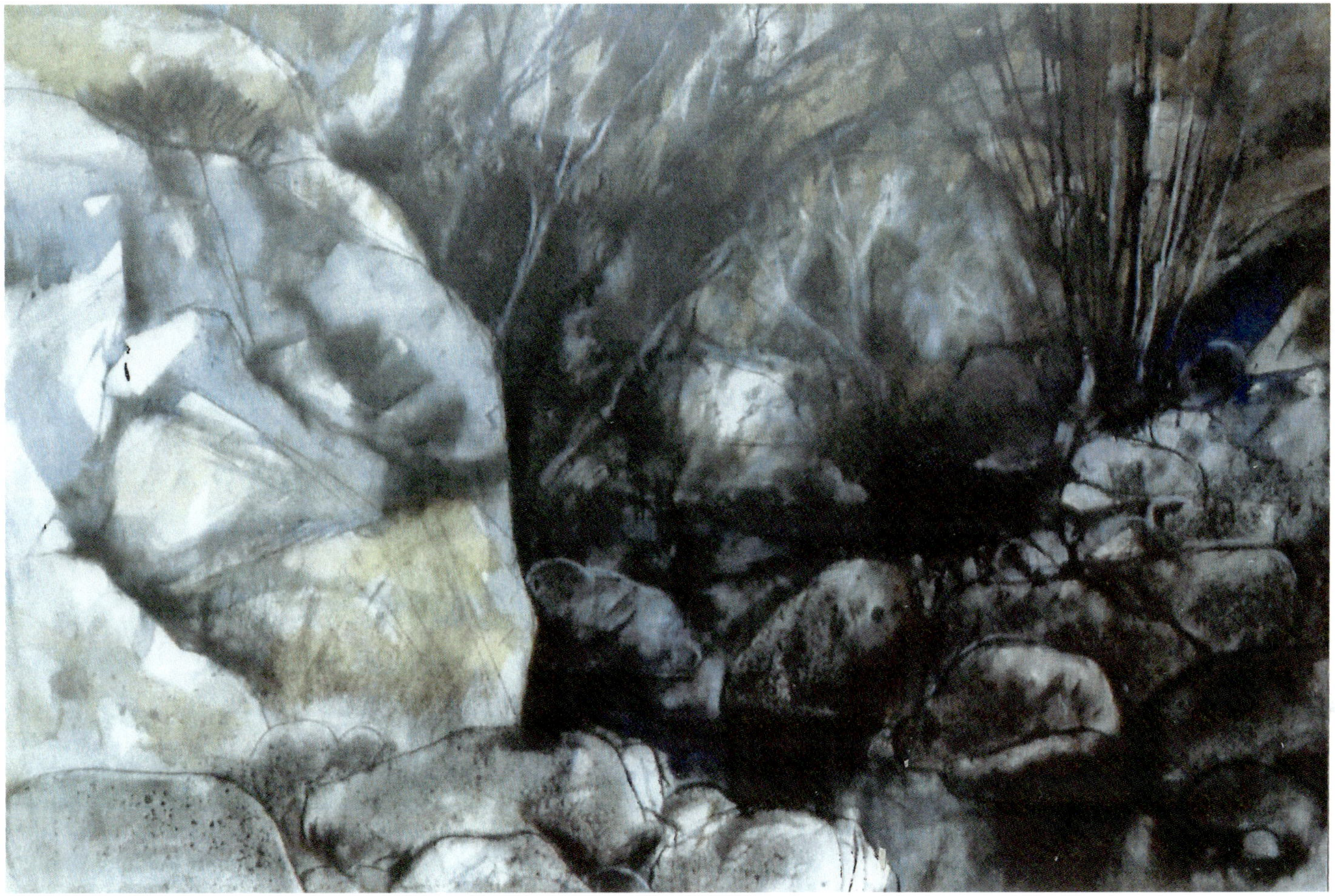

ROCK & RITUAL (Charcoal & inks)

From various finds it seems clear that water was a place in which items such as swords and spears were deposited possibly in some kind of ritual sacrifice or as votive offerings.

It is well known that the Romans placed silver, coins and other items, in the post-holes of the supports for their bridges and river crossings.

The rivers in north Northumberland such as the Glen, the Till and (here) the College Burn, have, I feel, a certain atmosphere and form the basis for some of my drawings.

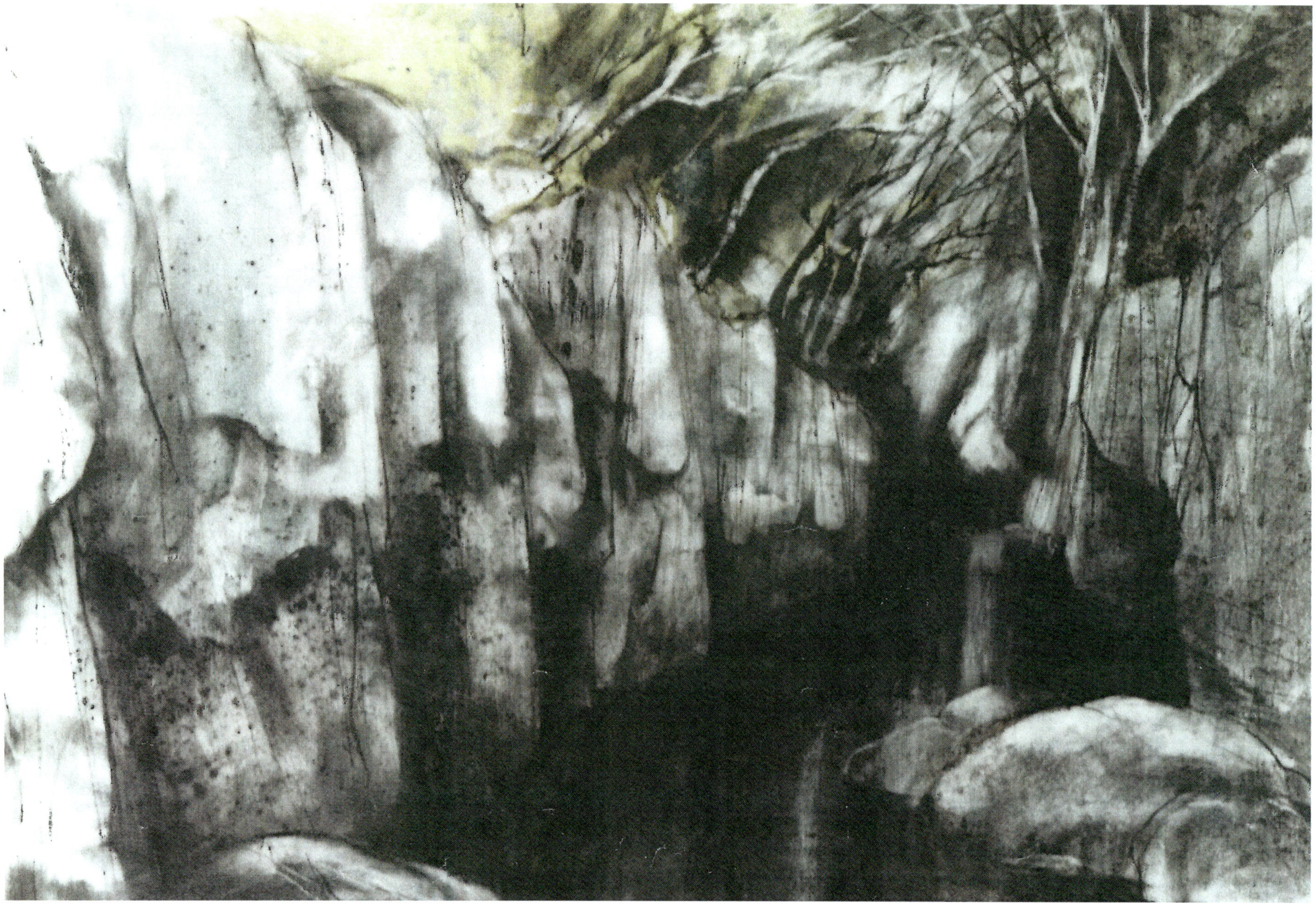

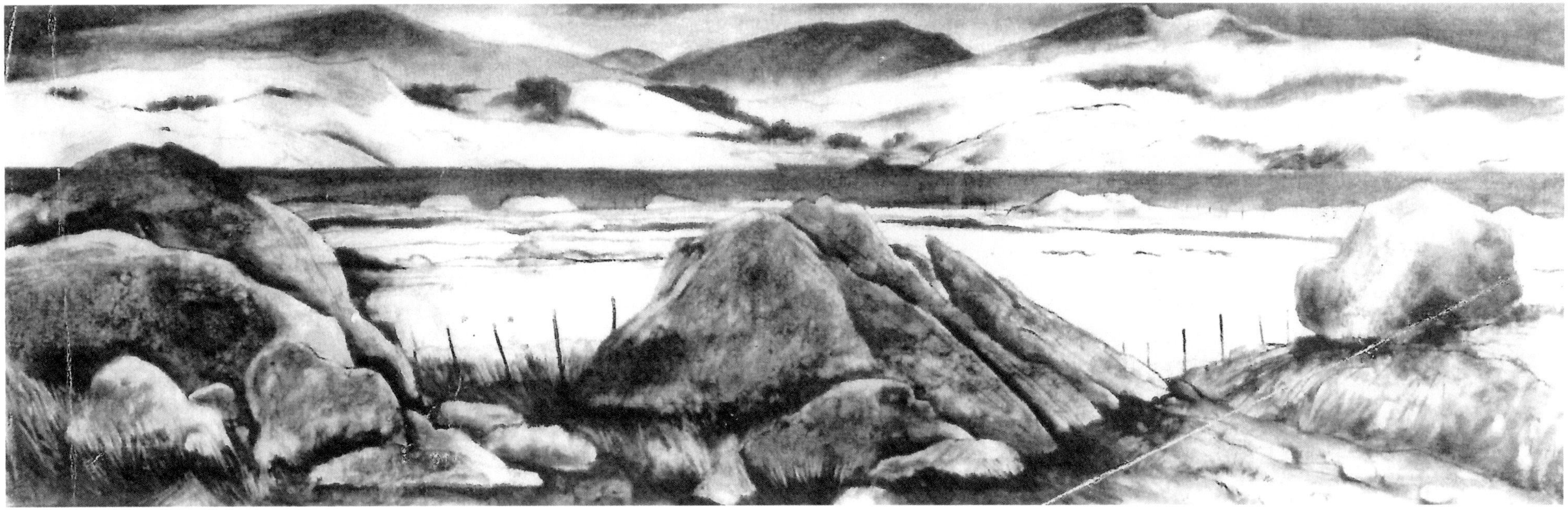

SUMMER SCHOOL WORK (Charcoal)

Drawings made on various summer schools, mostly on the Isles of Mull and Iona.

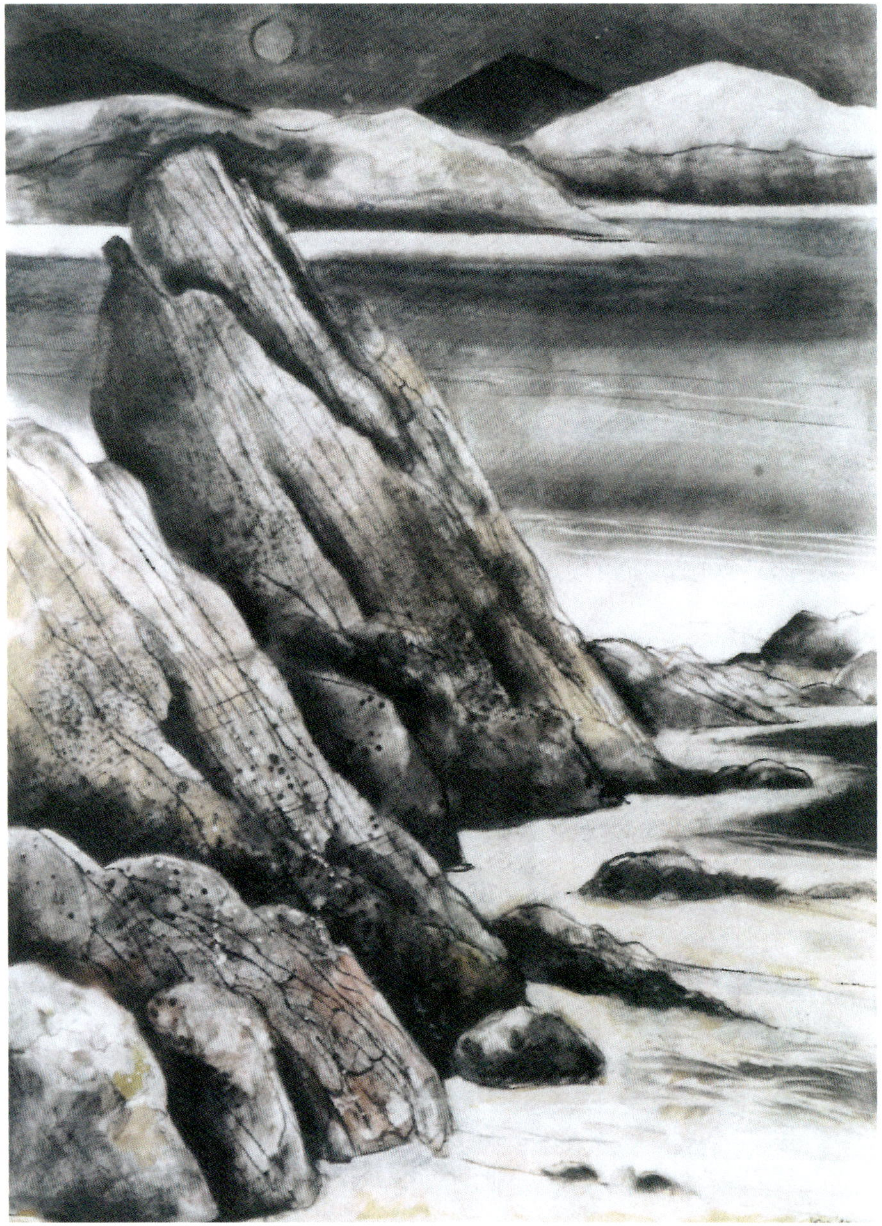

SUMMER SCHOOL WORK (Charcoal)

The island of Iona where we often worked, contains, besides a unique "spirituality", what is probably the most wonderful shore and rock scenery in Britain.

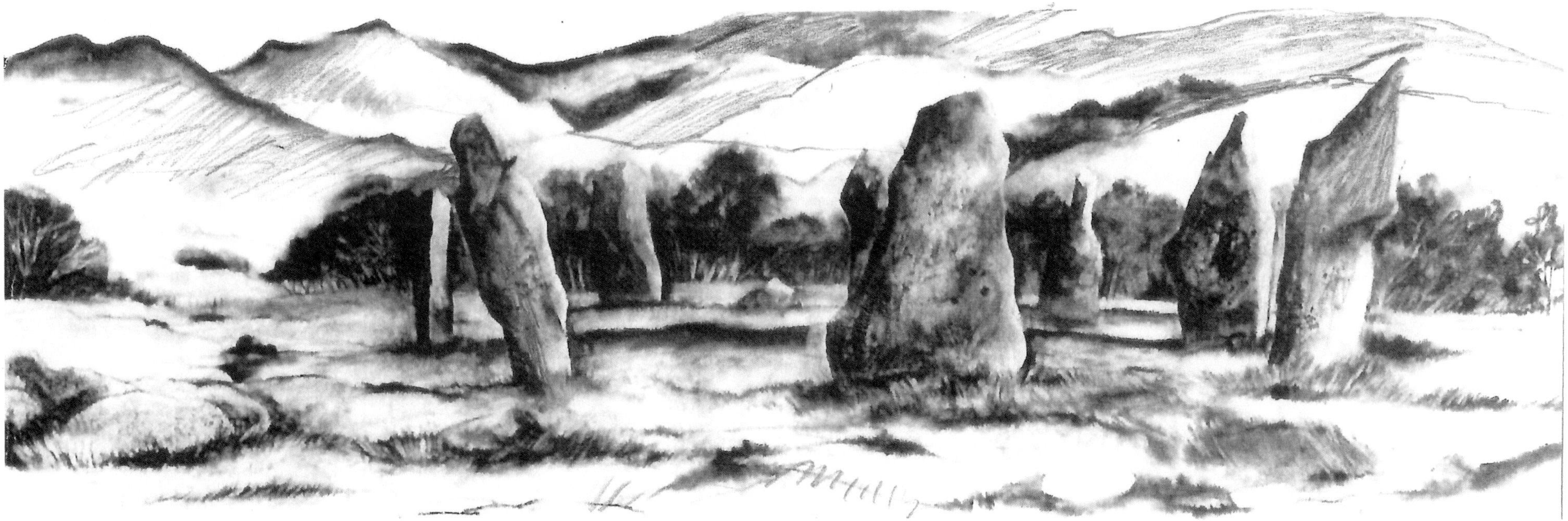

SUMMER SCHOOL WORK (Charcoal)

Drawings made on various summer schools, mostly on the Isles of Mull and Iona.

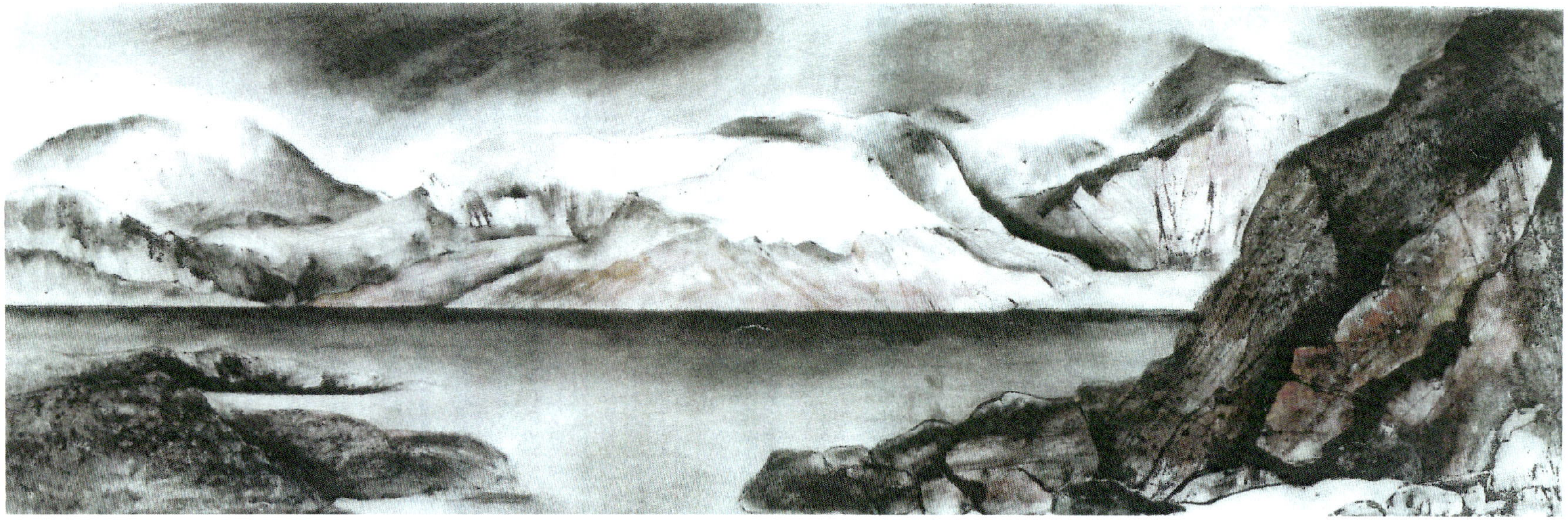

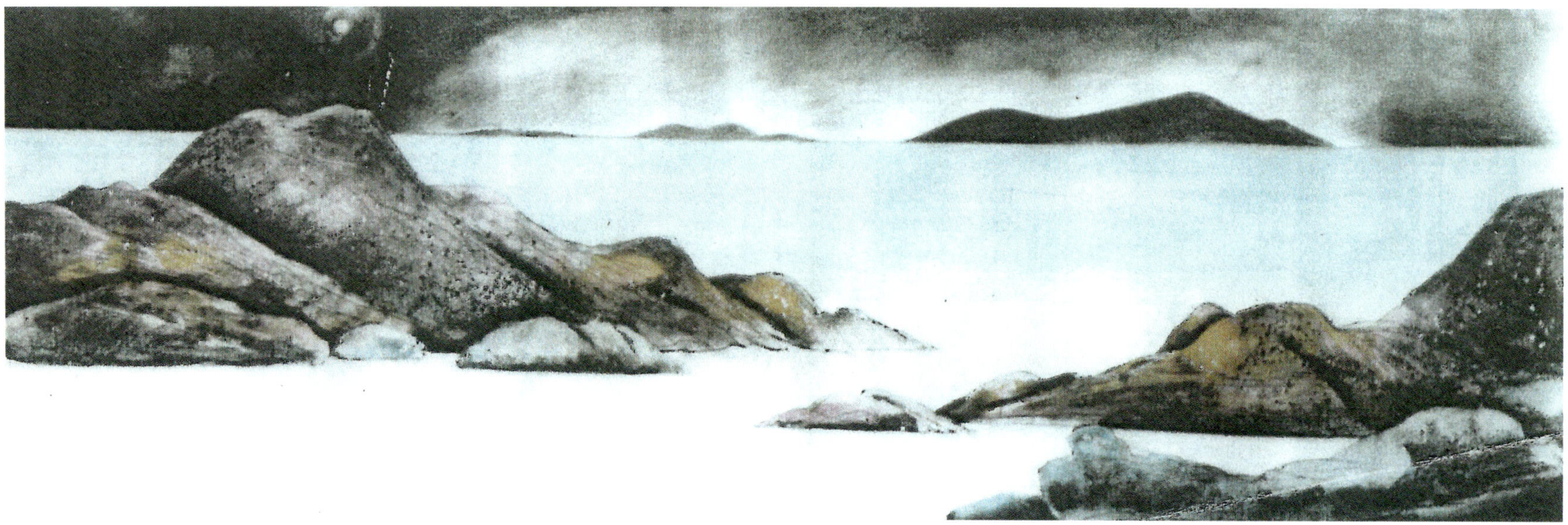

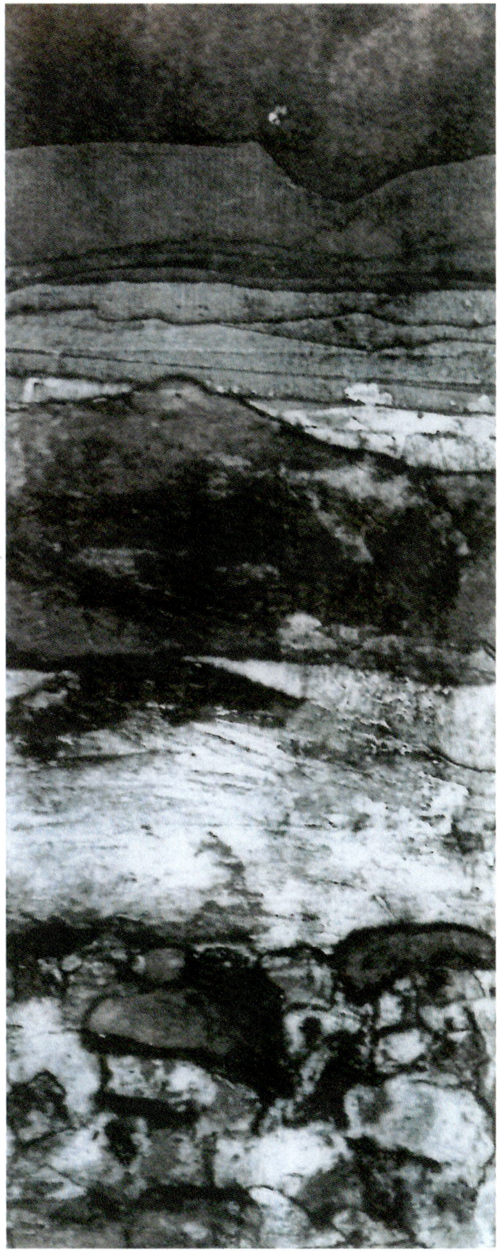

COLLOGRAPH

I found collograph to be the kind of medium which would allow me to make multiple prints of my work (the number of 'editions' depending on the quality of the materials used).

This, my first attempt, is made up from card, various papers and car body-filler, before being "inked" and printed as in a traditional etching.

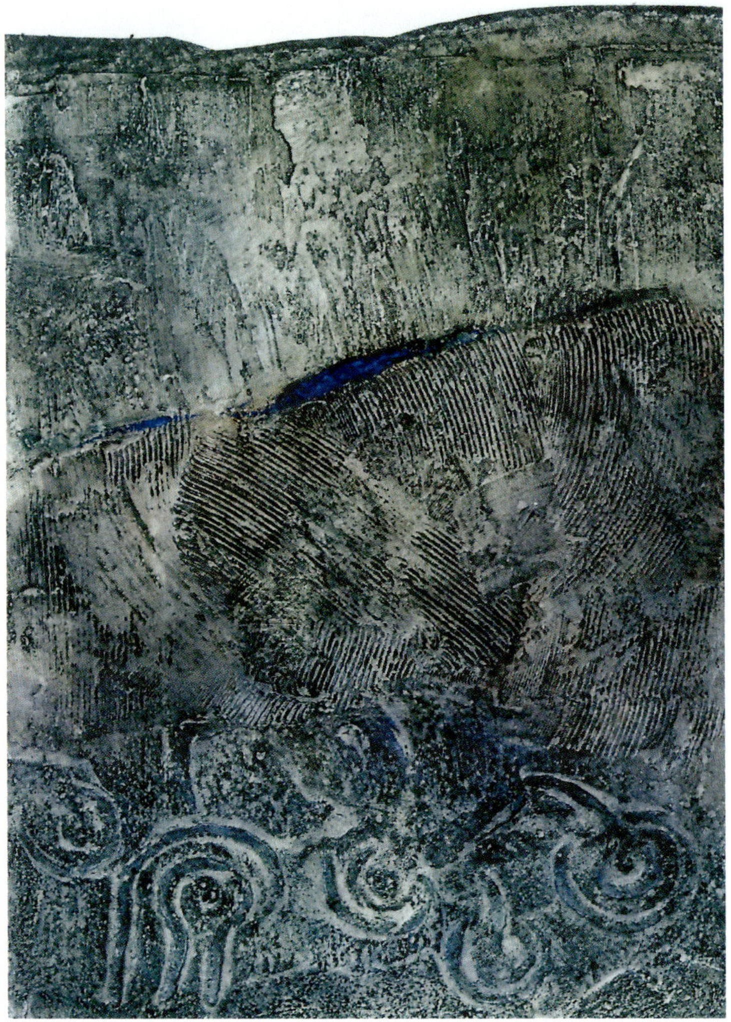

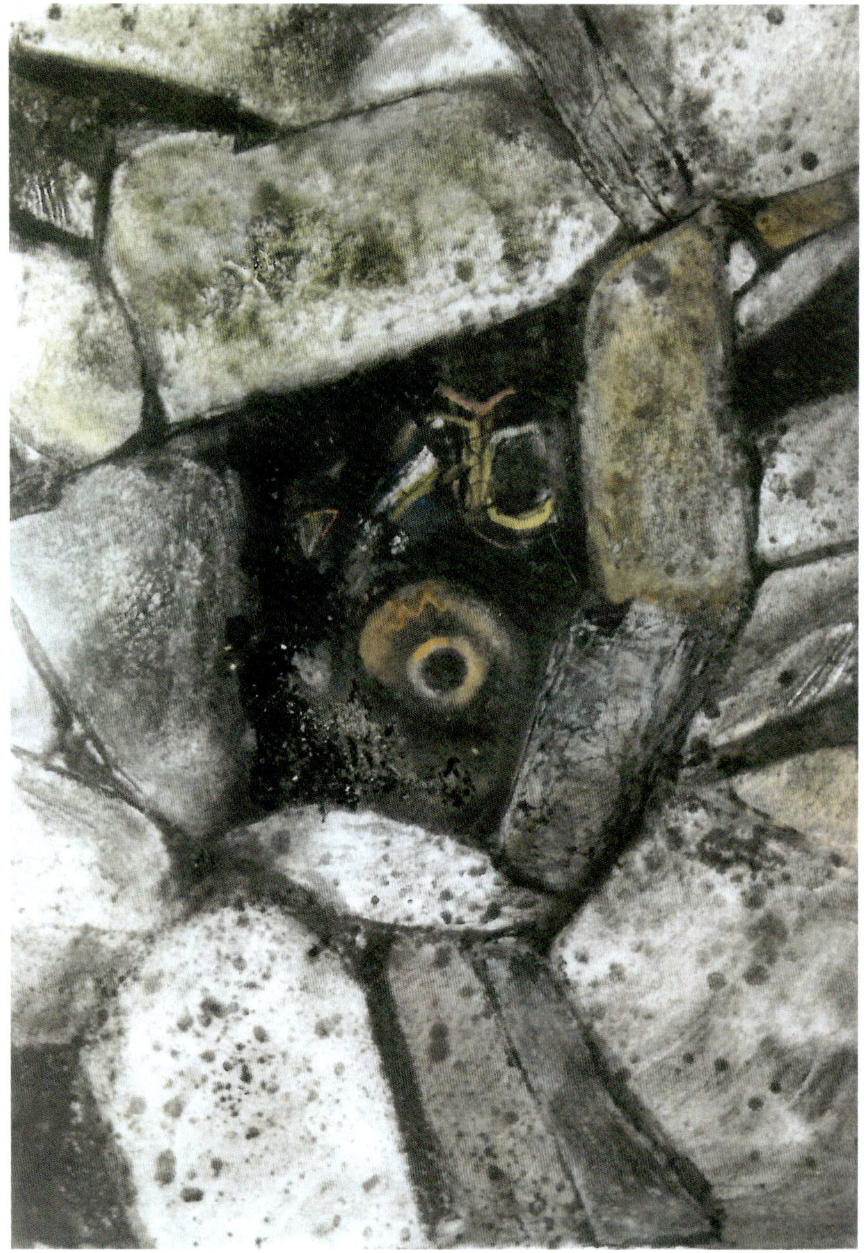

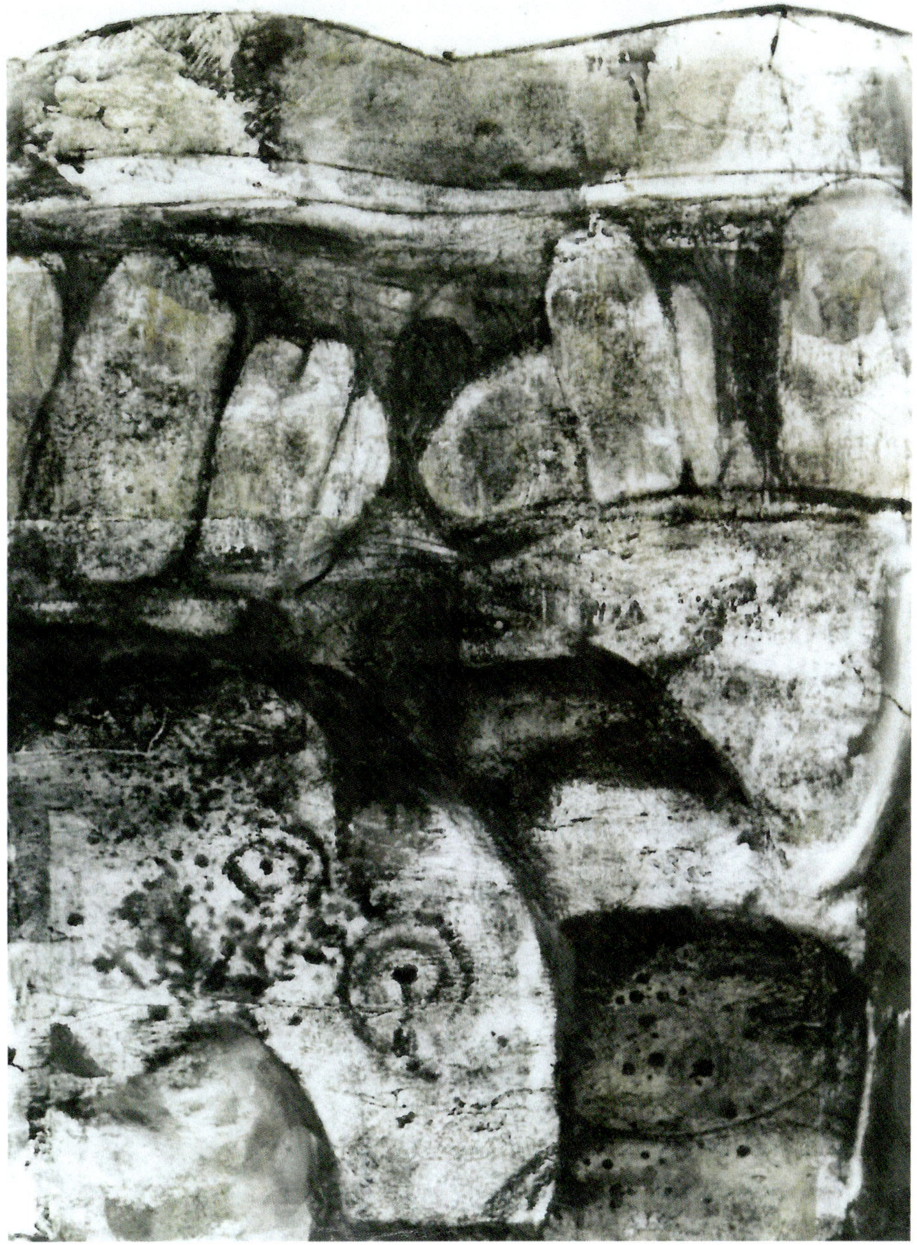

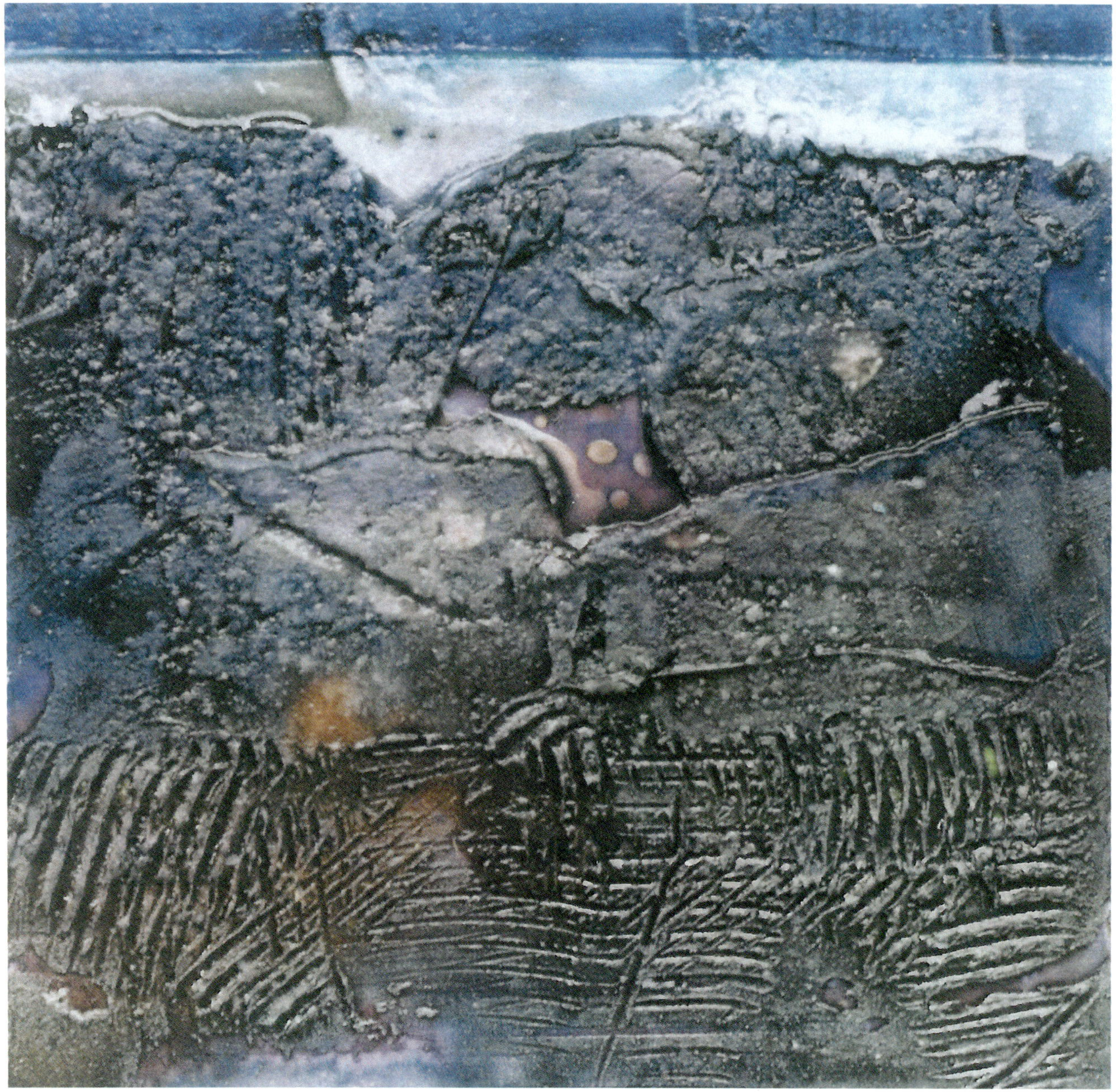

BOOKS ON ARCHAEOLOGY

Although I was aware of his work in discovering and charting the 'cup and ring' phenomenon in the north of England I had no inkling of the extent of both his knowledge and his wisdom in this field. Later I had the pleasure of working with Stan when we taught at a summer school in art and archaeology at Ford Castle after which he asked if he could use some of my work in his books, a request I was honoured to agree to.

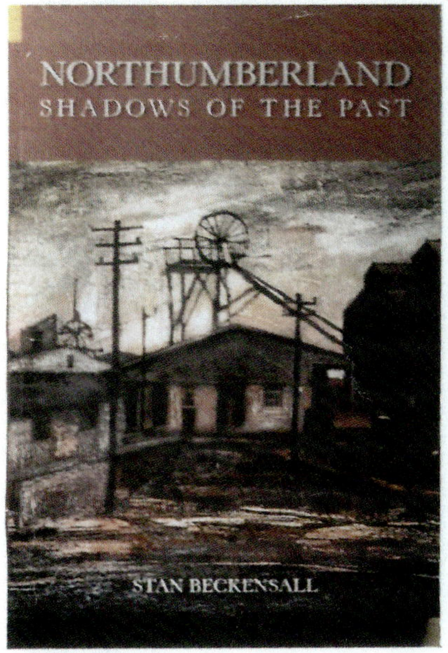

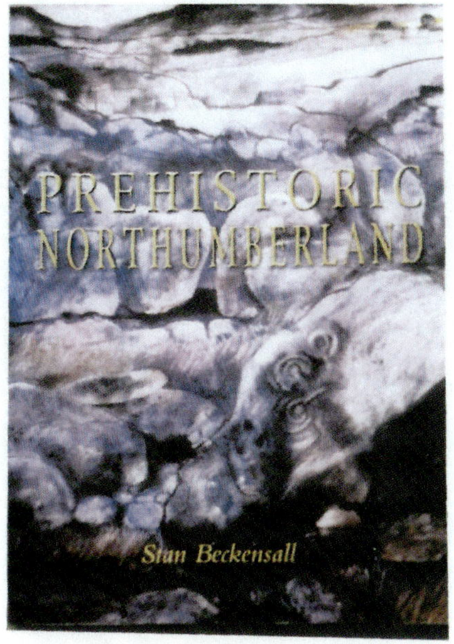

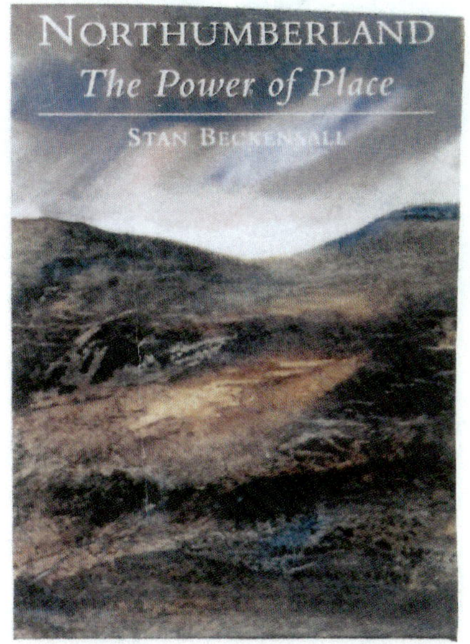

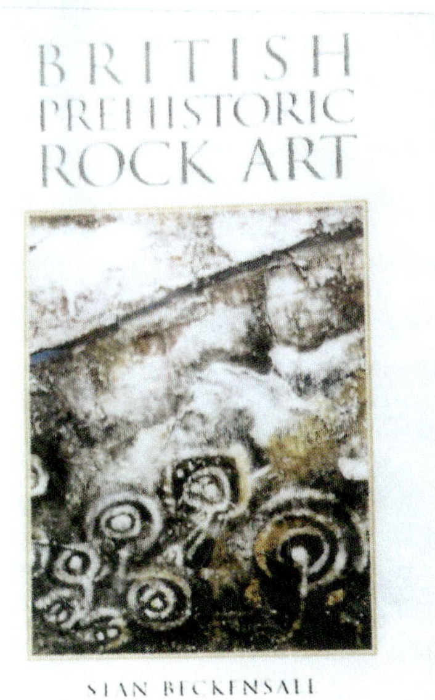

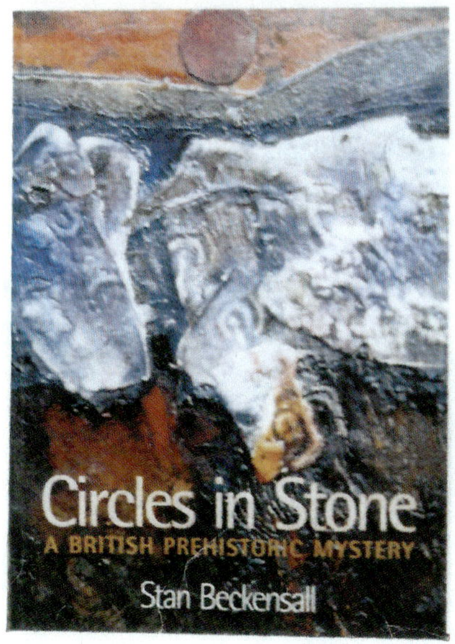

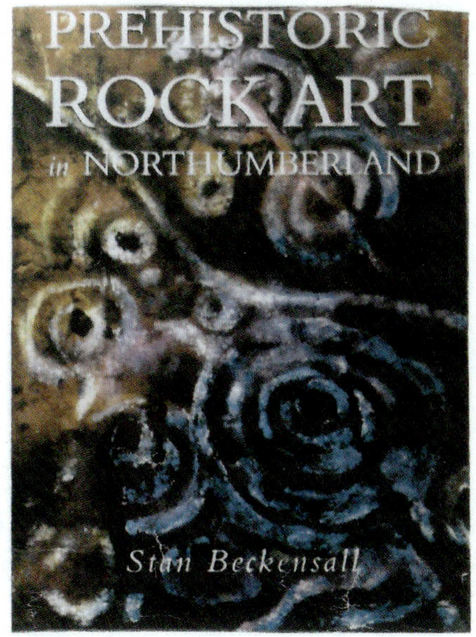